Developing an Effective Business Plan

- A Business Model Path to Success

by enodare publishing

Bibliographic data
- International Standard Book Number (ISBN): 978-1906144944
- Printed in the United States of America
- First Edition: October 2016

Published by:	Enodare Limited
Unit 102
The Northumberlands
Lower Mount Street
Dublin 2
Ireland

Printed and distributed by:	CasmateIPM
22841 Quicksilver Drive
Dulles, VA 20166
United States of America

For more information, e-mail books@enodare.com.

Copyright

"Developing an Effective Business Plan" © Enodare Limited 2016. All rights reserved. No part of this book shall be reproduced, stored in a retrieval system, or transmitted by any means—electronic, mechanical, photocopying, recording, or otherwise—without written permission from the publisher.

Trademarks

All terms mentioned in this book that are known to be trademarks or service marks have been appropriately capitalized. Enodare cannot attest to the accuracy of this information. Use of a term in this book should not be regarded as affecting the validity of any trademark or service mark.

Warning and Disclaimer

Although precautions have been taken in the preparation of this book, neither the publisher nor the author assumes any responsibility for errors or omissions. No warranty of fitness is implied. The information is provided on an "as is" basis. The author and the publisher shall have neither liability nor responsibility to any person or entity with respect to any loss or damages (whether arising by negligence or otherwise) arising from the use of or reliance on the information contained in this book or from the use of the form/documents accompanying it.

IMPORTANT NOTE

This book is meant as a general guide to business planning. While considerable effort has been made to make this book as accurate as possible, laws and their interpretation are constantly changing. As such, you are advised to update this information with your own research and/or counsel and to consult with your personal legal, financial and business advisors before acting on any information contained in this book.

The purpose of this book is to educate and entertain. It is not meant to provide legal, financial or advice. The authors and publisher shall have neither liability (whether in negligence or otherwise) nor responsibility to any person or entity with respect to any loss or damage caused or alleged to be caused directly or indirectly by the information or documents contained in this book or the use of that information or those documents.

ABOUT ENODARE

Enodare, the international self-help publisher, was founded in 2000 by a group which included lawyers, entrepreneurs, business professionals, authors and academics. Our aim was simple - to provide access to quality business and legal products and information at affordable prices.

Enodare's Will Writer software was first published in that year and, following its adaptation to cater for the legal systems of over 30 countries worldwide, quickly drew in excess of 40,000 visitors per month to our website. From this humble start, Enodare has quickly grown to become a leading international self-help publisher with legal and business titles in the United States, Canada, the United Kingdom, Australia and Ireland.

Our publications provide customers with the confidence and knowledge to help them deal with everyday issues such as setting up a company, running a business, preparing a tenancy agreement, making a last will and testament and much more.

By providing customers with much needed information and forms, we enable them to help protect both themselves and their families through the use of easy-to-read legal documents and forward planning techniques.

The Future….

We are always seeking to expand and improve the products and services we offer. However, in order to do this, we need to hear from interested authors and to receive feedback from our customers.

If something isn't clear to you in our publications, please let us know and we'll try to make it clearer in the next edition. If you can't find the answer you want and have a suggestion for an addition to our range, we'll happily look at that too.

USING SELF-HELP BOOKS

Before using a self-help book, you need to carefully consider the advantages and disadvantages of doing so – particularly where the subject matter is of a business, legal or tax related nature.

In writing our self-help books, we try to provide readers with an overview of a specific area. While this overview is often general in nature, it provides a good starting point for those wishing to carry out a more detailed review of a topic.

However, we cannot cover every conceivable eventuality that might affect our readers. Within the intended scope of this book, we can only cover the principal areas in a given topic and even where we cover these areas, we can still only do so to a moderate extent. To do otherwise would result in the writing of a text book which would be capable of use by professionals. This is not what we do.

It goes without saying (we hope) that if you are in any doubt as to whether the information in this book is suitable for use in your particular circumstances, you should contact a suitably qualified professional advisor for advice before using it. Remember the decision to use this information is yours! We are not advising you in any respect.

In using this book, you should also take into account the fact that this book has been written with the purpose of providing a general overview of business planning. As such, it does not attempt to cover all of the various procedural nuances and specific requirements that may apply from country to country indeed state to state. It therefore remains possible that your location may have specific requirements which have not been taken into account in this book.

Another thing that you should remember is that the law changes – thousands of new laws are brought into force every day and, by the same token, thousands are repealed or amended every day! As such, it is possible that while you are reading this book, some of the legal references in it might well have been changed. Let's hope they haven't but the chance does exist.

Anyway, assuming that all of the above is acceptable to you, let's move on to exploring the topic at hand...............developing an effective business plan.......

TABLE OF CONTENTS

Important Note 4

About Enodare 5

Using Self-Help Books 6

Part I - Introduction and Overview 1

Chapter 1 Your Business Model and Business Plan — What's the Difference? 4

What is a Business Model? 4
Why Should I Spend My Time Creating a Good Business Model? 5
The Business Model Canvas: What is it and Why is it the Best Modeling Technique? 6
    Customer Segments 10
    Value Proposition 11
    Channels 12
    Customer Relationships 12
    Revenue Streams 12
    Key Resources 13
    Key Activities 13
    Key Partnerships 13
    Cost Structure 14
Why Should I Create a Business Plan as Well as a Business Model? ... 14
What are the Components of a Good Business Plan? 18
    Executive Summary 18
    Description of the Business and Business Model 19
    The Business Environment 19
    The Marketing Plan 19
    The Operations Plan 20
    The Management Team 20
    The Financial Plan & Projections 21
Case Study - Introduction 22

Chapter 2 - Laying a Foundation for Success 28
Getting Up to Speed: Conducting Your Initial Market Research 30
    Secondary Research 34
    Primary Research 36
    Who Should Do the Research? 38
    Forming Your Business Modeling Team 38
Case Study - Getting Started 41

Chapter 3 How to Use the Business Model Canvas 48
Downloading the Business Model Canvas 49
Getting in the Right Frame of Mind 50
Brainstorming and Idea Generation 52
Selecting Your Initial Business Model Hypothesis 53
Testing Your Business Model Hypothesis 55
    What is the Best Sequence for Testing and Validating Your Business Model? 56
    Developing Tests for Your Hypothesis 58
    Generating a List of Potential Customers for Face-to-Face Meetings 61
    Contacting Potential Customers for Face-to-Face Meetings 62
    Meeting with Potential Customers, Presenting Your Hypothesis and
    Obtaining Feedback 63
Learning from Customer Feedback—Revising Your Hypothesis - Iterating Testing 64
Validating Your Business Model 65
Executing Your Business Model and Iterating Once Again . . . and Again 67
Case Study - The Business Model Canvas 69

Chapter 4 Customer Segments 76
What Important Problem Do You Intend to Solve? 77
What is Your Market? 81
What is a 'Customer Segment' and Why is Segmentation so Important? 82
Identifying Your Target Customer Segment 82
Creating Target Customer Profiles 84
Testing and Understanding Your Customer Problem and Customer Profile Hypotheses 85
Revising, Iterating, and Validating Your Customer Profile Hypothesis 89
Case Study - Customer Segments 92

CHAPTER 5 VALUE PROPOSITION	100
What is a Value Proposition?	101
Creating Your Value Proposition Hypothesis	103
Gathering Customer Feedback on Your Value Proposition	106
Assessing, Revising and Iterating Your Value Proposition	112
Validating Your Value Proposition	114
Case Study - Value Proposition	115

CHAPTER 6 CHANNELS	120
Types of Channels	122
Making Your Channel Hypothesis	123
Promotion of Your Product/Value Proposition	123
Sale and Distribution of Your Product	124
Customer Service and Support	129
Which Channels Should I Choose?	129
Gathering Customer Feedback on Your Proposed Channels	131
Revising, Iterating and Validating Your Channels	132
Case Study - Channels	133

CHAPTER 7 CUSTOMER RELATIONSHIPS	138
Creating Your Customer Relationship Proposition	139
Keep Your Focus on Acquiring, Retaining and Growing Customers	142
Acquiring Customers	142
Retaining Customers	144
Growing Customers	145
Gathering Customer Feedback on Your Customer Relationship Proposition	146
Revising, Iterating, and Validating Your Customer Relationship Proposition	148
Case Study - Customer Relationships	149

CHAPTER 8 REVENUE STREAMS	154
How to Create a Revenue Stream Hypothesis	156
Pricing Your Product Offering	157
Single-sided versus Multi-sided Markets	160
Integrated Revenue Streams	161

Generating Customer Feedback and Revising Your Revenue Stream Proposition 162
Revising, Iterating, and Validating Your Revenue Stream Proposition 163
Case Study - Revenue Streams 165

CHAPTER 9 KEY RESOURCES, ACTIVITIES AND PARTNERS 170

Key Activities 170
Key Resources 173
Key Partnerships 175
Case Study - Key Activities, Key Resources and Key Partners 177

CHAPTER 10 HOW MUCH WILL ALL THIS COST? 182

Identifying Costs 182
Fixed Versus Variable Costs 184
Cost Driven Versus Values-Driven Business 185
Economies of Scale and Economies of Scope 185
Cash Flow and Costs 186
Case Study - Cost Structure 187

CHAPTER 11 - GETTING STARTED ON YOUR BUSINESS PLAN 194

Strategy and Goals 195
SWOT Analysis 196
Operational Planning 200
The Audience 201
Length of Your Business Plan 203
Case Study - Getting Started on Your Business Plan 205

CHAPTER 12 - THE EXECUTIVE SUMMARY 210

Contents of the Executive Summary 211
Length and Style of the Executive Summary 215
When to Write the Executive Summary 216
Case Study - Executive Summary 218

Chapter 13 Description of the Business 226

Company Background 226
Vision, Mission and Values Statements 227
Nature of the Business 228
Core Competencies and Competitive Advantages 230
Description of the Value Chain 231
Financial Business Model 232
Strategic Goals and Objectives 233
Critical Success Factors 234
Funding Requirements 234
Business Ownership 235
Case Study - Description of the Business 236

Chapter 14 Discussion of the Business Environment 250

    Industry Analysis 251
    Market Analysis 254
    Competitive Analysis 257
Case Study - The Business Environment 260

Chapter 15 - The Marketing Plan 266

Conducting Market Research and Analysis 267
Setting Marketing Goals 267
Developing Strategies and Tactics to Acquire, Retain and Grow Customers ... 269
Product 269
Price 270
Place 271
Promotion 271
    Advertising 272
    Public Relations 272
    Sales Promotion 273
    Personal Selling 273
Internet Marketing 275
Budget and Analytics 278
Case Study - The Marketing Plan 280

Chapter 16 Website and E-Commerce Plan 286

Creating a Website 286
    Domain Names 287
    Websites 288
    Web Site Design and Development 289
    Buying a Website 291
Engaging in E-commerce 291
Case Study - Website and E-Commerce Plan 294

Chapter 17 Operations 298

Product Design and Development Plan 300
Production 301
Suppliers 302
Distribution 303
Service and Support 305
Service Businesses 305
Organization 306
Location and Facilities 308
    Choosing the Right Location 309
    Property Lease 310
Capital Equipment 311
Legal Environment 311
External Influences 311
Case Study - Operations 312

Chapter 18 The Management Team 316

Forming Your Management Team 317
    Sales 319
    Marketing 319
    Product Development 320
    Technology 320
    Finance and Accounting 321
    Human Resources 322
Board of Directors 322
Case Study - The Management Team 324

Chapter 19 Financial Plan and Projections 329

Types of Financial Statements and Reports 330
Balance Sheet 331
    Current Assets 331
    Fixed Assets 331
    Intangible Assets 331
    Other Assets 331
    Current Liabilities 331
    Long-Term Liabilities 332
    Owner's Equity 332
Income Statement 332
    Sales 332
    Cost of Goods Sold 333
    Gross Profit 333
    Operating Expenses 333
    Operating Profit 333
    Depreciation 333
    Other Income and Expenses 333
    Net Profit Before Taxes 333
    Net Profit After Taxes 334
Cash Flow Statement 334
    Net Cash Flow from Operating Activities 334
    Net Cash Flow from Investing Activities 334
    Net Cash Flow from Financing Activities 335
    Net Change in Cash and Marketable Securities 335
The Financial Planning Process 335
Assumptions 335
Financial Forecasts 336
Revenue Forecasts 336
Expenses 338
Gross Profit Margin 338
Net Profits 339
Case Study - Financial Plan and Projections 340

Chapter 20 Funding Sources 344

How Much Cash Do I Need? 345
Should I Raise Money? 346

Who Should I Raise Money From?... 347
Friends and Family.. 348
Angel Investors 348
Venture Capital Investors... 349
Banks and Other Lending Institutions 349
SBA Loans.. 350
Basic 7(a) Loan Program.. 350
CDC/504 Loan Program.. 351
7(m) Microloan Program 351
Crowdfunding.. 351
How Much Money Should I Raise and When?... 352
Seed Financing.. 353
Series A Round 353
Series B Round 354
Series C Round 354
What Ownership Interest Should I Give to Equity Investors? 355

PART I

INTRODUCTION AND OVERVIEW

CHAPTER 1:

YOUR BUSINESS MODEL AND BUSINESS PLAN —WHAT'S THE DIFFERENCE?

Chapter Overview

What is a Business Model? 4
Why Should I Spend My Time Creating a Good Business Model? 5
The Business Model Canvas: What is it and Why is it the Best
Modeling Technique? 6
      Customer Segments 10
      Value Proposition 11
      Channels 12
      Customer Relationships 12
      Revenue Streams 12
      Key Resources 13
      Key Activities 13
      Key Partnerships 13
      Cost Structure 14
Why Should I Create a Business Plan as Well as a Business Model? 14
What are the Components of a Good Business Plan? 18
      Executive Summary 18
      Description of the Business and Business Model 19
      The Business Environment 19
      The Marketing Plan 19
      The Operations Plan 20
      The Management Team 20
      The Financial Plan & Projections 21
LinksBuddy Case Study 22

CHAPTER 1

YOUR BUSINESS MODEL AND BUSINESS PLAN—WHAT'S THE DIFFERENCE?

What is a Business Model?

A business model is your unique recipe for making sufficient sustainable profits. A business plan is your strategy for developing and running each major aspect of a business that successfully executes your business model.

The goal of every business is to:

- Create a product that a large group of people value

- Convince those people to buy the product

- Make a sufficient profit on the sales, and

- Sustain all of this for a long period of time

In order to realize this goal, you first need to identify an important problem or need of a defined group of customers. Then you must develop a product that will solve their problem and/or fulfill their need, and by doing so create value that a customer is willing to pay for. Finally, your business needs to produce the product, communicate with potential customers and convince them to buy your product instead of one offered by the competition, deliver your product to the customers, receive a price for your product and run your business in a cost-efficient manner such that in combination they produce a sustainable profit, and develop customer loyalty so they come back to buy more.

A good business model must address each of these components, or "ingredients." And just like any good recipe, if any ingredient is lacking, or if all the ingredients don't blend well together, then this will eventually drag down the entire enterprise. In fact, the business model recipe is the defining factor in whether any business succeeds or fails. Every successful business has a business model that works well, both in its parts and in its whole.

Why Should I Spend My Time Creating a Good Business Model?

Every company has a business model whether they know it or not. The question is whether you have identified a model that you believe, based on verified facts, will be profitable and sustainable, and one that you can consciously execute to give you a high probability to achieve good results, or whether you have a business model that simply emerged based on educated guesses that you will test for the first time when you launch your product—if you ever get there. Even if you already have a decent business model, you want to try and optimize it as much as possible—so its components should be tested, verified and revised throughout the life of your business.

Taking the time to create a business model before diving headfirst into business operations allows you to identify those key components that will not work and change them, identify the components that will work and improve them, and integrate all of the components so they work well together as a system, both in practical and strategic terms.

In addition, there are many other benefits, both tangible and intangible, that ripple through a business when its founder takes the time and effort to identify the components of the optimum business model.

For example, doing so allows you to:

- Test the model before fully implementing it

- Use the model as a benchmark going forward that can be iterated and improved upon

- Set a comprehensive strategy for your business focused on executing and exploiting your business model

- Zero in on and fully exploit competitive advantages

- Obtain focus and buy-in from your key employees and partners

- Make sure you have a product that truly fits a sizeable target market

- Focus on who will actually be your customers and what they really value—i.e. what are they actually buying when they pay for your product

- Obtain an initial sense of whether your "great product that customers will flock to buy" is also a profitable idea—because great products don't always result in great profits

- Lay a foundation for scalability and repeatability

- Innovate with respect to process as well as product—by creating a new business model that may in itself become your key competitive advantage

- Brainstorm and possibly discover a new product, unsatisfied need, or better process you hadn't thought of before

- Distill your entire business to its key ingredients, and effectively communicate those ingredients to employees, customers, partners, investors, etc.

The Business Model Canvas: What is it and Why is it the Best Modeling Technique?

Your business model will be the core of your business strategy and plan, and its key components must be identified and tested before spending time on how it will be implemented. With the proper modeling technique, you can quickly work through many iterations of a proposed business model—hypothesizing and testing and learning, then revising and honing, and then hypothesizing and testing and learning again, and so on. The important thing is to choose a single technique for creating your business model so that everyone working on and reviewing it has a shared understanding of the basis for the model.

Many such business modeling techniques have been developed, but almost all of them do the same thing: break the entire business process into component parts—from identifying a product that certain target customers value and are willing to pay for, creating that product offering, and then selling and delivering that product to customers at a high enough profit margin to be able to sustain and grow the business. Some business analysts break it into four components with many processes included in each component; some break it down finely into more than a dozen components. But at the end of the day most include the same business process elements—the product offering, business infrastructure, market and finance—somewhere in their system, and they are all intended to discover the best sustainable way to create and deliver value and make a good profit.

The "Business Model Canvas" was developed by a guy named Alexander Osterwalder, and it first gained broad attention in 2010. His technique breaks the business process down into nine component parts; or "building blocks" as he calls them. His building blocks and visual approach are very comprehensible and easy to work with for a new entrepreneur like yourself, and allow you to concisely and clearly describe your business model. The Business Model Canvas is also very flexible, allowing for the iterative process that all good modeling goes through. And it facilitates easy group comprehension and participations as well. But most importantly, we believe this system will lead to the best understanding of how to exploit your business idea, and therefore the best results.

The reason for this is that the Business Model Canvas requires the entrepreneur and his team to carefully focus on, understand and think through each component building block individually, but also to think through and understand how each building block relates to the others, and how the entire system integrates and works as a whole. If any piece is weak or will not integrate well with the others, it will often be quickly apparent, and if it isn't apparent on the surface, it will most likely come out in hypothesis testing—which is a critical part of the Business Model Canvas process.

Once weaknesses in a proposed business model are identified through testing, and their corrections are identified through learning and analysis, revisions can be quickly and easily incorporated into the model—and tested as well. In other words, creating a business model using the Business Model Canvas is a fluid, organic process—not a one-time event. And your entire modeling team will gain a clear understanding of how the model which is eventually adopted came into being, because all they have to do is look at the Business Model Canvas and how it evolves in order to understand the improvements being made.

Keep in mind that once a business model created using the Business Model Canvas has been adopted and becomes a starting point for your business, the process is not finished. It is just that, a starting point, and there will be more testing and iterations as the product enters the market and the hypotheses embedded in the model are truly put to the test.

The Business Model Canvas is literally, as the name suggests, a "canvas" on which to draw a business model. And as we just mentioned, the canvas is broken down into nine interrelated blocks.

The nine building blocks of the Business Model Canvas are:

- Customer segments
- Value proposition
- Channels
- Customer relationships
- Revenue streams
- Key resources
- Key activities
- Key partnerships
- Cost structure

The physical layout of the business model canvas looks like this:

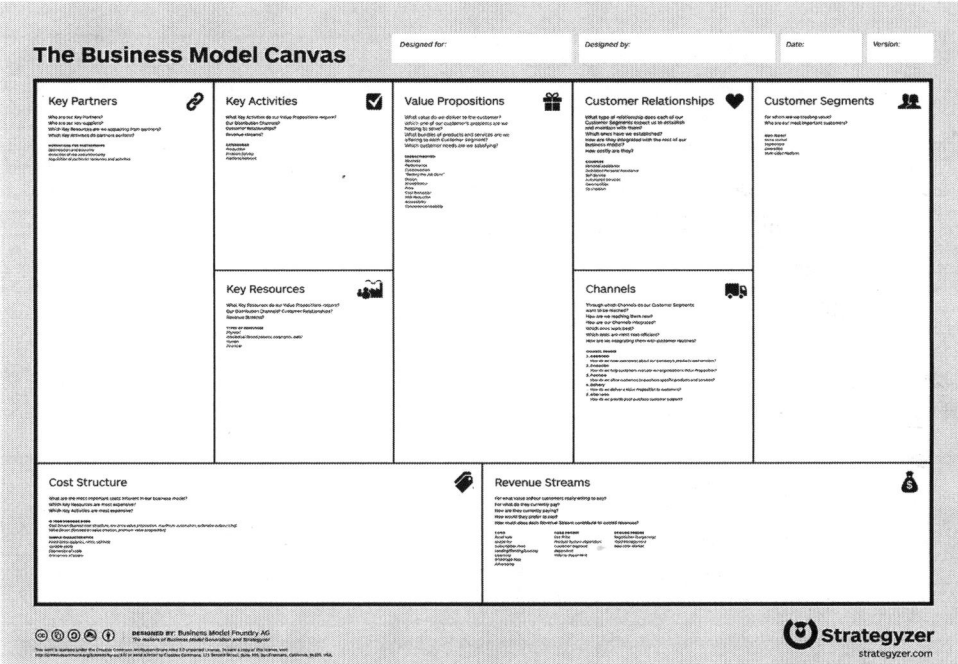

If you look at the Business Model Canvas, you can see that the value proposition is smack dab in the middle. On the right side of the value proposition are the components relating to which group of customers you will target, and how you will communicate with those customers and deliver the product to them. To the left of the value proposition are the components which will work together to produce your product.

The value proposition is in the center because it is the beating heart of the business through which everything flows, and without which the business would not exist. Finding the right value proposition is so important, in fact, that in 2015 Alexander Osterwalder and his team developed a companion to the Business Model Canvas, called the "Value Proposition Canvas."

This is the layout of the Value Proposition Canvas:

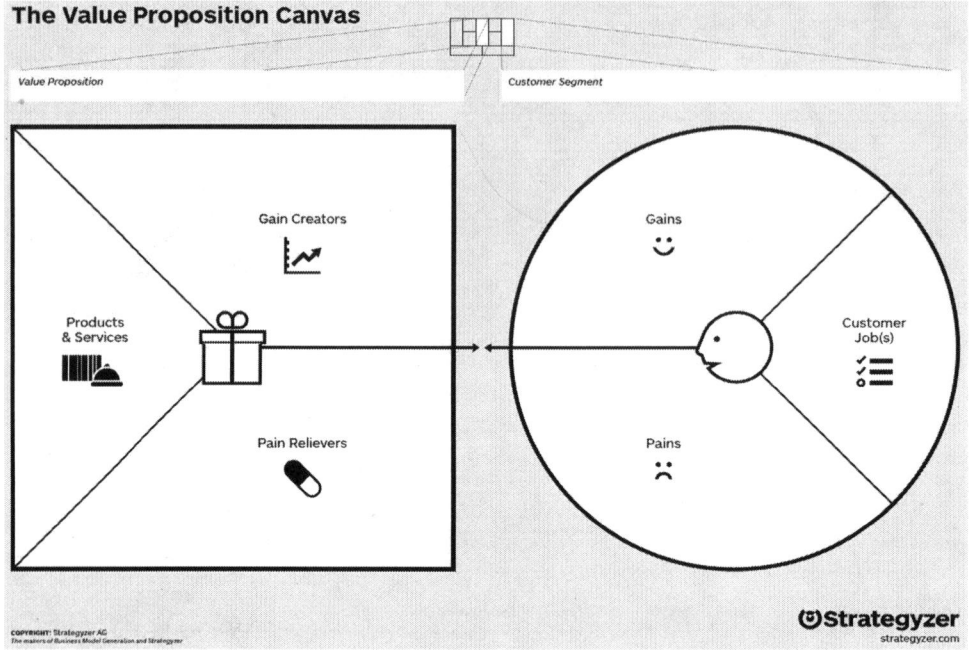

The Value Proposition Canvas is a tool used in conjunction with creating the value proposition and customer segment blocks of the Business Model Canvas, and achieving the proper integrated fit between them.

Let's take a brief look at each building block of the Business Model Canvas to give you an overview, and then we'll get into more detail on both the Business Model Canvas and the Value Proposition Canvas in Part II of this book.

Customer Segments

Most good businesses first identify an important problem or need which is shared by a large number of people, and then develop a product offering that solves their problem or meets their need. The right side of the Value Proposition Canvas is used to identify these problems and needs. "Customer Jobs" describe what customers are trying to get done in their work and in their life. A customer job could be the tasks they are trying to perform and complete, the problems they are trying to solve, or the needs they are trying to satisfy.

"Gains" describe the outcomes customers want to achieve or the concrete benefits they are seeking. "Pains" describe bad outcomes, risks and obstacles related to the customer.

Identifying customer problems and needs is not the only goal of the customer segment building block. An additional goal is to group potential customers into "customer segments" sharing similar characteristics in order to be able to target marketing and also product development efforts towards the specific segment or segments which are most likely to buy the product at a price that will produce the most profit. By targeting a specific customer segment, you are able to efficiently and effectively tailor your product offering to their problems and needs (i.e. pains and gains), and then communicate and distribute your product offering in the same manner to everyone within the targeted segment.

For example, Apple has targeted different customer segments for the iPhone 5, the iPhone 6 and the iPhone 6 Plus. Both the product and marketing message will be different and aimed at converting the target customer for each particular product. The key is to first identify the important need or problem to be solved, and then identify the group or groups of customers with similar relevant characteristics who share that problem or need.

Value Proposition

The group of benefits that you intend to offer your customers in order to solve a problem or satisfy a need that they have is called your "value proposition." These benefits can be either a tangible or intangible aspect of your product—most likely both. And your value proposition encompasses the entirety of the benefits that your business offers your customer, not just the actual product they purchase or service they use. In other words, your value proposition is your overall solution to your customer's problem or need.

On the Value Proposition Canvas, the value proposition is broken down into three parts as well. "Products and Services" are the bundle of products and services that you offer, which your value proposition is built around. "Gain Creators" describe how your products and services create customer gains. "Pain Relievers" describe how your products and services alleviate customer pains. The goal is to achieve "fit" between a customer segments jobs, pains and gains and the gain creators and pain relievers offered as part of your value proposition.

Look at the Evernote website for an example of a good value proposition, where they communicate their "one workspace" value proposition simply and very effectively—"Your life's work: For everything you'll do, Evernote is the workspace to get it done."

Channels

The "channels" referred to by this building block consist of two different types, which often overlap at some point. The first set of channels are the marketing platforms and vehicles by which you will communicate your value proposition to your customers and convince them to buy your product, and then continue to buy in the future. The second is the sales and distribution channels by which you will physically sell your product and deliver it to your customers, such as in-store sales, direct shipping, sales to wholesalers or an Internet download by the customer.

Customer Relationships

Business is all about forming long-term relationships with customers so that they trust your organization and your value proposition enough to make the initial purchase and then become loyal repeat customers over a long period of time. If the marketing "channels" are the vehicles by which you communicate with your customers, then "customer relationships" in this building block are the means and methods you use to form a relationship with customers using those channels. For example, a B2B business may rely on its sales force to develop personal relationships with key individuals at each of its accounts, while a large online retailer like Amazon.com may develop relationships without ever speaking directly to its customers through its website product "suggestions," promotions, online reviews, etc. In other words, this is the manner in which you get the attention of, convert, acquire, retain and grow your customers.

Revenue Streams

There are often many ways to generate revenue from the same product, and they can be both direct and ancillary. The key is to discover what all those potential "revenue streams" are, and then identify which are the most profitable, sustainable and scalable. As part of this process, you need to identify what benefits your target customer segment is willing to pay for, how much they are willing to pay, and when and how they are willing to pay. Examples of different types of revenue streams include revenues from the sale of a product, usage fees, subscription fees, advertising revenue, rental fees, and licensing fees. Remember also that you may have more than one customer segment and/or product offering, and completely different revenue streams coming from those separate groups of people or products.

Key Resources

These are the key physical, intellectual, human and financial assets necessary to produce, offer, deliver and support your product in a profitable and sustainable manner. For example, the "key resources" of the New York Yankees major league baseball team would include its star players (human resources), stadium (physical resources), source of funds to pay its players (financial resources) and brand used to market products such as hats and shirts (intellectual property resources).

Key Activities

These are the key activities that must be undertaken in order to develop, produce, offer, deliver and support your product in a profitable and sustainable manner. For an independent bookstore, these activities may include identifying and sourcing books that will sell the best, creating a website and driving potential customers to that site and then to your place of business, and participating in Amazon.com or other online selling opportunities.

Key Partnerships

No business is an island unto itself. In today's interconnected world, almost all businesses must work together with outside persons in order to create the most effective business model. This may come in the form of supplier relationships, manufacturing partnerships, strategic alliances and joint ventures, sales and distribution agreements, etc.

Cost Structure

Looking at each block in the business model, you need to identify the most important fixed and variable costs that will be incurred. Matching these costs against your revenue streams, you will then be able to assess the potential profitability of your business model. You should also determine the nature of these costs, such as whether they will decrease on a per customer basis due to economies of scale.

That should give you an initial understanding of the Business Model Canvas and Value Proposition Canvas. Just by looking at the canvases and what we've covered already, you can see how each of the blocks must be integrated with all of the others in order for a business model to work efficiently, effectively and profitably. And you can also see how easily you can "mix and match" and go through many iterations of the business model using this technique until you find the business model and value proposition you think will work the best.

Keep in mind, however, that any system is only as good as the way you use it. If you think you can just put your initial ideas in each block and immediately run with them to launch a new business, you would throw away the entire value of the Business Model Canvas technique. Remember, those ideas you have running around your head right now are just that—ideas. And those ideas need to be fleshed out, tested, adjusted, tested once again, and so on. If the process is not iterative and educative, then it has no meaning and is destined to fail, or at minimum not produce optimum results. We'll show you exactly how to do this throughout Part II of this book.

Why Should I Create a Business Plan as Well as a Business Model?

A business plan serves different purposes than a business model. A business plan is where you flesh out and document how you are going to execute your business model—i.e. how you are going to realize the hypothesis that you have proposed in your business model.

Business planning includes the process of setting goals for your business, adopting strategy and tactics to meet those goals, and making financial projections to test the feasibility of doing so. As such it addresses some important areas that are not explicitly considered in great detail during the process of creating a business model—even though there is some overlap between the two. And just like the business model, nothing in the business plan is set in stone. This is also an iterative, trial and error process that requires you to get out from behind your desk and test your assumptions. The business plan is a starting point and measurement tool, a blueprint if you will, but it also needs to be adjusted along the way based on the real world experience of your business.

Keep in mind that in today's business environment, what we term a "business plan" can take many forms, shapes and sizes depending on how it is intended to be used. If it's for a formal proposal to get a bank loan or angel investor capital from people unfamiliar with you or your business, then it may need to be presented in a classic format. But if you're pitching your idea to VCs who are already familiar with you and your business idea, it may take the form of a power point presentation and nothing more. The process is more important than the document. But the document forces an entrepreneur to take the step of getting the ideas out of his or her head and into some form of writing, and that has value as well.

Many people believe that the only reason to write a business plan is to obtain outside funding. However, the number one reason for writing a business plan is that it forces you to thoroughly analyze every important aspect of starting and running your business. It requires focus and clarity as to how you most effectively can realize the potential of your business model and where you want it to take you. This means developing a 3-5 year vision and strategy for your business—which once again will be subject to an ongoing iterative process. But you need to start with a destination in mind and a roadmap of how to get there in the future, otherwise you can easily get off track. The flipside of course is you cannot become too married to your business plan, or else you risk not being flexible and adaptable enough to jump on new opportunities or change course when required. The process requires judgment and balance.

In addition, in order to write a good business plan, you need to take a brutally honest look at the strengths and weaknesses of your business idea, yourself and your organization. During the business planning process, you will inevitably discover flaws in your initial concept, business model, and strategy and tactics that need to be addressed. Finding flaws at this early stage allows you to make any required changes before they become problematic. You will also uncover opportunities that may otherwise have been overlooked, providing you the chance to take advantage of unfilled gaps in the market that may prove to be the difference between success and failure. In addition, your business plan will give you a good estimate of how much cash will be required to run your business until it can generate its own positive cash flow, so you don't run your ship aground before it ever gets out to sea.

Your business plan will also provide clear direction to everyone involved in running your business, so they are all operating from the same playbook and running the same plays. By having a global understanding of the direction and objectives of your business, you will make it easier to achieve management "buy-in" with respect to the goals and strategies you have set out for the business, thereby ensuring that everyone is committed to following your plan for success. This is crucial at the start-up stage, where execution is critical to success and cash is limited. Everyone has to understand and support the strategic priorities and goals that have been adopted, or there is no chance of achieving the follow-through required. This is another good reason why putting these items in writing is such a useful process.

The business plan will provide practical benefits as well. The market research you perform as part of the business planning process, which will most often go beyond what you did in creating your business model, will allow you to gain an even deeper understanding of your industry, market and competition, and lay the groundwork for your all-important marketing plan and the message it will deliver to acquire new customers. Competition is worth a special mention here, because the lack of a specific focus on competition is one of the main criticisms of the Business Model Canvas. In preparing your business plan, you will spend a lot of time understanding the competition inside and out and determining the strengths and weaknesses of their product offerings and organizations, as well as your own with respect to your competitors.

Also, your business plan's financial projections—which will go beyond the rough projections you will make in creating your business model—can be used first as a confirmation that if all goes as planned, you will make the profit your business model hypothesized, and afterwards can provide the foundation for creating your first year budget. These projections can be made under different scenarios, and this helps you prepare for various "what if" situations, adapt quickly if they occur, and make sure you can maintain a viable business at the time. One of the best examples of this, and one which is not directly addressed during the process of creating a business model, is cash flow. Even if a business is profitable, if it doesn't have enough cash flow to pay its bills, it may find itself out of business. The business plan projects cash flows at the beginning, and then subsequent budgets and forecasts update those projections on a regular basis.

Last but not least, your business plan will in fact be your company's primary marketing document when it comes time to raise money from investors, borrow money from lenders, hire key management employees, and enter into strategic relationships. Even if you raise money from a business angel or venture capital fund that you are familiar with, you build credibility through the fact that you have thought through all areas of your operation, as required by a good business plan. Contrary to what you've been told, many will actually read it as well—especially with respect to your business model, financial projections, marketing strategy, management structure and key personnel—and even if they don't, the business planning process will help you convey what they need to hear and have answers for all of their questions.

As such, you need to tailor your business plan to your intended audience and make sure that it clearly and compellingly sells them on your business and answers all their key questions in a manner that convinces them to jump on board. For example, venture capital investors will want to see a clear "exit strategy," or manner in which they will be able to realize and pocket a sufficient return on their investment. Lenders, on the other hand, will be focused on the company's ability to generate enough cash flow to make the principal and interest payments on loans when due. And key hires and strategic partners will want to know that you are strategically and operationally on the same wavelength, and there is a blueprint for success.

The length and style of your business plan is open to debate and will depend on the nature of your business, the intended audience, etc., but because a business plan serves a different purpose than a business model, we highly recommend you write one to clarify the strategy and tactics necessary to implement your business model. And you'll almost definitely need a business plan if you want to raise money from investors or borrow from a bank.

What are the Components of a Good Business Plan?

There are many ways to organize a business plan. Both the layout and content of your plan should be individualized so that it best highlights the most important aspects of your business. And you don't want it to appear directly out of a mold. But regardless of the format you choose to best portray your business model or the strategy and plans you intend to use to execute that model, all good business plans include certain standard categories of information and analysis.

These categories include:

- Executive summary

- Description of the business—including the business model

- Business environment—industry background, market analysis, and competitive analysis

- Marketing plan

- Operations plan

- Management team

- Financial plan and projections

Executive Summary

The executive summary is the most important section of the business plan. It is not a "summary" as the subheading suggests—at least not in the classic sense of the word. The executive summary is a concise and compelling description of the business opportunity you have identified, the strategy, business model and other means you will use to capitalize on that opportunity, the resources you will require, and the potential payoff for those involved. It is the essence of the business plan condensed into 1-3 pages, and whoever reads it should come away with a very good understanding of exactly what your business is about and feel realistically excited about its prospects.

Description of the Business and Business Model

Once you've hooked the readers and given them a targeted understanding of your business in the executive summary, you can walk them through a more thorough review of each component of your business plan, starting with the exciting business opportunity you have identified and the way you intend to take advantage of that opportunity, i.e. a description of your business model and business strategy and the key factors underlying them. This will include a more detailed description of your product offering and overall value proposition, your core competencies and competitive advantages, your goals and objectives, and how you intend to achieve those goals and meet those objectives. Finally, you should describe the key success factors that will determine whether your goals and objectives can be achieved and growth targets met. And if your business will not generate sufficient funds to cover its initial cash requirements, then you need to identify what outside funds will be required, how you intend to raise them, how you intend to use them, and how the investors and/or lenders will be repaid.

The Business Environment

This section is sometimes broken down into separate sections for its three components: industry analysis, market analysis, and competitive analysis. The industry you will be competing in and the market for your products or services are not the same thing: an industry is a group of sellers, while a market is a group of buyers. It is possible for a market for a product to be attractive at the same time the industry supplying that product is not, and vice versa. So you need to understand both your industry and your market in order to assess the opportunities and challenges each present for your business. You also need to understand and describe who your real competition will be, including their strengths and weaknesses. This includes companies that sell the same or similar products to yours within your target market, products that meet the same needs as your product, and potential future competitors doing either.

The Marketing Plan

Once you have completed your industry analysis, market analysis, and competitive analysis, you can use the results to develop a plan that allows you to communicate effectively with the consumers in your target segment, convince them to buy your product, and retain them as loyal customers. Investors know that if you cannot explain how you will efficiently and effectively market your product, then your business will not succeed. You can have the best product in the world, but if nobody knows about it or the people that do know cannot be convinced to buy, the product has no meaning.

The Operations Plan

With respect to your business plan, "operations" consists of everything necessary to convert your idea into a product in your customer's hands. This includes product design and development, purchasing and supplies, manufacturing and production, physical sales and distribution, organization/personnel and accounting systems and controls. In this section of the business plan, you should demonstrate that you have a firm grasp of the process necessary to develop your product and bring it to market in an efficient and cost effective manner that ensures the level of quality and profitability you desire. But the main value of this section, and the analysis that goes into it, is identifying the areas that must be concentrated on to succeed in your business—in particular those areas where you can gain a competitive advantage. Conversely, you need to identify the areas where you may currently lag behind the competition, and develop a plan for either getting up to speed or compensating for your weakness.

The Management Team

When analyzing your company, investors will not only look to see whether you have a good idea and a large target market, they will closely assess whether you and your management team can execute on that idea and build a valuable business around it. They know that without the right people, even the best business idea will wither on the vines and their funds will go down the drain. You will begin this section by providing background on each member of your senior management team, including their educational and employment history. Your focus, however, will be on what their responsibilities are in your business and what qualities they bring to the table that will help you succeed.

The Financial Plan & Projections

Last, but definitely not least, is a description of your financial plan and financial projections. This is where you provide the projected funding needs and financial results of putting your business plan into effect, and discuss the meaning and ramifications of those numbers for your business. As with the rest of the business plan, the most important reason for putting together these financial projections is for your own internal planning purposes. They can serve as the basis for your budget, allow you to gauge how much extra cash you need to raise, and provide a measure of how you are doing with respect to your plan once actual results start to flow in.

In addition to becoming the primary barometer of your internal planning process, the financial projections you create for your business plan will allow potential investors and lenders to analyze whether your business model, if properly executed, will provide them with a sufficient rate of return on their investment. If the business will not generate sufficient cash, reach profitability soon enough, or create enough value to make an exit strategy viable, they will wish you good luck and move on. But if your forecasted financial results will achieve these three goals in a credible manner, you may find yourself with a feeding frenzy of investors at your door.

You should now be able to see that while there is overlap between the business model and business plan, they are not the same animal and serve very different purposes. Both of those sets of purposes are important. The key is to be fast and efficient, while at the same time smart and thorough, in discovering the best business model to use and then in creating a business plan to execute that model.

Now that you have an overview and can see how the business modeling and business planning process fit together, and what is involved in each, it's time to get busy and make these things happen. The sooner and faster you do so, the sooner and faster you'll be out there in the market.

But first, we'd like to introduce you to a case study that we will refer to throughout the book to demonstrate how the business modeling and business planning processes play out in actual practice.

LinksBuddy Case Study

Chapter 1
Introduction

Steven Duffer is a professional golf instructor who works in a prestigious resort located in Napa Valley, California. He is keen on starting a business of his own, but has yet to come up with a feasible idea that combines his love for golf and other sports with his experience and interest in the hospitality and tourism industry.

Steven has been invited to play a round of golf with a friend and client at the prestigious and very private San Francisco Golf Club. The invite has come from Peter Programmer, a successful software entrepreneur who frequents Steven's course. Like many of the other regular golfers at the resort, Peter lives and works in the Silicon Valley, about a two hour drive from Napa. Peter has also offered to put Steven up in his carriage house during the visit.

The weekend arrives and Steven makes the short trip from his home in Napa to the San Francisco Gulf Club. After a great afternoon on the links with Peter, they both retire to the clubhouse for a drink. While sipping a cocktail and looking out over the veranda, Steven thinks out loud how great it would be if avid golfers like him could travel around the world, stay in the homes of other golfing enthusiasts like Peter, share experiences and knowledge, and play all the best clubs.

"Make it happen!" Peter says.

"What do you mean?" Steven asks.

"You've been looking to start a hospitality business in the golfing niche, right?" Peter replies. "Maybe this is the idea you've been looking for?"

"Kind of like Airbnb for golfers?" Steven wonders.

Peter nods his head and rubs his fingers together in considered thought.

"Do you have any idea how much a business like Airbnb is worth?" Peter asks rhetorically. "A lot! I'll tell you what, give the idea some proper consideration, flesh it out and come back to me in a month with a business model. If it works, I'll help you write your business plan and introduce you to some of my investor buddies in the Silicon Valley."

Steven feels a rush of adrenalin and his mind races with visions of a worldwide golfing network. But he quickly catches himself and sinks back down into his chair.

"What's a business model?" he asks. "Isn't it the same thing as a business plan?"

Peter shakes his head, realizing that his new protégée has some getting-up-to-speed to do if he wants to enter the start-up business world.

"No, it's not," Peter says. "Tomorrow we'll go down to Half Moon Bay for another round of golf and dinner and I'll give you the low down on creating a business model. If you're still interested after that, I'm happy to meet with you once a week to walk you through what you need to know and do in order to create a good business model and write a good business plan. But you're the one who will need to go out and get it done. Nobody can do it for you ... you have to make it happen yourself."

The next morning Steven and Peter make a short trip down the coast from San Francisco, where they golf at Half Moon Bay Golf Links. Afterwards they dine at sunset on fresh local artichoke soup and wood plank Pacific salmon at a hidden gem of a restaurant.

"Local knowledge of restaurants, music clubs, attractions ... that's another benefit of staying with host golfers," Steven notes. "Not to mention the cultural exchange that takes place. Maybe this could become a highlight of my new business as well? But first things first Peter—what is this 'business model' you were talking about?"

"This restaurant is a good example," Peter says. "Here we are, 40 miles from any major population center, but the place is full every night. Why? Because they have a good business model that they execute with a good business plan."

Peter explains that the restaurant offers a combination of attributes that both tourists and local San Francisco Bay Area residents value enough to travel a long distance and pay a pretty penny to experience. It's value proposition includes a quiet, away-from-it-all location with a stunning ocean view, combined with gourmet local dishes made with fresh local products, and it's situated on a historical site that gives customers the sense of a unique Pacific Coast experience. In addition, the restaurant owners have hired a top chef and an experienced maitre d' who know their best customers by name, have effectively exploited the competitive advantage of a beautiful location steeped in local atmosphere, and have spent money refurbishing and maintaining the structure and its surroundings in order to do so.

"There are many excellent restaurants in San Francisco, but it's becoming harder to find a great dining experience in a unique out-of-the way setting that isn't too far from the city. This place has accomplished that and met important needs of a lot of people."

To communicate with and acquire customers, the restaurant has partnered with hotels and travel agencies in the Bay Area, and to obtain the best food products at a reasonable price, they have partnered with local produce sellers, who the owners have known since childhood—another competitive advantage. Finally, they have a sophisticated website and Internet marketing strategy and many promotions aimed at achieving repeat customers and word of mouth recommendations. And they track the data from this website and customer reviews on other sites, as well as conduct informal "interviews" with customers visiting the restaurant, in order to know their clients inside and out.

"All of these pieces are important," Peter says. "If you take any one away, the business may turn from highly profitable to unprofitable. The business model is the difference between this restaurant, where we had to book two days in advance to get a table, and the one a couple of miles down the coast that serves a great meal but is half empty right now and probably will be out of business in six months."

The restaurant they are sitting in, Peter continues, has fully exploited all of its core competencies and competitive advantages to its benefit, and to the detriment of competitors who either don't possess the same features or haven't managed to exploit them properly. These competitive advantages differentiate their business and convince customers to dine in their restaurant rather than others located nearby and/or allow them to make a better profit margin than their competitors can achieve. The specific advantages may lie in one or more particular components of the restaurant's business model such as the quality of their food or overall service; or it may lie in how each of the components interacts with each other, or ideally in both.

"Let me give you another example that you can relate to," Peter says. "Look at the components of a golf swing … and think about them as an analogy for the components of a business model. The club selection, the set-up, the takeaway, the backswing, the downswing, the follow-through, and the player's overall course management are all important aspects of producing a 'profitable' and repeatable swing each and every time and over the duration of many rounds of golf over many years. All of these components need to work together, and if any is deficient then the swing will be less profitable and less sustainable."

"In order to create the most profitable golf swing," he continues, "a true professional uses an iterative learning process. First he or she will analyze the swing in relation to their own physical attributes and determine the areas where each component can either be changed or improved. This is their blueprint for success, the equivalent of creating a business model for their golf swing. Then they will first practice and test that model, making changes and improvements where necessary. After they think they have a good working model, they will test it once again in competitive rounds of golf. This will undoubtedly reveal other areas where improvement is possible, and they will go back and tweak the model as necessary, or overhaul it if it just isn't working. Once you have your swing model down and tested, then you can start to plan how to use that swing to score well and win tournaments on the golf course."

"I think you can see clearly that if a golfer just goes out on the course and plays competitive rounds without taking the time to establish a swing model and test that swing, then the chances of success are much lower—and the process will take much longer with many more severe failures along the way. The same goes for starting a new business. First you need to test and validate your model, then you can develop a plan to launch in the marketplace."

"OK, I get it," Steven says. "So how do I go about figuring out my business model? Can we do it this afternoon? I've got so many ideas already!"

"I like your enthusiasm," Peter says. "And the fact that you have a lot of ideas is one of the reasons you need to go through the process of identifying the best business model for your initial concept. Let your ideas flow—and give them some more thought. Then come back in two weeks and I'll tell you about the Business Model Canvas, which, in my experienced opinion, is the best technique for generating a business model. After that you can get started on your own model."

Fast but smart, Peter advises Steven, is the best way to proceed.

"The first thing I want you to do is immerse yourself in your business idea," Peter says. "In the next two weeks I want you to do some research and learn everything you can about the business you want to start, the industry you want to dive into and the market you want to attract."

CHAPTER 2:
LAYING A FOUNDATION FOR SUCCESS

Chapter Overview

Laying a Foundation for Success 28
Getting Up to Speed: Conducting Your Initial Market Research 30
      Secondary Research 34
      Primary Research 36
      Who Should Do the Research? 38
      Forming Your Business Modeling Team 38
LinksBuddy Case Study 41

CHAPTER 2

LAYING A FOUNDATION FOR SUCCESS

At this point you are likely eager to dive right into creating your Business Model Canvas. But before you do so, there are certain steps you should take to ensure you are prepared to successfully complete your business model and business plan, as well as launch and run a successful business.

To begin with, prior to starting to create a business model you should have a firm idea in mind of the type of business you want to create and your personal goals for that business, as well as a firm understanding of the market you are entering. This means taking a thorough look at what you want to accomplish with your business and the values you want to employ when doing so. It also means putting in the time and effort to perform research and educate yourself on the business you are getting involved in. Each of these steps will save you a lot of time and frustration during the business modeling and planning process.

Writing Your Vision, Mission and Values Statements

A good starting point for the business modeling and planning process is to express in concise written statements exactly what your business is about, what it intends to achieve and the value it intends to provide its customers, and how it intends to go about doing so.

These statements are called the vision statement, mission statement, and values statement.

Your "vision statement" signifies the type of business you intend to create, i.e. what you want your business to become. Think about the reasons you are going into your particular business and the primary goals you want to achieve. Then put those goals into a single sentence—or a few at the most—that encapsulates your vision.

One good example is Amazon.com's vision statement: "Our vision is to be earth's most customer centric company; to build a place where people can come to find and discover anything they might want to buy online."

The "mission statement" is customer oriented. Here you state precisely what your line of business is, the benefits you will provide to your customers and the manner in which you will satisfy their needs which sets you apart from the competition.

CVS Corporation, which has thousands of retail pharmacy stores in the United States, boiled their mission statement down to one simple sentence: "We will be the easiest pharmacy retailer for customers to use."

Can you see how every aspect of their business can be focused on and built around this statement? Your goal should be to write a mission statement upon which you can do the same.

Sometimes, by the way, companies combine their vision and mission statements into the same statement.

A "values statement" identifies an organization's core set of beliefs and the qualities that it prioritizes over all others. You can use your values statement to clearly identify the manner in which you want to realize your vision and accomplish your mission.

Most often, values statements will have both ethical and performance components, creating a corporate culture based on qualities that foster success, while at the same time setting ethical guidelines for accomplishing such success.

For example, the global pharmaceutical company Merck has adopted the following values statement:

"At Merck, we do business on the basis of common values. Our success is based on courage, achievement, responsibility, respect, integrity, and transparency. These values determine our actions in our daily dealing with customers and business partners as well as in our teamwork and our collaboration with each other."

You will most definitely hone and adjust your vision and mission statements as you discover the best business model and write your business plan, but your values statement should remain constant.

Once your vision, mission, and values statements are finalized, you can shine every other aspect of your business through their collective prism in order to create your business model, set your goals and strategies, and write your business plan. And on the flipside, everything contained in your model, goals and strategies, and plan should be in sync with and designed to achieve what is contained in your three key statements.

In other words, these statements though brief are very important and should be considered extremely carefully.

Getting Up to Speed: Conducting Your Initial Market Research

Once you've given some initial hard thought as to the type of business you want to create, before you start working on your Business Model Canvas you should take a crash course in the market and industry you want to enter. As we mentioned in Chapter 1, the building blocks of the canvas are actually a series of hypothesis, or guesses. It's much more efficient to make your initial guesses as educated as possible. So now is a good time to immerse yourself in as much relevant knowledge as possible regarding your chosen line of business.

Market research is not a one-time event—it is an ongoing process of different levels undertaken at different times when creating a new business. In general, this can be broken down into four different phases of market research:

- **Phase I: Initial Market Research**—This is where the founders and initial employees learn as much as possible about the market and industry they are entering in order to efficiently develop the best business model possible.

- **Phase II: Hypothesis Testing**—Nearly every item listed in one of the nine building blocks of the Business Model Canvas will be a hypothesis that needs to be tested by some form of market research. During this phase, the founder and his or her team will design tests, and then get in direct contact with potential customers and business partners in order to either validate their initial hypotheses or collect feedback allowing them to learn, gain valuable insights, and make proper adjustments to the hypotheses.

- **Phase III: Marketing Plan Research**—Once the business model is decided upon, a marketing plan must be created to execute that business model. A good marketing plan will require in-depth knowledge of the customer segments, the market, the industry, the competition, and every aspect of the business model. Much of this information will already have been acquired during the initial market research in Phase I and the hypothesis testing in Phase II, but additional market research is most often necessary.

- **Phase IV: Ongoing Market Research**—Market research, including testing, does not end once the business is launched and the product is being sold. It is a continuous process of staying abreast of the customers' problems and needs, the competition, trends, etc. in order to keep the business model optimized and be able to pivot quickly when the environment changes.

Market research can be broken down into two categories: primary and secondary market research. Primary research is material that you directly acquire yourself or hire someone else to directly acquire for you. Secondary research is material that others have collected and published. Both types of research can be based on quantitative data (can be measured in numbers) or qualitative data (descriptions and opinions that cannot be measured in numbers).

Primary research will give you information directly from potential customers about such matters as who they are, what problems and needs they have, what type of solution they would be interested in buying to solve their problems and/or satisfy their needs, what they would be willing to pay for that product, how they can be reached, and how they would expect to purchase the product.

Secondary research will give you the information needed to analyze the market you are entering and the competition you will face, such as the market share held by companies already existing in the market, their marketing strategies, etc.

Right now you're just in the beginning phase of initial market research. So you need to perform your research with the goal of collecting and analyzing as much information as possible about the industry your are entering, the market for your product, your potential customers, and your competitors to allow you to productively begin work on creating your business model using the Business Model Canvas. This means that at this point, before you begin working on your Business Model Canvas, your research will be mostly secondary—although it never hurts to get out and speak with as many people as possible to get initial direct feedback as well.

A threshold question that should be answered during your initial market research is: *what is the estimated size and growth potential of the market you wish to enter.* If you discover that the market for your products will not be big enough to make it worthwhile producing and selling the product you have in mind, then now is a much better time than later to reassess, pivot and revise your business and product idea. One way to make this initial assessment is to determine your total addressable market (TAM), serviceable available market (SAM), and serviceable obtainable market (SOM). TAM is the total market demand for your product. SAM is the segment of TAM which you will target and is within your geographical reach. SOM is the portion of SAM that you can capture. These quantitative pieces of data will give you the upside potential of your market, as well as its ceiling.

Once you've answered that threshold question, the secondary research you conduct during first phase of initial market research will be geared towards obtaining the background necessary to make well-informed initial hypothesis for your Business Model Canvas, as well as properly formulate questions for your primary research and target the right subjects during the Hypothesis Testing phase. Therefore, you need to become as much of an expert on the line of business you wish to enter as possible.

The operative question now is: *what do I need to know in order to generate good initial hypotheses for our Business Model Canvas?* The type of information you should gather in your Phase I initial market research effort includes the:

- Problems and needs of your potential customers and the solutions available to them

- Size and nature of the overall market for your product

- Size and nature of the market segments within that overall market

- Size and nature of the customer segment(s) that you think you will target

- Demand for your product within each segment, and the nature of that demand (e.g. is it a "must have" product)

- Growth potential of the overall market and each market segment

- Demographics, tastes, expectations, and buying habits of your target customers, such as:

  - Their personal characteristics, including age, gender, level of income, etc.

  - Their spending habits

  - Where they live; how you can get their attention; and what convinces them to buy

  - What product they want; when they want it; where they want it delivered; and at what price they will buy it

- Unique selling points that you can use to differentiate your product from the competition

- Price elasticity of your product

- Proven viable business models for profitably creating and selling your type of product

- Direct and indirect competition, including how they perform on all of these same questions

- Market share held by each competitor

- Potential market share for your product

- Barriers to entry

- Trends in the market and external trends that will affect the market

- Resources required to enter the market

- Strengths and weaknesses of your potential business, as well as the opportunities and threats you will face

Gather and absorb all the information you can, particularly about the size of the market, the characteristics of your potential customers, and the competition—such as competing value propositions and the business models already in use by other companies in your line of business. Then during the business modeling process, you can use this information to drill down and identify the best target segment to pursue, the product features that will convince consumers in that segment to buy from you, and the best way to create a business that generates a sustainable profit.

As an overview, here is a more detailed description of the type of secondary and primary research you may want to conduct during the four phases of market research. The methods you use, and balance between primary and secondary materials used, will depend on the phase and the goals of your research.

Secondary Research

The purpose of secondary research in Phase I initial market research is to learn everything you can about your industry, your market and potential customers, and the competition. Doing so will answer threshold questions, such as market size and potential, that will give you a strong indication as to whether or not your business idea is worth pursuing. It will also allow you to make the most educated guesses possible when creating your initial Business Model Canvas.

Sources of information can be found on the Internet and in local and university libraries, particularly business school libraries. Material can also be ordered from government departments, industry and trade associations, and business data providers. If possible, you should also obtain material from specialists who follow the industry, such as research reports written by analysts working for securities brokerage firms.

Here are some secondary research resources available on the Internet:

- Business.Com—www.business.com

- Fuld & Company—www.fuld.com

- Standard & Poors—www.standardandpoors.com

- Small Business Administration—www.sba.com

- Hoover's—www.hoovers.com

- Dun & Bradstreet Reports—www.dnb.com

- Thomson Research—http://research.thomsonib.com

- Value Line—www.valueline.com

- The U.S. Census Bureau—www.census.gov

- The U.S. Securities and Exchange Commission ("SEC")—www.sec.gov

- The Federal Trade Commission ("FTC")—www.ftc.gov

In addition, track down as many relevant business periodicals as possible, whether online or in hard copy, and look to resources such as: *Dun & Bradstreet Industry Handbook*; *Encyclopedia of Global Industries*; *U.S. Industry and Trade Outlook*; *Handbook of North American Industry*; *Statistical Abstract of the United States;* and *Encyclopedia of Emerging Industries.*

To locate a trade association that reports on your proposed business, look to the *Encyclopedia of Associations* (Gale Research) and the *Encyclopedia of Business Information Sources* (Gale Group). You should also seek out academics who are experts with respect to your industry and highly regarded professionals in the field.

At first glance, conducting market research among all of these dry sounding publications may sound like a dreary proposition. But not only is this a highly beneficial exercise, it is a test of whether you are truly passionate about your business idea and becoming an entrepreneur—because if you are, you will devour every piece of related information you can find.

As a starting point for all of this, you can perform simple Internet searches to gather information on similar products that are already on the market, the size of the market you wish to enter, and the nature and number of potential competitors.

Once you've determined who your competitors will be, visit their websites to gain information on their products, services, customers, pricing, and positioning. Don't be satisfied, however, with performing online research as your only source of information on competitors. Get out and visit their stores, go to trade shows, and speak with their customers, vendors, and other people they do business with. Also look at their advertisements, which will reveal quite a bit about their business strategy, value propositions and target customers.

Using the secondary research material you have gathered as a base, you can first make the hypothesis for your Business Model Canvas. Afterwards you can turn to primary research and meet with your potential customers to validate or iterate your Business Model canvas hypothesis, determine whether there will be high enough and enthusiastic enough demand for your product, find out what particular solutions/product characteristics they value most, discover at what price they are willing to buy, etc.

Primary Research

Once you've obtained a good understanding of your market and industry through secondary research and filled out your initial Business Model Canvas, it will be time to interact a large number of potential customers about whether they would buy your product, under what circumstances, and at what price.

As we will discuss in detail in the following chapters, this will be a critically important piece of the business modeling and business planning processes.

The keys to primary research are properly designed tests and questions to be used in interviews, experiments, surveys, etc. If you ask the wrong questions of the wrong people in the wrong way, you will receive information that is worse than useless—it will form the foundation of bad decisions at the critical stage of starting your new business. As the old adage goes: garbage in, garbage out.

Primary research consists mainly of:

- Interviews
- Experiments (tests designed to validate or invalidate a hypothesis)
- Surveys and questionnaires
- Focus groups

Real-time interviews can be conducted in person, over the telephone, or online. Experiments can be designed to measure relationships, causality, etc. Surveys and questionnaires, and questions asked during interviews, may be closed-ended or open-ended. Closed-ended questions provide users specific answers to choose from for each question—the old multiple choice we've all been familiar with since grade school—whereas open-ended questions allow the participant to choose their own response, which may provide valuable insights going beyond what a closed-ended question would elicit.

Focus groups can be sophisticated and formal, conducted in a controlled environment by trained behavioral specialists, or unsophisticated and informal, consisting of an entrepreneur exposing family, friends, and business associates to a potential product, service, or message. One advantage of focus groups is that they are interactive. You can give participants hands-on experience with your product, give them your marketing pitch, throw out different product features or pricing options, and then observe and record how they react. In general, however, one-on-one interviews are a preferred form of direct interaction if possible.

For example, if you've developed a new mosquito repellant, give it to 20 people and ask them to track where and when they used it, and how effective it was. Then interview each of them about their experience, documenting exactly what they liked and didn't like about all aspects of the product. And that means all aspects. Interviews and focus groups allow you to discover the problems and needs customers really care about and the features, design, positioning, and marketing message that will best appeal to them.

Who Should Do the Research?

A key decision is whether to conduct the primary and secondary research yourself or hire a market research specialist to do the work. Good research firms and consultants do not come cheap, with the price escalating if more detailed, current, and local knowledge is sought.

As a new business, it is very important that you and your fellow founders have direct contact with customers in order to get feedback from them personally. In addition, you will probably not have the resources to hire a professional outside firm to perform extensive and detailed primary research, so you'll need to get creative in order to gain an adequate sense of your target customers' characteristics, tastes, and buying habits.

One possibility is to get students from a local university business school to help out. Another alternative is to hire a data collection firm that conducts the interviews and prepares, distributes, and collects the surveys and questionnaires, but then simply hands you the raw data to analyze yourself. You can also conduct online surveys in many different formats. Many companies now provide the service of either conducting online research for you or providing the tools for you to conduct your own online survey.

But these options should be used for data collection tasks that would be impractical for you to perform yourself. When it comes to getting in front of customers, direct personal contact is an absolute must while you are creating your Business Model Canvas.

Forming Your Business Modeling Team

One key action you will need to take before beginning the business modeling process is deciding who will constitute your initial team which takes part in creating your Business Model Canvas. Don't take this decision lightly. Who you bring on board at this point will not only impact your business model, it could have long-term implications for your business. So you need to make your choices carefully and wisely.

Much of this will depend on the size and nature of your business. If you are starting a very small business, then you and your fellow founders (if any) may be able to do the business modeling and planning on your own. But even under these circumstances, you may want to bring an experienced hand or two on board to help you brainstorm and act as a sounding board when it comes time to make key decisions. In the event you have a co-founder, then the decision of who to involve at this stage will be made for you. But again, depending on each founder's level of experience, you may want to enlist someone with experience in your industry and market to advise you during the process.

But the real choice you need to make is whether it is a good idea to involve individuals who may constitute your key employees going forward. This is not as straightforward a decision as it may seem. The reason, as we will discuss in Chapter 16 dealing with management personnel, is that the nature and timing of key hires when starting a business is often critical. On the one hand, you want the right people on board to form your business and develop and launch your product, while on the other hand, you want to be lean and cost-efficient, not top heavy and costly, during the start-up phase—i.e. not loaded down with expensive personnel until after you've tested your business model in the actual marketplace and are now ready to scale your business. This is very important, as scaling to soon can drag the entire enterprise down.

The other thing you need to make sure of is that if you hire someone to fill a critical position for your business, you absolutely get the right person. So while if you know a certain individual will be involved in your business going forward at a senior level, then it is good to have them involved in creating your business model and business plan. But you don't want to jump to soon and hire the wrong person. Then you may end up creating a business model together with someone who is not involved at the launch of your product!

Welcome to the world of business. Nothing is black and white—everything is some shade of gray. It is all about judgment, decision making, timing and action.

That being said, when forming your initial team at the business modeling and planning stage, you should keep a couple of things in mind. First, the experience, talents, skills and temperament necessary for key employees in startup businesses are not the same as those required for larger mature businesses. Individuals must be able to deal with a fast-paced, often-changing environment where decisions are made and acted upon quickly. Second, look to create a team that brings a diverse experience, knowledge and skill set to the table.

In addition, you want to stock your team with individuals that balance the customer development and product development sides of the ledger, and who are willing and able to interact with their counterparts. On the customer development side, you want people who are able to interact personally and with an open mind with customers, and then have the ability to analyze and incorporate the information they receive into an improved business model. As you will see in Part II, this will be crucial when testing and validating the hypothesis in your Business Model Canvas and Value Proposition Canvas. On the product development side, you of course want people who have the technical and operational ability to execute—to develop the desired product on spec, on time and on budget. But you also want individuals who are willing and able to buy into the business modeling process, taking input from the customer development team based on what they learn when testing the hypothesis with real customers.

In other words, your business modeling team must integrate as well as your business model.

> **LinksBuddy Case Study**
>
> ## Chapter 2
> ## Getting Started
>
> Steven did his homework, and two weeks after their last meeting he arrives at Peter's home office with a big smile on his face. He has spent every moment of his free time researching the golf tourism industry and market, thinks he's really onto something with his concept, and can't wait to get started on creating his business model.
>
> "I was completely wrong," Steven says. "Within a day I realized that I actually knew almost nothing about the business I was getting into and what companies in this business have to do and contend with to succeed."
>
> "Such as?" Peter asks.
>
> "To begin with, my business sits at the intersection of a number of different industries and they're all going in different directions right now," Steven replies. "There's the golf industry, the hospitality industry, and the travel and tourism industry, which all come together in the golf tourism industry. And then there's the peer-to-peer marketplace industry and the sharing economy, which is really what I want to tap into and where my main learning curve is going to be."
>
> "What about your market?" Peter asks. "Is it big enough to justify your leaving your career as a golf pro and jumping into this business? Would you be able to convince an investor that the market is big enough to justify financing your company?"
>
> Steven tells Peter that he sees his Total Available Market (TAM), as being every person who travels and plays golf as part of their trip, regardless of whether they are traveling primarily to play golf or for multiple purposes. Each of these persons could potentially use the LinksBuddy platform to find their accommodation for the trip. This is a very large market, and despite the economic challenges of the last few years and the stagnancy in the overall golf market in the US during that time, the market continues

to grow. If Steven could capture even a small percentage of this market he could have a viable business.

"That's the key question," Peter says. "You're talking about a diverse world-wide market. So what portion of that market to you think you have a fighting chance to capture? Do you really think that all golf tourists would be willing to stay in a private residence on their excursion? Do you really think your business would have worldwide reach?"

"Initially," Steven replies, "the answers to those questions are no and no. But I believe in the future that can change to yes and yes."

Certainly not every golf tourist would be willing to stay in private accommodation, Steven acknowledges. For many reasons, a large percentage will continue to prefer to stay in hotels and resorts: some will want to maintain privacy, many will travel in groups too large to stay in someone's home, some will desire resort destinations where private accommodation isn't available, etc. But Steven does believe that there will remain a large enough market of persons who would be willing to stay in a fellow golfer's home to build a sizeable business around, and that his market will expand as peer-to-peer travel expands.

"Especially since other companies in the peer-to-peer accommodation sector, namely Airbnb, are making this type of travel a normal option in many people's mind," Steven says.

Geography, however, will be another challenge. Steven is unsure how his business idea will play across different countries and cultures. And he is beginning to glimpse that building this business will probably require him to focus on a few select geographic areas at a time, at least initially, rather than attempting a world-wide roll-out. He will also be competing with golf tour operators and accommodation providers who will fight tooth and nail to make sure that what Airbnb has done to the hotel industry overall does not happen to them in this niche.

So initially, his Serviceable Available Market (SAM), will be much smaller than this TAM—although his potential SAM will be quite large if he ever reaches critical mass and can operate nationally and then internationally. Similarly, his Serviceable Obtainable Market (SOM) will be very limited at the beginning, but potentially quite large if his business takes off.

"The bottom line," Steven says, "is that I believe there is a sufficient market for this business if I can make it happen. But I've also realized that I'm going to need help … I can't do this on my own."

Steven tells Peter that he'd like to bring a close friend, Martin Marketer, on board as his co-founder. Martin is the director of marketing at Steven's resort in Napa and has extensive experience in the golf tourism industry and hospitality industry, as well as in internet marketing. Steven would also like to approach a sales professional he is acquainted with, and a partner in the resort's public accounting firm, to round out his initial team.

"Get Martin," Peter advices. "But he's all you need right now. You need to prove your concept first; prove that you can create a business model that will drive a profitable, repeatable, and sustainable business in this space. Only after that should you start thinking of building a full-blown management team to execute your business model."

Steven reluctantly agrees to limit the size of his initial team, and turns his attention to the Business Model Canvas, which he wants to complete ASAP.

"The good news," Steven says, "is that my initial market research has given me an exponentially greater number of ideas about how to model my business. I can't wait to get started on the canvas. With all my new knowledge, I think we can knock this out in an afternoon."

Peter once again sinks back down into his chair.

"You could do that," Peter replies. "In fact, you could do it in an hour if you really wanted. But that would defeat the entire purpose of the Business Model Canvas, and you'd really be no further along towards finding the optimum business model for your business—or validating the one you apparently have in your head already."

"I don't understand," Steven says. "It all seems pretty straightforward and I've got most of it worked out in my head already."

"It is straightforward," Peter says. "And that's the beauty of the Business Model Canvas. But it's not easy, it's not linear, and it's not a one attempt, one afternoon process."

To lift Steven's confidence once more, Peter points out everything he has accomplished in a short period of time. In fact, Steven already has all the preliminary pieces in place that are necessary to begin filling out the Business Model Canvas: he has a business idea he is passionate about, has visualized the type of business he wants to create and the values he will bring to the table, has educated himself on the industry and market and the competition, and has put himself in the right frame of mind.

PART II

CREATING A BUSINESS MODEL USING THE BUSINESS MODEL CANVAS

CHAPTER 3:
HOW TO USE THE BUSINESS MODEL CANVAS

Chapter Overview

How to Use the Business Model Canvas 48
Downloading the Business Model Canvas 49
Getting in the Right Frame of Mind 50
Brainstorming and Idea Generation 52
Selecting Your Initial Business Model Hypothesis 53
Testing Your Business Model Hypothesis 55
      What is the Best Sequence for Testing and Validating Your Business Model? 56
      Developing Tests for Your Hypothesis 58
      Generating a List of Potential Customers for Face-to-Face Meetings 61
      Contacting Potential Customers for Face-to-Face Meetings 62
      Meeting with Potential Customers, Presenting Your Hypothesis and Obtaining Feedback 63
Learning from Customer Feedback—Revising Your Hypothesis—Iterating Testing 64
Validating Your Business Model 66
Executing Your Business Model and Iterating Once Again . . . and Again 67
LinksBuddy Case Study 69

CHAPTER 3

HOW TO USE THE BUSINESS MODEL CANVAS

The Business Model Canvas is the best tool available to help you visualize and work through a creative and iterative process intended to discover and validate the optimum business model—which 99 percent of the time is not the first one that pops into your head. While you want to achieve the end result as fast as possible without getting bogged down in over-analyzing and over-researching, you can't take shortcuts or you won't get the desired outcome.

In order to illustrate what is meant by iterative, as well as how the creative business modeling process unfolds and is validated, it is helpful to get a bird's eye overview of the proper way to use the Business Model Canvas. To give you that overview, in this chapter we'll walk you through the following phases of using this business modeling technique:

- Downloading the Business Model Canvas
- Getting in the right frame of mind
- Brainstorming and generating ideas
- Selecting your *initial* business model hypotheses
- Testing your business model hypotheses
- Learning from customer feedback
- Revising your business model hypotheses

- Testing your revised business model and iterating once again … and again

- Validating your business model

- Executing your business model while continuing to test and iterate

Remember that this chapter is just an overview. We will get into more detail about each phase in the subsequent chapters, which will cover the individual building blocks of the Business Model Canvas.

Downloading the Business Model Canvas

The first practical step to take is to obtain an actual Business Model Canvas to work with. There are three easy methods of downloading and using the Business Model Canvas, as well as the Value Proposition Canvas:

- **Sticky notes:** download, print out and enlarge the Business Model Canvas and Value Proposition Canvas; then use sticky notes to fill in the building blocks in a flexible and visual manner

- **Download free applications:** search the internet and download a free Business Model Canvas and Value Proposition Canvas application which allows you to fill in the building blocks on your computer

- **Purchase the Strategyzer Web App:** this application provides the most sophisticated and flexible method of filling in the building blocks and using both the Business Model Canvas and the Value Proposition Canvas—but it's not free

Founded by the creators of the Business Model Canvas and Value Proposition Canvas, Strategyzer creates tools to help you design, test and manage value propositions and business models. All three of the above methods of using the Business Model Canvas and Value Proposition Canvas can be accessed at the Strategyzer/businessmodelgeneration.com websites: https://strategyzer.com/ and http://www.businessmodelgeneration.com/.

The advantages to the "old-fashioned" method of a poster and sticky notes are that the canvases are easy to create, there are no computer applications to be learned, it leads to a creative and engaging environment for groups, and it's free other than the cost of pen and paper. The main disadvantage is that you will likely go through quite a few iterations of your canvases, as you will see throughout this chapter, and will want to keep track of each iteration to see how your business model evolves. This will be cumbersome using the large poster and sticky note method.

The advantages of the computer-aided canvases are the ease in which you can create, revise and compare many iterations of the canvases along with accompanying notes and information. They also allow your team to work from separate locations if necessary. And the more elaborate Strategyzer package will allow you to use design and analysis tools to assist in your business model creation process.

Once you have a Business Model Canvas and Value Proposition Canvas to work with, it's time to begin brainstorming and filling in those building blocks. But we recommend first taking a short amount of time to make sure you are approaching this process with the right perspective.

Getting in the Right Frame of Mind

In order to get the most out of the Business Model Canvas from the word go, you should visualize the process and what you want to accomplish. This may sound obvious, but it's important to have that sense of the whole, the direction you want to go and what you want to accomplish.

The first thing to do is to review your vision, mission and values statements that we covered in Chapter 2, and then keep them firmly in mind throughout the process of discovering your business model. When writing these statements, you made personal decisions about the type of enterprise you want to build. Your business model is one of the primary means for you to achieve the desired results, but if you don't keep in mind the ends you are trying to achieve, you may end up with a business that does not match your personal goals and values. That being said, your vision and mission statements are not written in stone. As we said in Chapter 2, they can be revised as well, and most likely they will change as you learn more and more about the business while discovering your business model.

The next exercise is to step back and take a long look at the Business Model Canvas and each of the building blocks, and visualize how they form the key components of a business enterprise. Then visualize how all of those components must in the end be integrated and work together. As we said in Chapter 1, if you look at the Business Model Canvas, you can see that the value proposition— including your actual product offering—is in the center. To its right are blocks relating to who your targeted customers will be, and how you will communicate with those customers and deliver the product to them. To the left are the key considerations involved in producing your product.

Take another look at the Business Model Canvas below, and imagine the workflow of your business and product through all of these categories.

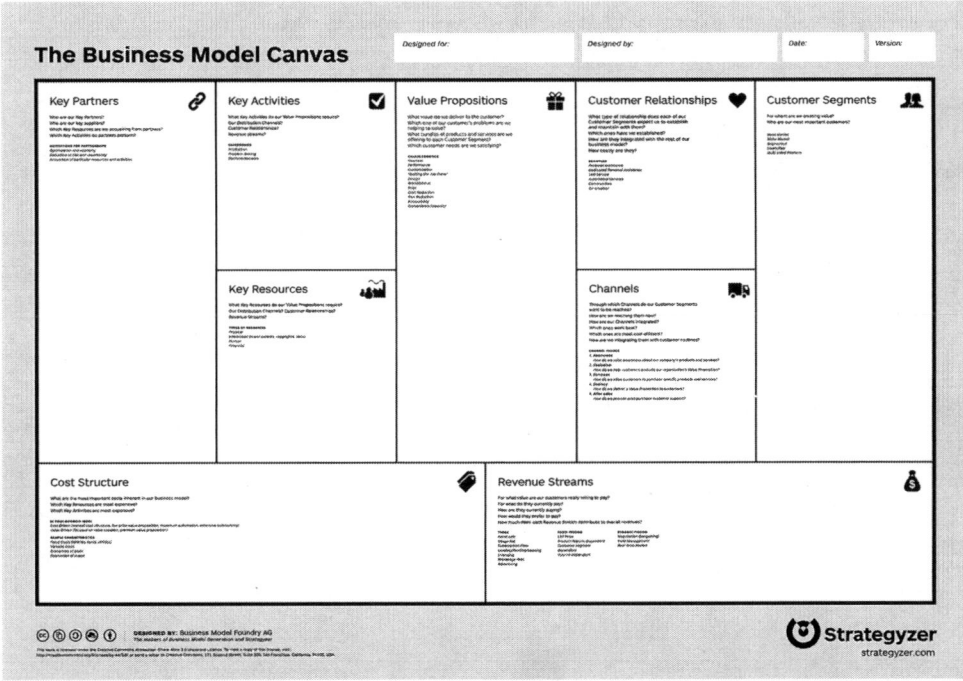

Finally, remind yourself that the goal of the business model canvas is to discover the best manner for you to create value for your customers by solving an important problem or satisfying an important need, and then produce, sell and deliver your product in a manner that results in your business capturing value and generating acceptable, sustainable profits.

In other words, you need a business model that will:

- Create and deliver value to your customers

- Create and capture value for your business and its owners and employees

Always keep these things in mind as you are filling out the canvas so that you achieve an integrated model that serves the proper purpose and achieves the desired results.

Your mantra at this stage should be: *Keep an open mind and remain flexible.*

This is especially true if you think you already know how you will initially fill out most of the building blocks. While your initial vision is an important guiding light, you should not let that get in the way of generating new ideas and thoroughly testing your initial ideas. Otherwise you risk blocking the type of creative thinking that is required at this point, as well as the ability to test and revise your building blocks in the following phases of business model discovery. At this stage everything, even your business idea itself, is simply a guess—a "*hypothesis*"—that must be subjected to challenge, discussion, and testing before it becomes a validated fact.

Brainstorm! Brainstorm! Brainstorm!

Brainstorming and Idea Generation

Now it's time to get started filling out your Business Model Canvas, as well as your Value Proposition Canvas. Go through each building block of the canvas and list its potential features in an entirely creative and open-minded fashion. Nothing is off the table. Freethinking and open discussion are the rules. Idea generation is the goal. Don't limit yourself to a specified number of hypotheses for each building block. Don't worry if your hypotheses conflict. Don't spend time analyzing what you come up with—you will do plenty of that later. That is what is meant by brainstorming.

In the next step, when you select an initial business model—or prototype—to test, you will discard many ideas and options that don't stand a chance of survival. That's to be expected. But the creative thought process often acts in unexpected ways, and one of these dismissed options may provide a stepping stone to something valuable. So don't be limited by anything at this point, including what other people in the same line of business are already doing. In fact, with respect to each building block, try to think of innovations that other businesses have yet to try. You may come up with an entirely new business model that is even more important and valuable than your product idea.

Selecting Your *Initial* Business Model Hypothesis

At some point you will have to cut off the brainstorming session and look at what you have come up with. You will probably have an instinctive feeling when you hit the point of diminishing returns. At that point, going block by block, you should sift through each of the hypothesis you have listed and try and make them as specific as possible. Avoiding generic statements is important, because if what you list is too vague you will neither be able to test nor implement the item in question.

After separating the potentially good ideas from the obviously unworkable, your business modeling team should discuss and debate each potential hypothesis before settling on which items to select as part of your initial Business Model Canvas. Throughout this process, always keep in mind that the business functions described in each block of the canvas must in the end integrate well with all of the others.

Ask yourselves questions:

- Does this hypothesis meet, or contribute towards, our stated criteria?

- Will each hypothesis work? What will have to happen for it to do so?

- Do these hypotheses integrate well together?

- What's missing to make this business model work?

- Does any item appear unnecessary?

- Where will my competitive advantages come from?

- Is this business model scalable and repeatable?

- Would this business model be disruptive?

Once you have selected a list of items for each component of the canvas, do some more deliberate, second-level brainstorming to refine your ideas, and then revise the canvas accordingly. At this stage, you may also want to more formally incorporate some of the initial market research you previously performed if you haven't done so already. Go back and review successful business models that other companies have used in the same or similar industries, and see if it makes sense to cherry pick certain items that you've left out. But challenge these business models as well, and see where there are areas where you can do better.

Ask yourself over and over again: *What if I tried this?*

Ultimately, however, you will have to do what every entrepreneur must do every day of his or her business life: make a choice and run with it—with one important caveat. The caveat is that at this stage, you could and probably should actually choose not just one but several Business Model Canvas prototypes to test.

When selecting your initial business model prototype(s), keep firmly in mind this second mantra:

Everything on the Business Model Canvas is a hypothesis to be confirmed . . . or not.

In other words, you know nothing for a fact at this point. Everything you have written down so far is simply an educated guess that will either be validated or invalidated by testing. This is where the Business Model Canvas process gets the most difficult, because this is where you first have to deal with your predictions not working as planned.

Be prepared—many if not most of your initial hypothesis will not survive intact. This is not failure. It is your first true initiation to the real world of business. The customers collectively know more than you . . . and in discovering your business model, your most important job is to learn from your customers exactly what they want and what they will pay to have, and then either improve your business model accordingly or pivot to an entirely new one.

Testing Your Business Model Hypothesis

In order to efficiently and effectively test the hypothesis contained in each building block of your initial Business Model Canvas, as well as the business model prototype as a whole, you need a strategy and method for doing so.

The best overall framework involves the following steps:

- Prioritize your hypothesis
- Decide on a testing sequence
- Develop tests for each hypothesis
- Generate a list of potential customers to contact
- Contact potential customers and get their agreement to participate
- Conduct your test and obtain feedback

While you will be testing and questioning each individual hypothesis, here are the overarching questions you are looking to answer with respect to your business model prototype:

- Have we identified a target group of customers who have an *important* problem that we thoroughly understand?
- Do we have a value proposition that provides a solution to our target customers' important problem?
- Do we have evidence that there is a sufficient number of reachable customers who have this important problem, are highly enthusiastic about our value proposition, and are willing to purchase our product at an acceptable price?

- Have we learned enough about those customers to efficiently and effectively sell them our product?

- Do we have a business model that will be scalable and sustainably profitable?

Keep these questions in mind throughout the process of discovering your business model. You will revisit these exact questions when it comes time to determine whether you have validated your model and can begin thinking about sales and execution.

What is the Best Sequence for Testing and Validating Your Business Model?

While all of the components of the Business Model Canvas are important, the most critical are the value proposition at the center of the canvas, and the related "customer problem" embedded in the customer segment block of the canvas. We will discuss these items in detail in Chapters 4 and 5, but they entail identifying the important problem shared by an identifiable group of customers, and then creating value for those customers by finding a compelling solution to their problem. If you have not accomplished these goals, then the other components of the Business Model Canvas may be revolutionary, but your business and business model will most likely fail.

Therefore, we recommend that you first test your hypothesis about what the important problems and needs you believe your target customers have, and next test your value proposition hypothesis—i.e. how you will solve those problems and/or satisfy those needs. Then you can make any necessary revisions to your Business Model Canvas before you test the hypothesis you have come up with for the other building blocks.

When it comes to testing the remaining components of your Business Model Canvas, it also makes sense to prioritize and first test those that will be most critical to your business. Identify those items that are absolutely necessary to the success of your business, rank them in order of importance, and test them first.

Therefore, we recommend that you follow this overall sequence:

- **First step:** test, understand and validate the customer problem
- **Second step:** test, understand and validate your solution
- **Third step:** prioritize your remaining business model hypothesis
- **Fourth step:** test, understand and validate your entire business model

In the first step, you are testing the circle of your Value Proposition Canvas—seeking to validate the jobs your customers need to perform, as well as the most important pains they most want to avoid and most important gains they want to achieve. If you don't have enough customers who care deeply about the problems you're trying to address and feel they are urgent, you won't have enough customers who care about and will purchase the solution that you offer. So here you need to test and collect evidence about which jobs, pains and gains matter the most to your customers.

In the second step, you are testing the square in the value proposition canvas—seeking to validate whether the manner you intend to solve your customers' problems or satisfy their needs fits what they really care about, i.e. that your solution will kill pains and create gains that matter to customers in a way they are enthusiastic to purchase. Here you will test to validate both the "problem/solution fit" and the level of enthusiasm customers have for your solution, the "product/market fit," which we will discuss further in Chapter 4.

In the third step, you will determine which of the other hypothesis in your business model are the most crucial, i.e. those that have to be true for your business model to work, and in the fourth step you will test each of these hypotheses. Remember, even great value propositions can fail without a sound overall business model. So you need to validate that if you execute your business model then all of the components will work both individually and as a whole, resulting in a sustainably profitable business.

We should emphasize once again that this process will not be entirely linear. At every step you will be gathering feedback and information that will help you understand, iterate and validate various aspects of your business model. But following this sequence in general is the most efficient manner of creating the best business model possible.

Developing Tests for Your Hypothesis

Now it is time to design methods of accurately testing your business model prototype and each of the hypotheses contained therein. Before beginning this process, take time to review your initial Business Model Canvas and make sure you and your team members have a full and consistent understanding of the meaning and implications of each hypothesis you are proposing for each block. We recommend that you write a short explanation of the hypothesis contained in each building block, keeping these explanations to 1-2 pages at most and using bullet points where possible. Write the explanations clearly, as if you were trying to communicate them to a third person, to ensure that everyone on your team has the same understanding.

Then ask these two critical questions with respect to each hypothesis:

- What needs to be true about my hypothesis in order for it to work?

- What do I need learn from my customers in order to confirm this hypothesis as a fact in the real world marketplace, rather than an educated guess made by me in my office?

Based on the answer to these questions, devise a method of testing your hypothesis with customers that will allow you to gather the information you need and learn enough to either validate or revise the hypothesis.

Your tests can be broadly categorized into those that require your direct personal interaction with customers, such as interviews, and those that don't, such as creating prototype landing site tests for a web-based business. The type of test you conduct and the amount of direct personal customer interaction you require at any given point in time will be driven by what it is you need to learn, the cost in terms of time and money, and the level of reliability you require in your data.

Remember that direct personal contact between the founders of a business and potential customers is invaluable. By meeting with your customers and getting direct personal feedback, you will obtain insights and achieve an understanding of your customer's problems and desired solutions that can never be achieved through indirect testing.

On the other hand, there are some drawbacks to tests that involve direct personal contact with customers. The first is that some tests you may want to conduct would require a prohibitive number of meetings, or would involve the customer interacting with your product in a manner that precludes direct customer contact, or both. The second drawback is that your presence may influence how a customer responds, and the related fact that what customers tell you they will do and what they actually do when away from your presence often don't match.

Therefore, you should design some tests that involve getting you face-to-face with potential customers, and others that allow customers to answer questions, interact with a product prototype, respond to call for actions, etc. without any person from your team present.

When devising questions to ask potential customers during face-to-face interviews, keep in mind the following:

- Don't ask for opinions: use questions that cause the customer to respond with facts that will help you build a pass/fail case for your analysis

- Use visual aids: give the customer something to see, touch and feel, ranging from simple product prototypes, power point slides, etc. at the beginning of the testing process to more complete product prototypes at the end—and observe how your customers react when interacting with these aids

- Include calls to action: ask the customer to take action that confirms there is a match between what they are telling you they will do and what they will actually do

Calls to action could include e-mail sign ups, referrals and introductions, responses to surveys, etc., all the way up to pre-orders of the product. In the testing phase, they are intended to show that the customer is interested enough in your value proposition to take further action and receive further information. Generally, the further along you are in the testing/iteration process, the more involved your calls to action.

The same is true with respect to the visual aid or product prototype you use in your test—the closer you get to nailing down your business model, the higher the level of product prototype you use in your testing. However, keep in mind that the purpose of these prototypes is not to sell products. They need to be specifically designed to test specific hypothesis, confirm or not the validity of the hypothesis, and obtain valuable customer insights that allow you to improve your business model. At each stage, use the simplest prototype possible to obtain the information that you need and iterate quickly. For example, you can build a prototype with only one or a limited number of features to test only those features. Remember as well that at the beginning you can test several prototypes; you are not limited to one version, and this is yet another reason not to make your prototype any more complicated than necessary.

Here are some examples of product prototypes and visual aids that you can use in both personal interviews and tests, ranging from the simple to the more complex:

- **Data Sheet or power point slide:** create a spread sheet or slide showing the problems you intend to address, the benefits of your value proposition, etc.

- **Brochure:** make a sample brochure for your customer to read, containing information that allows you ask follow-up questions, request a call to action, etc. to test a particular hypothesis

- **Storyboard:** sketch a storyboard that demonstrates how your customer's daily life or workflow would take place both with and without your product

- **Landing page:** set up a website page that allows you to capture a visitor's information through a lead form that includes a call to action which will give you the information you require

- **Wireframe:** this could involve a homepage or other webpage—mock-up or functional—which gives the reader the hypothesis information you want them to respond to; again including a call-to-action

- **Sample package:** produce a mock-up of the product package, give it to the customers and see how they respond

- **Video:** create a simple video that highlights the business model hypothesis that you want to test

- **Product prototype:** these can range from a simple model at the beginning to a near finished product at the end of testing, keeping in mind that the prototype should only include the features necessary to run your test and obtain the information you desire

With respect to any type of test, whether involving direct personal contact or not, design experiments that produce evidence that is measurable and allows you to make a pass/fail decision on your hypothesis. This could, for example, include a certain percentage threshold of positive responses to calls to action involving your value proposition. For example, if you ask each customer to list their three most important problems, you may set a threshold stating that 70 percent of customers must a problem for you to retain that problem as part of your customer problem hypothesis. Keep in mind, however, that you also want to collect qualitative data that gages customer enthusiasm and provides an opportunity to learn helpful insights.

Generating a List of Potential Customers for Face-to-Face Meetings

Once you've devised your testing methodology, you now need to find a group of potential customers willing to participate in the test. The key here is to find as many potential customers as possible that can give you high-value feedback.

With respect to finding customers with whom you can have direct personal contact and interview, start with people you know. Ask yourself: who am I familiar with that likely has the type of problem that I think my product will solve, or need/desire that it will satisfy, and who are likely to give me some of their time? This will form your initial list of people to contact.

Next ask friends, family, peers and other contacts if they personally know people who have the type of problem you think your product will solve, etc. who may be willing to spend some time with you. Finally, use LinkedIn, Facebook and other social media, and other sources you can think of to generate potential contacts.

This process will hopefully yield about 200 people who you can approach and propose a meeting.

Contacting Potential Customers for Face-to-Face Meetings

For most persons on your direct contact list, email is probably the best way to initiate contact. First write the sample text of an e-mail requesting a meeting with your target potential customers. Even if you will contact some persons you know well less formally, this draft email will be a helpful guide on how to approach them.

Be honest about your intentions, and keep firmly in mind—as well as tell your contact—that the purpose of your meeting is not to sell your product, but to familiarize them with your business idea and get their informed feedback. That being said, you do need to pique everyone's interest in your product if you want to get them to agree to meet with you. Therefore you want to emphasize the problems you intend to address and the solution you are proposing.

If you obtained the contact through a reference, always mention that reference right away. Better yet, send the email to your reference and ask them to forward it directly to the contact person. Once again, in the email, make sure the contact understands that you are not trying to sell him or her anything—what is intended is an exchange of information. You simply want to understand if they have the same or similar problem and how they address that problem currently, as well as get their insight about issues surrounding the problem and solutions they would be interested in.

Now contact the potential customers you know personally and set up as many meetings as possible—with in-person meetings being highly preferable. Then ask persons who can act as references for you if they will forward your e-mail to potential customers who they know, and follow up with a phone call to those persons.

This process will hopefully yield at least 50 potential customers for you to meet with and test your hypothesis. To do this will inevitably take some time. Don't be discouraged, even if it takes a week to set up the meetings. The payoffs in terms of understanding your customers, testing your hypothesis, and gaining insights will be invaluable.

Meeting with Potential Customers, Presenting Your Hypothesis and Obtaining Feedback

As you walk in the door, remind yourself once again that your initial goal is not to sell your product. You are there to either confirm your hypothesis or obtain information and insights that allows you to revise and improve your business model. Therefore, after succinctly presenting your hypothesis you should spend this valuable time primarily listening and observing, rather than speaking and explaining.

Using a product prototype or one of the visual devices we described under "hypothesis testing," present your hypothesis as quickly and comprehensibly as possible, then go directly into listening mode. Keep a very open mind. Follow-up on statements by your customers with questions that may lead to unexpected insights, possibly even pivots to new solutions or solutions to problems you had never thought of.

You can conduct interviews in teams of two, with one person taking the lead in asking questions and another taking notes—but no more than two so you don't overwhelm the customer. You can also use a recording device, but ask permission first and realize that this may inhibit some customers from speaking freely.

As we discussed earlier, you are looking for concrete insights—facts and experiences—into attitude and behavior that will help you learn as much as possible and refine your business model. Opinions don't help you much in this function.

Also, you cannot simply ask the customer what their problems are or what solutions they desire, and leave it at that. You need to learn what really matters to them and what they are really purchasing when they look for a solution. As any good salesperson knows, what their real problems and desires are lie below the surface of their stated problems and desires. Ask a lot of questions that begin with "why" in order to uncover true motivations.

At the end of the interview, ask your customers if they'd be willing to let you contact them again. This serves two purposes. First, you will inevitably go through several different iterations of testing. Second, it serves as a call to action to gage customer interest, acting as a test in and of itself. In this same respect, always ask your customers if they would be willing to make an introduction to people who might be interested in your product and/or would be willing to participate in future tests.

Learning from Customer Feedback—Revising Your Hypothesis—Iterating Testing

Once you have finished testing your hypothesis, you will need to closely analyze all of the information you have received to see what it has validated and what it has raised questions about with respect to your original hypothesis . . . and then most likely start the entire process all over again.

Begin by creating a one page summary of the results of your hypothesis testing that can be compared to your original hypothesis and accompanying explanation. Try to glean as many valuable insights as possible from the data you received. Then engage in another round of informed brainstorming and analysis. Once again, be open to all ideas and willing to challenge everything you had previously assumed and listed on your canvas.

The key question after each round of testing will be this: *Based on the data, should I revise my hypothesis, or should I discard it and pivot to an entirely different hypothesis or business idea?*

If your hypothesis has been validated by data you consider sufficiently reliable, great, move on to test your next important hypothesis. For example, when you have validated an important problem shared by a critical mass of customers, proceed to test your solution to that problem. But if the answer comes back at the other end of the spectrum—that your initial hypothesis was incorrect and/or simply will not work, then you can use your data to pivot to a new hypothesis to test.

Most often, however, the data will suggest that you just need to make adjustments to your initial hypothesis. If this is the case, then now is the time to revise your Business Model Canvas. Outline the specific changes you will make to your hypothesis and write a new hypothesis description. Be as specific as possible in your items for each building block, and note which hypothesis have been validated and which have yet to be validated. It is *very important* not to discard your original, or any iteration of, your Business Model Canvas. It will be very valuable for you and your team to be able to review all of the iterations and observe how your business model evolves throughout this process.

After you have revised your Business Model Canvas, it is time once again to take each item which has yet to be validated outside the building to test in front of customers. Design and conduct further tests and present them to customers. This may be the last time you do so, but more than likely it will not.

Iterate! Iterate! Iterate!

The goal of all of this is to obtain as much concrete evidence as possible, so that the items listed in your building blocks move from the realm of educated guesses into the realm of objectively verified facts. So even if your initial tests come back positive, you should assess the reliability of the data, and maybe design further tests that confirm what the first tests indicate. In addition, initial tests may beg questions as to why the data came back the way it did. If so, follow-up with qualitative interviews designed to deepen your understanding and obtain additional insights.

Remember once again, that although in this chapter we are walking through the Business Model Canvas process in a linear fashion, in reality it will not be linear. The iterations and revisions will not always happen simultaneously. Things may appear a little messy and uncoordinated. But have faith that through testing, learning, and iteration, creative solutions will ultimately emerge that lead to the best business model possible.

Validating Your Business Model

After you've been through several rounds of hypothesis creation, testing, revision, and iteration, you will hopefully reach a point where most of your current hypotheses have been validated by potential customers.

Now you must stop and assess the results of the experiments you've conducted and verify that you have validated your entire business model fully enough to move forward. The questions you should ask in determining whether you have enough hard facts to validate your business model are those we mentioned previously:

- Have we identified a target group of customers who have an *important* problem that we thoroughly understand?

- Do we have a value proposition that provides a solution to our target customers' important problem?

- Do we have evidence that there is a sufficient number of reachable customers who have this important problem, are highly enthusiastic about our value proposition, and are willing to purchase our product at an acceptable price?

- Have we learned enough about those customers to efficiently and effectively sell them our product?

- Do we have a business model that will be scalable and sustainably profitable?

At this point you should have spoken to a large number of potential customers who have identified the problem now listed on your business model as an urgent problem that they place a high priority on solving—with a premium being placed on customers who are already in the process of actively trying to find a solution for themselves.

These customers have also been presented with your most recent value proposition, agree that it would solve their problem, and have indicated through tangible calls to action that they would enthusiastically purchase your product at an acceptable price if it were available to them right now. In other words, you have accumulated evidence of both a product/solution fit and a product/market fit. The customers have also indicated that your product offers distinct advantages such that they would purchase your product at this price over any competing products available.

Based on your projections, the evidence you have obtained indicates that the number of customers in your target market that would share this enthusiasm for your product and who would be within your sales and distribution reach is large enough to signify a sustainably profitable business opportunity. You have also obtained sufficient data to be satisfied that you are now highly educated on who these customers are, where you can find them, what motivates them, and how you can convince them to buy your product.

Finally, you have sufficient evidence to show that if you execute your business model as it has evolved to exist, you can scale your operations and grow a sustainably profitable business. This means that all of the components of your business model will work as planned and will integrate together into a coherent unit. It means that each of these components will be cost-effective, efficient and effective in achieving your goals. It means that you will have access to necessary resources and can perform necessary activities on a cost-efficient basis. It means that you are confident in your ability to generate revenue from confirmed revenue streams. And of course it means that you will capture more value for your business than the cost of creating and capturing that value.

Once you are satisfied that this has been achieved, it will be time to create a strategy and plan for executing your new business model.

Executing Your Business Model and Iterating Once Again . . . and Again

After you've made a choice on the initial business model that you intend to execute, it will then be time to come up with a strategy and write a business plan to help you do so in the most efficient and effective manner. While writing the business plan, you will have additional thoughts and conduct additional research that may lead you to further revise your business model canvas. This will include a very close look at the current competitive environment, which is inherent, but not overt, in the Business Model Canvas. It will also include more detailed financial modeling than you did while putting together the canvas.

Finally, you will be ready to launch your product in the marketplace. And in essence, this is nothing more than the ultimate market research—a truly real world test of your business model. As such, you will receive the best possible feedback on how your business model is working.

What should you do with that feedback? Take it back to your Business Model Canvas, and iterate and revise once again.

LinksBuddy Case Study

Chapter 3
The Business Model Canvas

Martin agrees to become Steven's co-founder, and for the next week the two partners work on establishing a shared vision for their new business. They begin with their *values statement*. While Martin is not a professional like Steven, he is an avid golfer, and both men want to create a business that reflects what they believe is the best part of the game: its integrity and ethics. Golf is a game where serious players pride themselves on knowing both the written rules of golf and unwritten rules of golf etiquette, and conduct themselves within both the letter and the spirit of those rules with the utmost integrity. Both Steven and Martin want to run their business with the same code of ethics. They agree that this may rule out certain strategic options that other companies might pursue, but also believe it will attract fellow golfers who respect the fact that they are running their business the same way as they conduct themselves on the course.

In that same vein, Steven and Martin agree that their *vision* is to create a worldwide network of golfers who can meet, play golf together and directly share experiences, information and knowledge. The LinksBuddy platform will allow them to communicate, socialize and share the game of golf both online and in the comforts of their living rooms, club houses, and home golf courses. Developing a worldwide golfing "community" is the key to their vision.

In order to realize this vision, their *mission* will be to create an online platform which provides its golfing customers with the most efficient and cost effective way to discover fellow golfers who they would like to meet in any desired location; then to befriend, lodge with and play golf with their new links buddies on their host's home course.

Steven and Martin share a passion for the vision, mission and values they have laid out, and can't wait to get started filling out their Business Model Canvas. But when they download their canvas and begin brainstorming, they immediately realize they have a significant challenge that many types of new businesses don't face: their business will be solving different problems by offering different value propositions to different people. In other words, their business will be multiple businesses and accompanying business models wrapped into one package.

What Steven and Martin intend to create is called a multi-sided market platform, which will facilitate a peer-to-peer ("P2P") marketplace. In doing so, they will tap into the relatively new and rapidly growing "sharing economy." A multi-sided market provides value by bringing together two or more customer segments, with very different problems and needs, and facilitating their ability to directly interact and create and exchange value on an online platform. At its core, there is normally a "provider" segment on one side who offer goods or services, and a "user" segment on the other side who purchase the goods or services. In addition, some multi-sided platforms have more than two sides—for example providers, users, and advertisers—with several different types of interactions. While in many cases persons utilizing the platform will be both providers and users, one of the key challenges is that multi-sided markets often require a different value proposition, channel, customer relationship, revenue streams and/or pricing strategy for each side.

Some very familiar and successful examples of multi-sided markets that Steven and Martin came across in their initial market research include:

- Visa credit card, which links merchants with cardholders

- Microsoft Windows operating system, which links hardware manufacturers, application developers, and users

- Facebook, which links advertisers with users

- Financial Times, which links advertisers with readers, and

- Wii game console, which links game developers with players

- And then of course there's Google . . .

The most relevant examples of multi-sided marketplaces for Steven and Martin, however, were those that were P2P, meaning the providers were individuals rather than businesses. And the most relevant P2P multi-sided marketplace is Airbnb, which offers an online platform that directly connects travelers to people with an underutilized asset—available living space—which they want to rent. Other examples of recent P2P marketplaces that they researched include Uber and Lyft, Etsy, TaskRabbit, ELance and ODesk, and Skillshare.

Each of these P2P platforms combine three basic functions: a value proposition that attracts the different participants from each side; a place where the participants can both create and exchange value; and a "matching" function that curates the participants allowed on the platform and then matches them with the best potential participant on the other side.

The success of each of these P2P market businesses is extremely encouraging to Steven and Martin, but the challenges each business had to overcome in obtaining its success is daunting. First and foremost, P2P marketplaces face two primary and interrelated challenges: what is called the "double company problem" and the "chicken and egg problem."

The double company problem means that in creating a P2P marketplace, Steven and Martin will in essence have to build two different companies at the same time—one company offering accommodation and golf playing partners to traveling golfers, and another company offering a matching service to persons wishing to rent space to traveling golfers. Each will require a different business model, including different value propositions, customer relationships, revenue streams, etc. And each side's business model must succeed or the entire platform will collapse.

The chicken and egg problem means that for a P2P marketplace to work, it needs both providers and users on the platform—which means the double companies must both be created and be successful in a relatively simultaneous timeframe. The problem is that providers won't be interested in listing what they have to offer unless there is a sufficient user base, and users won't be interested in coming to the website platform unless there are a sufficient number of providers to find what they are looking for. With Airbnb, for example, renters wouldn't visit the platform unless it has enough accommodation options in the desired location, but providers won't make the effort to list their properties unless there are enough potential renters. The first question for Steven and Martin will be whether they can attract one side or the other first through some secondary incentive, and if so which side do you focus on. The alternative is to find a way to attract both sides at the same time. One way to attract enough users, they discovered in their research, is by offering a value proposition either for free or for a subsidized amount. The problem with this approach is that it then becomes necessary to attract enough paying customers on the other side quickly enough to cover the cost of those subsidies. Many businesses, Steven and Martin find out, have crashed and burned due to their failure to solve this "chicken and egg" problem.

In studying Airbnb's history, Steven and Martin can see that one of their biggest challenges in overcoming the double company problem and the chicken and egg problem will be establishing the trust of both their providers and users. Reputation, they can see, will mean everything in the success of their P2P marketplace. If they can't find a way to get their participants to trust in the safety and quality of using their platform and the services it offers, then they will have no participants on either side. In addition, they will likely have to face similar legal issues as those Airbnb is currently dealing with on a broad scale. These include consumer protection, taxation, health and safety, and zoning regulations that apply to businesses offering accommodation.

Last but not least, Steven and Martin have learned that it is not enough to solve the chicken and egg problem on a small scale—to succeed they will need to attain "critical mass," which in the P2P business is referred to as "liquidity." True liquidity in a P2P platform business happens when each provider has the reasonable expectation of selling what they list and each user has the reasonable expectation of finding what they want to purchase. Therefore, there is no value in the platform unless a critical mass is obtained on both sides of the platform. On the other hand, as the platform grows and the more providers and users it has, the closer it comes to liquidity and the more value it provides to participants. This is due to a phenomenon called the "network effect," pursuant to which the value of participating in a network depends on the number of people already participating.

In combination, all of these challenges add up to an additional hurdle for Steve and Martin: the sheer complexity of running a P2P business. The different sides not only require different business models, they can also lead to conflicting interests whereby satisfying one customer segment may mean disappointing the other.

"It's going to be more difficult than I thought," Steven says.

"Difficult … but not impossible," Martin replies. "Otherwise, there would be no Airbnb."

"And when we succeed, we will succeed big time," Steven adds.

CHAPTER 4:
CUSTOMER SEGMENTS

Chapter Overview

What Important Problem Do You Intend to Solve?	77
What is Your Market?	81
What is a 'Customer Segment' and Why is Segmentation so Important?	82
Identifying Your Target Customer Segment	82
Creating Target Customer Profiles	84
Testing and Understanding Your Customer Problem and Customer Profile Hypotheses	85
Revising, Iterating, and Validating Your Customer Profile Hypothesis	89
LinksBuddy Case Study	92

CHAPTER 4

CUSTOMER SEGMENTS

Every good business idea has four basic components. First, it identifies an important problem or a need shared by a significant number of potential customers. Second it provides a solution that solves the customers' problem or satisfies the customers' need. Third, the customers value the solution highly enough that they will buy the product or service at a price that supports a profitable business. And fourth, the solution contains a competitive advantage that will cause customers to choose the offered product over other similar products on the market.

So the first step in creating a good business model is to understand and define the important problem or need and identify the potential customers who share that problem or need. And the second step is to develop a solution that these potential customers value highly enough to pay good money for and will choose over other competing products in the market place.

If you look at the Business Model Canvas, those two steps fall under the categories of "Customer Segments" and "Value Proposition."

A *value proposition* is a solution that comes primarily in the form of a product or service which provides benefits and value to a group of customers by solving their problems or satisfying their needs better than available alternatives. That group of people with the same or similar problems or needs constitutes a *market* for the product. And that market can be further subdivided and targeted based on other shared characteristics. These subdivisions are called *customer segments*.

The process of identifying which customer segment to target includes the following:

- Identify and understand the customer problem you are going to solve and/or need that you will satisfy

- Identify and understand the characteristics of the people who have that problem or need

- Subdivide those people into smaller groups—customer segments—that will allow you to efficiently communicate with and deliver the solution to their problem or need

- Prioritize the customer segments and determine whether the most relevant ones will constitute a large enough market to support a profitable business

Afterwards, you can tailor your value proposition—your product or service together with all of the other benefits you intend to provide the customer—so that it solves the exact problem or satisfies the exact need of the customer segment (or segments) that you have targeted, and does so better than your competitors. This is called a *problem/solution fit*.

The ultimate goal is to get your product to become a "must have" solution for a sizeable portion of a large target segment of customers. This is called a *product/market fit*, and will be the key to a successful business because it will result in demand for your product being sufficiently high to scale production. Many other things have to happen in order for you to capitalize on a business opportunity, but without a good solution to an identifiable problem that ultimately results in a good product/market fit, all of the other activities have no meaning. In other words, even if you have a good solution to a problem, if not enough people want to buy your product then you don't have a business.

What Important Problem Do You Intend to Solve?

When determining the important "problem" that your business solution will solve or the "need" that it will satisfy, keep in mind that most often this will consist of a bundle of related problems or needs and not just one. Also realize that a customer's needs include their strong desires, such as the desire for social status that comes from wearing an expensive piece of jewelry. To assist in the process of accurately identifying, categorizing and understanding customer problems and needs, it is now time to turn to the "customer profile" portion of the Value Proposition Canvas.

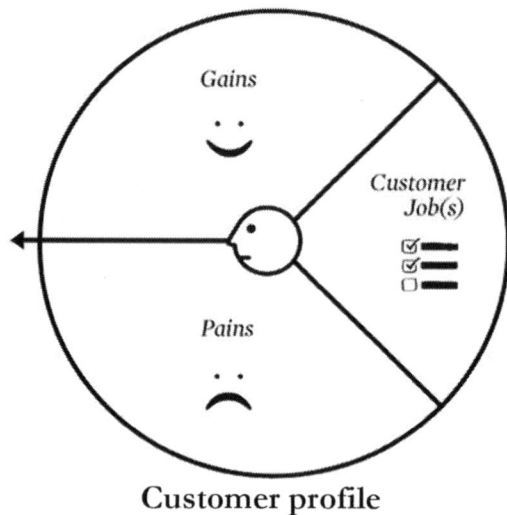

Customer profile

As you can see from the graphic, the customer profile identifies the customers' jobs, pains and gains:

- **Jobs** are the things your customers want to get done in their work or in their personal life, such as performing a task, solving a problem, or satisfying a need

- **Pains** are negative outcomes and obstacles related to the performance of a job

- **Gains** are positive outcomes and benefits related to the performance of a job

"Jobs" in this context is a term that goes beyond the word's traditional meaning. You should identify not only the functional task your customer wants to perform, but also the social and emotional tasks as well. Sometimes a person is performing all three at the same time. For example, a person who joins a new health club might want to perform the functional task of exercising to improve their health, the social task of losing weight to improve their appearance and satisfy their need to look good in public, and the related emotional task of solving their problem of poor self image. When you fill in this category on the Customer Profile, include all of the relevant jobs your customer wants or needs to perform.

"Pains" are the negative things that happen either during the performance of a job or as a result of a job not being satisfactorily accomplished. They include problems that make a job more difficult or impossible to accomplish, things that create stresses or risks that the job will not be satisfactorily completed, and the negative effects of a job not being properly completed. Once again, pains are not limited to the obvious functional aspects of a job, but include social and emotional pains as well. Pains experienced by target customers of a health club would be poor health, low energy, poor physical appearance and low self esteem due to lack of exercise—i.e. not satisfactorily performing the job of taking care of their physical and emotional health. Pains involved in attempting to perform the job include the physical pain and effort involved in working out, the cost of paying for a health club membership, the time and effort it takes to reach the health club, the potential embarrassment of working out in public environment, etc. All of these pains may be relevant when it comes time for a new health club to design a solution for their customers' problems and needs.

"Gains" are the positive results and benefits your customers want or need. What you are looking for is to identify not just the surface level gains that your customers' desire, but those that aren't immediately apparent. Dig deep to discover what really motivates them to perform a job. "Why?" is the operative question that you should ask over and over. Continuing the above example, ask yourself: Why do people join health clubs? What are *all* of the underlying motivations? Most health club customers want better health, better social perception and better self-perception with as little effort, cost and hassle as possible. But beyond that, different customers may be seeking different types of gains. Some might enjoy the social aspect of working out with other hard core fitness buffs, others like doing light aerobics with people of similar age and fitness level. Some may consider it a gain to have a broad range of activities available including a swimming pool and basketball court; others may want to be in a small gym where they can pump iron using free weights surrounded by other bodybuilding enthusiasts. Some might want a cheap and convenient local gym while others might be looking for an exclusive club. Once again, identifying exactly what gains your target customers desire is a key to designing a solution your target market will pay for.

As with the Business Model Canvas, the first step in filling out the Value Proposition Canvas is to brainstorm—so be creative in your first round of identifying customer jobs, pains and gains and don't limit yourself by getting too analytical at the beginning. In all likelihood you will identify many pains the customers experience and many gains that they desire. Try and be as specific as possible in your descriptions of the jobs, pains and gains. And don't list only jobs, pains and gains that apply to the value proposition you have in mind. Remember, that value proposition is also a hypothesis at this point, and if you identify problems you had never thought of before your value proposition may change for the better.

After brainstorming, and throughout the process of completing your Value Proposition Canvas, rank your customers' jobs, pains and gains in order of importance to the customer. You will first do this based on your best educated guess, and later based on customer feedback received when you test your hypothesis.

Ask yourself now, and your customers during testing, these questions:

- What jobs have the most serious consequences, the most severe pains, if they fail to get done?

- Which gains will the customer care about the most?

- Which are essential and which are simply nice but not necessary?

- What jobs and pains occur most frequently?

Ranking jobs, pains, and gains is critical. If you design a solution to a problem your customers do not feel strongly about, then nobody will buy your product. If you want to achieve product/market fit, you need to design a solution to problems your customers feel that they *must* solve.

Once you have created your initial customer profile hypothesis, you can use it to identify your market and create your target customer segment hypothesis. We want to strongly emphasize that after you have broken your market down into customer segments, you will want to circle back and create a separate customer profile for each segment identifying the jobs, pains and gains that are specific to that segment.

What is Your Market?

A market consists of a group of consumers having the desire and ability to buy a product to satisfy a particular type of need, or to solve a particular type of problem. Take music, for example—the market for the music recording industry consists of everyone who wants to buy recorded music and will pay money to do so, a very large market indeed as long as a record company has the ability to reach all of those customers. The market for nursing uniforms, on the other hand, would obviously be limited to a smaller number of people in a specific occupation.

It is important to identify your overall market for a number of reasons. First, it will give you an idea of the revenue and growth potential of your business, as well as their restrictions. In addition, it is the starting point for drilling down and identifying the segments of customers in that market that you want to target.

In Chapter 2 we discussed one method of identifying your overall market, and recommended you do so before beginning work on your Business Model Canvas. At this juncture you should revisit your market analysis, because it may change based on insights you gained while completing your initial Business Model Canvas.

In analyzing your market, it is important to be realistic. For example, if you are opening up a local organic food store, then your market will most likely be limited to local customers as well. But don't overly restrict yourself either. If you develop a great new business model for delivering organic produce to customers, then you may be able to scale your single store into a citywide, regional or national chain—in which case your market analysis becomes entirely different. In addition, it's important to identify the total market for your product, even if realistically you would never be able to reach everyone in that market, so you can identify trends in the market that may affect your local business.

What is a 'Customer Segment' and Why is Segmentation so Important?

Now it's time to look at your market and identify the group or groups of people most likely to buy your product. For many reasons, this is one of the most important activities you're going to engage in, both in creating your business model and business plan, and in operating your business.

Within almost every market for a product, different consumers have different specific problems and needs, will perceive and receive different benefits from the product, are willing to pay different prices for the product, have different motivations for buying, respond positively to different marketing messages, are in different locations, have different levels of enthusiasm for a product, etc. As a result, it would not be efficient to communicate with and sell to each potential customer in the same manner. So it's in the interest of every business to segment the market into manageable groups of people with similar problems and needs that can be efficiently targeted with a specific marketing message and mix, reached through a specific sales and distribution method, and offered a product with specific features and benefits—and then choose the best segment or segments to target.

The goal is to develop a target customer segment that consists of the people most likely to buy your product on the most profitable basis for your business who are within your marketing and distribution reach. Properly identifying this target segment will be a key to your business success. If you understand who your primary potential customers are, what they want, and how and when they buy, then every component of your business—from product development to marketing to sales to distribution to customer service—can be geared towards satisfying their needs, solving their problems, and convincing them to purchase what you have to offer at a price that allows you to make an acceptable and sustainable profit.

Identifying Your Target Customer Segment

In general, a customer segment consists of a group of potential buyers of your product who have similar:

- Needs for the product, and/or

- Characteristics (demographic, geographic, behavioral, and/or psychographic), and/or

- Responses to messages

An example of market segmentation based on needs would be toothpaste: some customers desire tooth paste for teeth whitening, some for cavity protection, some for tartar control, etc. In other words, different toothpaste customers want to perform different jobs, avoid different pains, and achieve different gains, and can be grouped accordingly. These customer segments could be further subdivided based on age demographics and responses to marketing messages, such as children versus young adults versus senior citizens. Another example would be automobiles—a jaguar is clearly targeted to persons with different pains and gains, income demographics, and marketing message responses than a mini-van.

Therefore, in order to determine which customer segments to target in your business model, you should:

- First determine the type of person whose needs your product will most satisfy/problems your product will best solve—or if different customers have different needs to be satisfied or problems to be solved, you can break them down that way

- Afterward, identify the common characteristics of that group, focusing on those characteristics that are most related to the buying decision

- Then further subdivide that segment into groups who will respond to similar marketing messages, would be reached through similar channels and customer relationships, would require different pricing strategies, distribution mechanisms, etc.

In selecting a market segment to target, you should keep the following criteria in mind:

- The segment should be measurable

- The segment should be relatively distinct from other segments

- The segment should be sustainable—the trends in the segment should be positive

- The segment should be reachable from a marketing, sales and distribution standpoint

- The segment should respond to a distinct marketing mix

- The segment should be large enough, enthusiastic enough, and willing to buy at a price point high enough to support a profitable business

Once you have identified a target segment of customers, place its description on your Business Model Canvas. Then go back to your Value Proposition Canvas and create a separate customer profile for each key customer segment. Keep in mind, however, that these profiles are still hypotheses subject to testing and validation.

Creating Target Customer Profiles

In business, it is always better to have in mind a specific person for whom to develop a value proposition and create a marketing message. So now that you've determined what will be your target segments of customers and identified and ranked each segment's problems and needs, your next task is to create a customer profile of a representative individual for each segment—i.e. a profile of the individual who will most highly value and therefore most likely buy your product or service.

It is very important that you understand this person inside and out, including their:

- Daily life routines and work flow

- Relevant jobs, pains and gains

- Demographic characteristics: age, gender, marital status, children, friends, occupation, earnings, discretionary income, home location, work location, free time locations, transportation, hobbies, etc.

- Buying habits: what they buy, where they buy, why they buy, how they buy, how much they spend, etc.

- Communication habits: Internet, mobile, television, friends, etc.

- Personal preferences: likes and dislikes, what causes pain and what brings happiness, what motivates them, who influences them, etc.

If you are selling to a business, then you need to answer similarly relevant questions and create a similar profile of your business customers. This means both about the business organization itself and the individuals who will buy your product on behalf of the business.

The other important thing you need to do at this point is to think about whether the economic buyer, purchasing decision maker, and user of your product will be more than one person. For example, if you are selling to a business, the person who buys your product may be one person, the person who chooses what product to buy another, the person who approves the purchase another, and the person who uses the product yet another. The same is true in a household: a ten-year old may use and even choose a product, but a parent will approve the purchase and pay for the product. This needs to be thoroughly understood and reflected in your customer profile analysis.

Testing and Understanding Your Customer Problem and Customer Profile Hypotheses

Remember, all you've done so far is make educated guesses about your potential customers and their problems and needs. Now it's time to test those hypotheses and gather real-world feedback that will either validate your guesses as true, or give you the information necessary to either revise them or pivot to a new idea.

As we discussed in Chapter 3, the very first test you should conduct with respect to your initial Business Model Canvas prototype is the customer problem you propose to address with your value proposition. This means testing whether you have accurately described your customers' most important jobs, pains and gains on your Value Proposition Canvas. What you are looking to find out is whether you really understand your customers' problems and needs, and whether the problem you can solve is important enough to a sufficient number of people to make your business viable and sustainably profitable.

In the process, you want to get as much information as you can about the characteristics and lifestyle details of the people who have this problem or need—or organization, workflow and product needs if your customers will be other businesses. You want to know who they are, why they will or won't buy a product that solves their problem, what they are looking for in a solution, and if they will buy, then where, how, for how much, and how often they will do so. You also want to know what they think about other similar products on the market already.

Most likely, you will be shocked at what you find out. After all, this is the first time you will meet real customers after creating your initial business model prototype, and the learning curve is likely to be steep. Don't be surprised or too disappointed if some of your hypotheses turn out to be way off the mark. After all, you and your team (if you have one) represent only a very small sample of people who may be interested in your product. So you really are only *guessing* about your customers and their problems. Talk to hundreds of people, thousands if possible, and then you can say you actually *know* something.

For example, you may find that many people do not care at all about the problems you thought you would address, but in fact have their own set of pains and desired gains you never even considered. In addition, the type of person you thought was your most likely customer may not be so at all, and people who for one reason or another you thought would not be interested in your product may turn out to be highly interested for reasons you hadn't thought of.

Testing your customer profile hypotheses involves five key steps:

- Designing experiments for customer tests

- Inviting and getting customers to participate

- Testing your problem hypothesis in order to gain understanding of the customer problem and assess its importance to customers

- Testing your customer segment hypothesis and gaining understanding of your target customers' characteristics, lifestyle and motivations

- Capturing competitive and market knowledge

As we discussed in Chapter 3, you can and should test your customer problem hypothesis both by conducting personal interviews with customers and using experiments in which you are not present. For a new restaurant, this may mean interviewing fifty people and then following up with blind taste tests for that same group. For a new website or mobile application, this may mean interviewing fifty people and then engaging with thousands of people via a landing page test.

The first step is to devise a series of interview questions that allow you to efficiently gather data and insights directly from potential customers regarding what they consider to be their most relevant problems and needs, as well as to gather the necessary details to group them into customer segments and create customer profiles. It is helpful to have at least a basic product prototype or visual aid to use in the interview. Remember, use the simplest and easiest prototype necessary to achieve the level of feedback you require.

When you meet with a customer, we recommend the following procedure:

- First summarize your hypotheses about customers' problems and needs (jobs, pains and gains), including the severity of those problems and needs

- Next present your understanding of how customers are currently solving those problems and meeting those needs

- Then offer some potential solutions

- Finally present a call to action to confirm the accuracy of what the customer has told you

After each step of the presentation, stop talking other than to ask questions. You are there to gather information and insight, not to sell your proposed solution. Most of your time spent in the interview should be listening and observing.

You can encourage discussion by asking questions such as these:

- We think these are the five top problems facing the industry. How would you rank them as they affect your company?

- If you have three major problems to solve (in this area) in the year ahead, what are they and why do they make the "top three"?

- How does your company evaluate new products? (price? performance? features?)

- What's the biggest pain in how you work?

- If you could change anything about how you perform tasks in your personal life/perform your job, what would it be?

When you think you have a handle on what the customer you are interviewing believes are his or her main problems or needs, you can get them to discuss what solutions they are aware of today, which ones they use, if any, and what their evaluation of those solutions. Get answers that are as concrete as possible. For example, have them rank their problems and rank the available solutions.

Afterwards, you can introduce your solution and see how the customer reacts. Gage their level of enthusiasm. Identify customer concerns—why they feel it would or would not solve their problem, etc. Ask how your solution compares with the current solutions you just discussed.

Once you've conducted a critical mass of customer interviews, you should confirm the responses you received by inviting customers to interact with a simple product prototype outside of your presence and respond to a call to action. This could be a basic website or landing page that presents much the same information that you presented in your customer interviews, combined with a request that customers participate in a survey, provide their e-mail address to learn more information, refer the product prototype to friends, etc. You may also want to consider using multiple prototypes to test different problem descriptions. For example, you could develop multiple basic websites to test different problem descriptions.

Try and get as many people as you can to engage in these tests, and measure everything possible, especially what percentage of people care about the problem or need, how deeply they care and whether they know and would recommend others with the same problem or need. One of the keys in gauging this information is the call to action, which can escalate from a simple sign up to learn more, to a request for referrals, to an agreement to participate in a future interview. Remember: the more a customer is asked to do, the more valuable the feedback.

Also, just as it is important to confirm information you receive in interviews with experiments that take place outside your presence, it is a good idea to confirm the results of these experiments by following up with interviews. Online feedback should be a supplement, not a substitute for talking directly to customers. Direct interviews can also give you feedback on whether your prototype is adequately communicating the need or problem.

Revising, Iterating, and Validating Your Customer Profile Hypothesis

After gathering your first round of customer feedback, it's now time to analyze the information you've received and revise the customer profile portion of your Value Proposition Canvas and customer segment block of his Business Model Canvas accordingly.

As the first part of this process, summarize your test results and compare them to your initial customer profile hypothesis. You should now be able to mark some of your propositions as validated, revise others that were in the ballpark but not entirely accurate, eliminate some that were either incorrect or have proved irrelevant, and add items that you had previously never thought of. Try to drill down in detail as well as accuracy. Remember don't be generic. And don't throw away your initial canvas—generate a new revised canvas so you can see how they evolve over all of the iterations you will go through, which at minimum should be several.

What if a customer tells you that the issues you thought were important really aren't? Instead of feeling as if you've failed, realize you've just obtained great data. While it may not be what you wanted to hear, it's wonderful to have that knowledge early on.

With the customer feedback summaries completed, analyze:

- What problems did customers say they have?

- How painful are these problems?

- How are they solving these problems today?

- What percentage of customers shared the same important problem or need?

- Would these people be willing to pay a lot to solve this problem or satisfy this need?

Consider the Scalability: Not only is finding customers who care a daunting challenge, you need lots of them to be successful. The ability to attract large numbers of customers will make or break the business. A lucrative business opportunity requires either a large number of people willing to pay a sufficient amount to solve an important problem, or a lesser number of people willing to pay a large amount.

One other thing you should do with your test results is to build a day in the life, or work-flow, for a typical customer. You can use this information to show the customer's personal or work routine both with and without your solution. You can also present this workflow to the customers in the next iteration of customer profile tests, and use it in creating your value proposition hypothesis, and in your value proposition test.

After drawing the customer workflow with and without your product, analyze how great the difference would be. Did customers you tested indicate they would be enthusiastic about paying for that difference?

In addition, you now want to refine your target customer segment hypothesis. Analyze the shared characteristics of customers with the same important problem who were enthusiastic about similar solutions. In addition, how large is each market segment you have listed? Can you begin to prioritize segments you think you should target? Are there some you should eliminate even though they contain potential customers?

Finally, now would be a good time to look at your customer segment list and customer profiles and take into account some important matters that the Business Model Canvas does not specifically address—competition and market size. For example, do the persons in each customer segment you listed purchase the same competing products? Do they spend their discretionary spending on other products that may compete indirectly with yours? Or maybe compliment yours? What are the strengths and weaknesses of those competing products?

Taking all of this into account, revise your customer profile and your customer segment block to hone your guesses based on the feedback you received, then go and test again and again until you validate your customer profile hypothesis. At the same time you're doing this, you'll be revising your value proposition to reflect an improved hypothesis about the best solution to your target customers' problems, and then honing that solution/value proposition based on customer feedback as well.

> **LinksBuddy Case Study**
>
> ## Chapter 4
> ## Customer Segments
>
> Finally, it's time for Steven and Martin to begin filling out their Business Model Canvas. They start with the "Customer Segments" section, where their initial focus is on identifying the customer problems and needs they wish to address with their new business venture. In order to do so, they turn to the Value Proposition Canvas.
>
> To address their P2P "double company problem" right from the outset, Steven and Martin decide to make two versions of their initial Business Model Canvas and Value Proposition Canvas—one for their customer segment who will provide accommodation for rent (the "accommodation providers") and one for their customer segment who will travel to play golf and stay in local private accommodation (the "golf travelers").
>
> Steven suggests that they start with the accommodation providers, and he and Martin begin to brainstorm about the relevant jobs, pains and gains of this customer segment.
>
> The practical *jobs* that their providers will want to perform begin with the obvious: renting available underutilized space to a golf traveler. But in order to accomplish this job, there are many other jobs that accommodation providers will need to perform. These include discovering and communicating with a potential renter/golf traveler; determining whether that golf traveler is an acceptable renter; agreeing to rental terms and obtaining payment; ensuring and insuring the safety of their property; and handling all the logistics involved in receiving and accommodating the golf traveler. The other jobs that Steven and Martin believe the accommodation providers will wish to perform, and in fact will be key to their business model, are social and emotional—such as meeting, socializing and golfing with other golf enthusiasts from around the world.
>
> Next Steven and Martin look at the potential *pains* of the accommodation providers. They break this category down into two sub-categories: the pains associated with their current status quo of not renting out available space to golf travelers; and the pains associated with attempting to rent

out their available space to golf travelers. Under the current status quo, an accommodation provider's pains could include the need for additional income to cover home maintenance, fees and taxes; as well as the cost of a golf club membership and annual dues. In addition, they list as a "pain" the fact that an accommodation provider's available space and golf club memberships can be considered underutilized assets. Social and emotional pains include the difficulty in finding new golfing buddies with free time to play, meeting people with similar interest in golf and other matters, etc.

Pains associated with an accommodation provider's attempt to rent available space to traveling golfers are numerous. In the first instance, they include the difficulty of creating a network of golfers who may be interested in traveling and paying to rent their available space, as well as curating that network and matching with acceptable golf traveler candidates. The pains also include the time, energy and difficulty of presenting and marketing their rental offering, as well as actually hosting a traveling golfer in their home or other accommodation. In addition, there are the stress and potential losses involved with the trust and liability issues inherent in renting property to golf travelers who the accommodation providers likely will have met for the first time.

Steven and Martin believe that the types of *gains* their accommodation providers will be seeking are diverse. They range from the purely economic, such as gaining additional income by renting out underutilized space, to the purely social and emotional, such as meeting and playing golf with people from other parts of the world and becoming a "member" of a worldwide network of golfers. Other desired gains could include the educational benefits of expanding their experience and knowledge base of the game of golf, or even business-related benefits such as networking with potential business partners from other geographical areas while hosting them for a golf/work holiday.

Turning to the user/golf traveler side of their P2P platform, Steven and Martin identified numerous *jobs* that they believe their golf travelers will want to accomplish. These include all of the tasks which must be performed in order to arrange and travel to a desired location where they can play golf with a local person, including informational jobs such as researching potential destinations and discovering and matching with acceptable providers, and logistical jobs such as making payments and arranging transportation. In addition, they will want to perform the social job of meeting, socializing and playing golf with local golfers in their desired location who have extensive knowledge of the golf course, the community and its surrounding area. Finally, they want to become a member of a network of international golfers.

The *pains* associated with accomplishing all of these tasks include the costs in money, time and effort, as well as developing the necessary technology and obtaining the necessary data. Among the costs involved in golf tourism are those of accommodation, transportation, meals, green fees, instruction, etc. The pains also include all aspects of planning and booking the trip that a golf tour operator would normally deal with, such as finding acceptable transportation to and around the desired location, finding and booking accommodation and tee times, etc. Pains involved in staying with a local provider, rather than a hotel, include finding an acceptable host and ensuring the safety and quality of accommodation. They also include finding a network of host golfers, and then screening and matching with the available providers with respect to level of play, motivations, age, income, personality, background, club memberships, etc. Steven points out that there are pains involved in staying in traditional golf travel accommodation as well, such as a sterile experience, lack of a golf buddy with local golf course knowledge, and having to research your own activities, restaurants, etc. for the trip.

The *gains* the traveling golfers hope to achieve are wide ranging as well. Some may want to achieve cost savings by finding accommodation that is cheaper than a hotel and with better atmosphere, but without any safety or quality concerns. Most traveling golfers, Steven and Martin believe and count on, will want to achieve social and emotional gains as well. These include renting space from a local golf enthusiast who could give them a new like-minded golf buddy with knowledge of the golf course, and a truly hospitable and unique local experience away from the course. On top of this, however, the gains they hope to achieve will likely include performing the jobs and minimizing the pains involved in golf travel in a manner that involve the least friction and allow them to communicate directly with their desired provider. Golf tour operators greatly minimize friction and

Steven and Martin's users will expect a similar experience. And finally, the golf travelers, like the accommodation providers, will want to become a "member" of a worldwide golf network that provides them information and a social platform for the game they love. In this sense, some users will want to feel that they are part of something relatively exclusive, the same as a golf club.

The next question Steven and Martin need to address is who are the people on both sides of their P2P platform who will most wish to perform the jobs, who most experience the pains and most desire the gains that they have identified. In other words, who will be the *target customer segments* of accommodation providers and golf travelers for their golf travel P2P platform?

For both the accommodation providers and golf traveler users, Steve and Martin first list the demographic characteristics that they think will be most relevant, and they want to identify when they test their customer segment hypothesis: With respect to golf, these demographics include golf skill level (low, medium and high handicap); golf interest level (serious, serious-social, or social); club member or non-club member; golf frequency; and golf travel frequency. Generic demographic characteristics that then want to identify are age, gender, marital status, income level, occupation type, home location, education level, ethnicity, computer literacy level, and level of participation in the sharing economy (especially Airbnb).

With respect to accommodation providers only, Steven and Martin want to know their motivation for renting out space, the type of space they have available, what available access they have to local golf courses, the amount of free time they have available to golf with guests, their level of desire to golf with guests, and their desired fees for renting out space. Regarding golf travelers, they want to identify their motivation for travel (purely golf, golf and culture, golf and relaxation, golf and education, golf and business, etc.), the golf course features they desire, the accommodation features they desire, the surrounding area features they desire, their average length of golf travel trip, the time of year they prefer for golf travel, the geographic area they prefer for golf travel, their budget for golf travel, who they like to travel with on golf excursions, etc.

Based on what they know from experience at their Napa Valley resort, Steven and Martin make their own educated guess of their customer segment profile for both the accommodation providers and golf travelers. Once they've done so, they list them on their Business Model Canvas. But now it's time for them to get out of the office and test their Value Proposition Canvas hypothesis regarding jobs, pains and gains, and their initial customer segment hypothesis.

Steven and Martin first develop a plan for testing their hypothesis that consists of the following series of escalating tests:

In-Person Interviews: They set up and conduct in-person interviews with dozens of golfers in the San Francisco Bay area. In these interviews, they seek to gauge the level of interest in their business concept, both from a golf traveler and accommodation provider perspective. They also elicit potential customers' views on the jobs, pains and gains involved from both sides of the equation, and then compare those answers to their own hypothesis. Finally, they collect as much information as possible on the persons interviewed in terms of demographic characteristics, lifestyle, golf and travel habits, and motivations. This information is used to refine their target customer segment hypothesis. As a call to action, they ask each person interviewed whether they could follow up with an e-mail once their project is further along.

Low-tech Homepage Test: Using the information they received in their interviews, Steven and Martin develop a basic homepage and several linked pages that include a dozen prototype accommodation listings, of different varieties for testing purposes, as well as dummy links for various other features designed to test which pains potential customers would be interested in solving and which gains they most want to achieve. They then invite the persons who positively answered their initial call to action to visit the home page, answer a follow-up questionnaire, and participate in a telephone or in-person follow-up as well. Finally, through their golf club and resort contacts they obtain the names and e-mail addresses of 200 golfers outside of the San Francisco area, and invite them to view the homepage, answer the questionnaire, and participate in follow-up telephone calls.

Sister-Cities Test: Now it's time to test how their business concept would play out in the real world, and to find out what the actual jobs, pains and gains their customers would experience while using their golf travel platform. Steven and Martin choose three golf courses in California where they are confident they will be able to enlist participants for their test: a highly-rated public golf course in San Diego, a private golf club in Los Angeles, and their own semi-private golf club in Napa valley. For each location they recruit at least a dozen persons who are willing to be accommodation providers for the test (attempting to choose a mix of different personal demographics, accommodation types, etc.). Then they invite each of those accommodation providers, as well as another dozen golfers from each location, to become golf travelers and visit one or both or their sister cities for a round of golf. They post very basic listings on their low-tech home page and a simple private chat function that will allow direct communication between two persons. Then they simply allow the golf travelers and accommodation providers to work out the other details by themselves during the following month-long test period.

Follow-up Interviews: After one month, Steven and Martin conduct follow-up interviews with each person who participated in their sister cities test. At the end of those interviews, they have collected a wealth of real-world experience from their test group about what their real problems and needs would be as customers on either end of the LinksBuddy platform, as well as who they're most valuable target segment will consist of. There will be further tests in this area, but they are now prepared to move on and first adjust, and then test, their value proposition hypothesis based on the information, analysis, and revisions they have made to date.

CHAPTER 5:
VALUE PROPOSITION

Chapter Overview

What is a Value Proposition? 101
Stating Your Value Proposition Hypothesis 103
Gathering Customer Feedback on Your Value Proposition 106
Assessing, Revising and Iterating Your Value Proposition 112
Validating Your Value Proposition 114
LinksBuddy Case Study 115

CHAPTER 5

VALUE PROPOSITION

Now that you have an idea of exactly who your target customers will be and what their problems and needs are, it's time to develop an overall product offering that solves those problems and satisfies those needs.

Once again, it's impossible to emphasize enough the importance of problem/solution fit with the ultimate goal being product/market fit. In fact, we could probably combine these two ideas into one: the "problem/solution/market fit." This is because your "product" will only form a part of your solution. Your customers aren't primarily concerned with what your product is, they're mostly concerned about having their problems solved and needs fulfilled. So your goal should be to find an overall solution that on the one hand solves the important problem, and on the other hand creates an offering that becomes a "must have" for the target market.

In order to accomplish this goal, you need to develop a "value proposition"—comprised of your overall solution, not just your product—that the customers in your target market desire highly enough (adds enough value to their lives) to convince them to purchase your product, rather than one of a competitor, at a price that will drive a sustainably profitable enterprise, and afterwards remain loyal customers.

A highly successful example is Uber, whose core value proposition is making it easier to get car transportation, no matter the time of day or location. But they also allow customers a choice of price and style, payment options, and choice of driver based on ranking of safety and efficiency. Further benefits now include WIFI in cars and even having the driver pick up your groceries on their way to pick you up. By supplying all these benefits together with the standard transportation "product" of getting their customers from point A to point B, they have created significant value for their customers by solving problems and satisfying needs that their competitors—especially traditional taxis—do not. And customers have responded by their willingness to pay for these added benefits.

What is a Value Proposition?

A "value proposition" is a concise statement of how your product offering benefits a target consumer and why they should buy your product over that offered by a competitor. It answers customer questions such as "What does your product offering do for me?" and "Why is your product offering better for me than competing product offerings?" You should be able to describe your value proposition in a relatively concise statement, and this statement should address what it is the customers are really buying. This means not just a description of your product, its key features, and the functions it performs, but also of the tangible and intangible benefits that the purchaser will receive from the product and your business. This includes why your product will add more value to their lives or better solve their problem than alternative offerings on the market.

For example, let's say that three friends with degrees in infant psychology wanted to open up a daycare center in a nice facility with a child pickup and drop-off service. Their product is the daycare center with the added features. But their value proposition to the customers includes convenience, significant time savings, peace of mind, pre-pre-school education for their children, etc. The product offering eliminates one pain point of many parents—getting their kids to and from daycare every day. And it reduces another—trust and qualification issues surrounding daycare providers.

The types of "value" that a customer may look for when buying a product include:

- **Cost savings:** these savings could come in the form of a lower priced product to that offered by a competitor, or a cost-saving alternative provided to a customer who otherwise would perform a task him or herself

- **Time savings**: in today's chaotic world, many people have way too much to do and way too little time to do it—time savings may be one of the most important benefits they look for in any product

- **Physical and mental energy savings:** almost as important as cost and time savings is the relief from having to spend additional energy to complete a task by paying for someone else to do it for you or for a product to do it more easily

- **Convenience:** once again, this could mean making it more convenient to pay for a service rather than self-performance, or could mean a variety of factors which make a particular offering the most convenient to purchase and use

- **Performance:** certain customer segments for certain products, such as gamers buying computer hardware and software, may place a premium value on performance and will shun inferior products that other segments may find satisfactory

- **Quality:** often going hand in hand with performance is quality; for example, the value proposition for a fine wine would be much different than for a cheap table wine (as would be the target customer segment)

- **Status:** some customers will purchase certain products primarily because the item itself confers a certain social status—Rolex watches and Gucci handbags, for example

- **Design:** all things being equal, and often even if they are not, many customers will buy a certain product because they believe it looks better than the alternatives—think Corvette

- **Entertainment value:** one of the most important but also intangible value factors is that a product makes a customer happy, or is fun or interesting to own and/or use—the primary benefit of something as basic as a kitchen utensil may be the "joy factor" it gives its owner

- **Customization**: a product that can be customized to suit a purchaser's needs may be much more valuable to them than an off-the-shelf product, such as the way Trek enables cyclists to build a bike from the ground up, giving it a competitive advantage with avid cyclers

- **Annoyance Reduction:** people often prefer products that reduce the pain of everyday annoyances and will buy those that do so the best—Uber eliminates the annoyance of having to stand on a curb and hail a cab, and millions of people are paying for that benefit

- **Risk reduction**: even if you are able to perform a task yourself, paying for additional technology or professional assistance, such as that provided by tax software, may be worth the peace of mind of knowing that the task will be performed correctly

The list is really endless. But as you can see, some of these items provide value in the form of tangible and intangible benefits, some of them create value by solving problems and others are valuable because they perform specific tasks. In addition, some are provided directly by the product itself, but others will come from a combination of product, pricing, customer service, distribution and the like.

Stating Your Value Proposition Hypothesis

So in order to start working on your value proposition, start with the obvious question of: What value will my offering provide my target customers? In other words, what ways will it benefit their lives? While doing so, always bear in mind the fact that the most important thing you are trying to do is not develop the best product, but to develop an all-around product offering that best solves

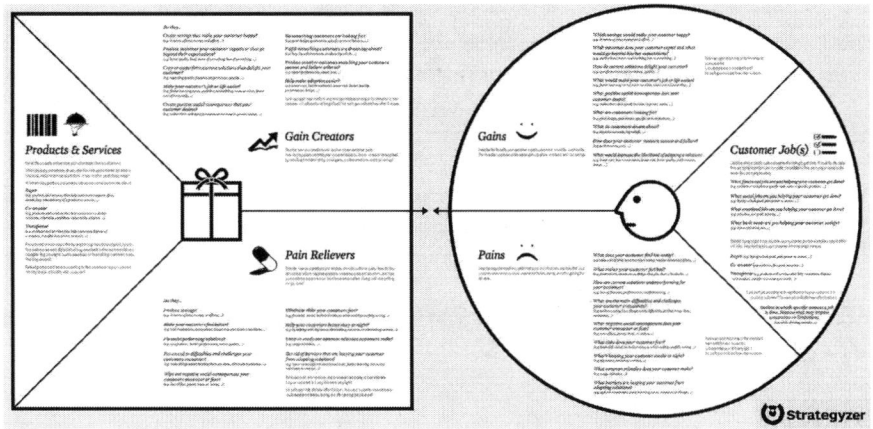

your customers' problems and satisfies their needs, as well as performs the desired functions of course.

To flesh out your value proposition in a structured and efficient manner, turn now to the left side of the Value Proposition Canvas.

As you can see, this portion of the Value Proposition Canvas breaks your value proposition down into:

- **Products and services**: a list of all the products and services included in your value proposition

- **Gain creators**: a description of how your products and services will create customer gains

- **Pain relievers**: a description of how your products and services will reduce or eliminate customer pains

Pain relievers and gain creators are not the same thing as the pains and gains you listed in your customer profile. You have the ability to choose what pain relievers and gain creators you will develop and offer to target specific jobs, pains and gains identified on the right side of the Value Proposition Canvas. In contrast, you have no choice over which jobs, pains and gains your customers have and consider important.

The "products and services" section of the Value Proposition Canvas is straightforward. List all of the products and services you will offer to the relevant target customer segment—remember you should have a customer profile for each major segment. Include everything that your product offering will consist of, including customer service, warranties, distribution options, etc. This collection of products and services should directly assist your customers in performing the jobs you listed on the right side of the Value Proposition Canvas. Once again, it is important to identify and rank your products and services in terms of importance to your customers. Some will be essential to your customers (if not then you need to immediately assess the viability of your value proposition), but others will be things which your customers consider nice to have but not critical.

"Pain relievers" address specific customer pains. Describe exactly how your value proposition will reduce or eliminate those pains by performing an important task and/or reducing or eliminating a pain point. You should now have your target customers' pains prioritized on the right side of your Value Proposition Canvas. In the pain relievers section, you need to describe how your product offering will address the most important pain points that your customers are experiencing. Don't be concerned if you don't address every minor pain, but if your product offering does not yet address each critical pain, or at least a sufficient number of them, then you've already gained valuable insight into how you need to improve your product. The more critical pains you relieve, the more value you provide to your customer.

In the "gain creators" section, describe the benefits and outcomes you will deliver to your customer that fulfill the expectations or desires listed in the gains section of your customer profile. Once again, focus on both tangible and intangible gain creators that your customers will most value, and be sure to include gain creators for functional, social and emotional gains that your customers will value.

Also, remember that each one of your customer segments may have different problems and needs, and may use your product in different ways. Therefore, you should create a Value Proposition Canvas with respect to each important customer segment—and you may have a different value proposition for each segment. And do not list all your products and services on every segment profile, only those targeted at the specific segment. You do not want to offer pain relievers and gain creators that have nothing to do with the pains and gains in the customer profile for that segment.

To continue with the health club example we used in Chapter 4, products and services offered to customers could include weight lifting and exercise machines, a gym and swimming pool, massage and physical therapists, a shuttle bus, discount memberships for seniors, medical exams, private fitness training, health food and power drinks, etc. Which products and services, pain relievers and gain creators you eventually choose to provide will depend in large part on the most important jobs, pains and gains of your target customer segment, as well as their enthusiasm for your proposed solutions.

However, make sure you start this process by brainstorming. List as many potential benefits that you will offer your customers as possible. Don't limit yourself at the beginning—because you may discover later that your best potential customers highly value things that you initially place a low priority on. Once you've come up with your initial list, you can sift through and eliminate some items that obviously don't belong. But wait to get customer feedback before you eliminate too much—you may find during testing that your customers value a pain reliever or gain creator in a vastly different manner than you expected.

At the end of the process, you will need to make hard choices about which jobs, pains and gains your value proposition will target. Trying to be all things to all people is normally a recipe for disaster. Do not offer pain relievers and gain creators that have nothing to do with the pains in the customer profile. Your goal should be to provide a very good solution to your customers most important problems. If you achieve this goal, you are a long way down the road to success.

Gathering Customer Feedback on Your Value Proposition

In testing your value proposition hypothesis, you want to find a combination of ways to ask potential customers some of the same questions you just asked yourself when filling out your Value Proposition Canvas. You want to find out what value your customers believe your product offering would add to their lives, what gains it would create and what pains it would reduce, what competitive advantages they see in your offering, what solutions and features they are really excited about and what they are ambivalent or indifferent to, etc. Once again, you need to create pass/fail tests that allow you to either validate or invalidate different aspects of your value proposition, while at the same time obtaining qualitative insights that help you learn as much as possible.

If you are following our recommended testing sequence described in Chapter 3, at this point you have already tested your customer profile hypothesis, gained valuable insights and understanding regarding your target customers' problems and needs and revised your customer profile accordingly. In addition, you have used your revised customer profile to revise your initial value proposition. Now it is time to present your product offering directly to your customer and confirm whether or not your revised value proposition hypothesis stands up to their scrutiny and is received with enough enthusiasm to buy your product.

What you are looking for in testing is concrete evidence showing whether or not your customers believe your value proposition will reduce or eliminate their pains and create their desired gains, and care enough to purchase your product. So you need to design tests that measure this. You are also looking for qualitative insight and understanding that will allow you to learn and improve your value proposition. So your tests need to elicit this information as well. Finally, you want to understand which features of your value proposition customers value the most, and which they value the least, so you can make sure you keep the important and eliminate the unimportant.

Once again, a key strategic question is whether you gather this feedback through the use of a product prototype, or simply by describing your offering, in an interview or otherwise, using a visual aid. In answering this question, keep in mind that the goal of initial rounds of Value Proposition testing is to get feedback on your hypothesis quickly so that you can learn, revise your value proposition, and test again. In addition, you want to be able to test the viability of several alternative value propositions. One technique to consider when testing more than one value proposition prototype is split testing, which allows you to compare two or more alternatives, such as two or more landing pages offering different value propositions, or two or more recipes for BBQ sauce.

The point is that spending too much time, money and energy on an initial prototype that may not survive the initial testing process does not make sense in most cases. In the first iteration, don't worry if you're not able to quickly and cost-effectively create a functional prototype of your product. On the other hand, you want your prototype to be sufficient to serve the testing purposes for which it was designed, otherwise your data may not be sufficiently reliable or complete. So if at all possible, at least create some kind of visual aid for them to look at to give them a visual sense of your product offering. You need to use your best judgment and strike a balance.

The nature and complexity of the prototype you use will also depend on the nature of your business. For example, Web/mobile startups find it hard for customers to visualize the proposed solution without a minimum viable product. If your value proposition will be offered on a website, try to create a simple homepage and two or three click-through pages for them to look at. If you're selling a physical product, a graphic design or simple mock-up is OK.

Try a combination of the visual aids we described in Chapter 3 to maximize your learning in the most efficient way possible. The following testing aids, shown in order of complexity from the least to the most, can be used to obtain valuable insight and feedback on your value proposition before you ever spend any time, money, and resources building a physical product or service.

- Data sheet or power point slides
- Brochure
- Product packaging
- Storyboard
- Video
- Landing page
- 3D product mock-up
- Product Prototype

Data Sheet or Power Point Slide: you can create a data sheet or 3-4 simple slides describing your value proposition, the customer problems it solves, and how the customer's life would look with and without your product or service. You may even want to create a stylized version of your Value Proposition Canvas to show customers who participate in the test.

Brochure: create a mock marketing brochure communicating in clear and simple terms the benefits and features of your value proposition.

Product Packaging: design a prototype of the packaging for product idea that effectively communicates your value proposition. This is a good way to see how they select and respond to different features or aspects of your value proposition.

Storyboard: create a graphic storyboard showing your customer's workflow or daily life without your product, and another using your product that demonstrates its benefits and features.

Video: create a video to showcase the elements of your value proposition and demonstrate how it works. This can even be done using available technology such as a mobile phone.

Landing Page: set up a basic webpage highlighting the elements of your value proposition you want to test. This gives a customer the illusion that your product exists, even if it is only a single page. Include a call to action that allows you to validate one or more of your hypothesis on a pass/fail basis, which could even be a simulated sale.

3D Product Mock-up: this will allow your customer to directly experience the look and feel, if not the functionality, of your product.

Product Prototype: as your testing and learning progress, you can create an actual functioning prototype of your value proposition. However, do not put the cart before the horse—until your value proposition is close to validation, only include the feature set required to gain the learning that you are seeking.

Once you have designed your test and your visual aid/prototype is ready, it's time to present your value proposition to customers and get their feedback. Your ultimate goal is to determine whether you have a product/solution fit and a product/market fit. So you want to get customer feedback on whether they feel your value proposition solves their most important problems, and does so in a manner that makes them very enthusiastic about buying your product.

In your presentation, cover only the product features you want to test and how they solve and important customer problem. Even if you are not using a storyboard as a visual aid, include a description of a customer's life without the product and with the product. Do not try and sell the product. This is not a sales call. You do now want to influence the responses you receive. What you are looking for are measureable responses regarding how the product would benefit their life, whether it solves their most important problem or satisfies their most important need, what the required features for them would be, and whether this is a product they would purchase and recommend to others. In an interview, stop often and obtain feedback. Also observe closely the customer's reactions and behavior during the presentation.

Here's a product/ solution presentation outline that you can use as a guide:

- Review the problem—start by reminding the audience about problems the product is designed to solve and why a solution is important if not urgent.

- Pause to have the customer re-validate the importance of solving the problem

- Describe the solution while allowing the customer to interact with your visual aid or prototype

- Pause to get feedback on whether your customer believes your value proposition solves their important problem?

- Show the customer his or her work flow before and after the new product

- Pause to have the customer validate the "before and after" work flow

- Describe who else in the customer's organization or circle of family and friends the solution might affect.

- Pause to validate whether the customer would recommend your solution to others

- Describe your revenue model and potential price points

- Pause to explore pricing boundaries and validate what benefits the customer would pay for and how much they would be willing to pay

- What do customers think about the proposed revenue model and pricing?

- What are comparable prices for this kind of product?

- What do they pay now?

After you've presented your value proposition and noted your customers initial reactions, now it's time to ask purposeful questions designed to elicit measurable responses and valuable insights.

For example, ask your customers:

- How they think your value proposition solves their problem?

- Which aspects of your value propositions create the most value for them?

- What is the value created?

- Which aspects should be saved?

- Which aspects could be discarded without affecting their purchase decision?

- What is missing that they would like to have in the product offering?

- What is missing that they would need to have before purchasing?

Keep in mind that when you ask about pain points and desired benefits, it's important to get some qualitative as well as quantitative feedback. Ask "why" questions as follow-ups to dig deep and capture insightful feedback. At the end of the day, you want to be able to rank aspects of your value proposition, i.e. the gain creators and pain relievers you will offer, in terms of how important each is to your customers. This will allow you to select the most important features to offer your customers—the ones that solve the most critical problems and which your customers are most enthusiastic about buying.

But you also want to understand why any particular aspect of your solution is important or unimportant. It may be that you still haven't nailed down the problem your customers have, and asking why the solution doesn't interest them may expose this, as well as give you insight as to what you were missing with respect to the problem. If you don't ask these follow-up questions, you may end up unnecessarily changing your product offering, or changing it to solve the wrong problem.

You also want to ask your customers about competing products. Find out what other businesses are offering to your customer segment that you will have to compete with and whether those other businesses have a perceived competitive advantage. Find out what benefits does your product offering gives your customers that the competitors' offerings do not. And find out why customers will or will not chose your company's product offering over others on the market.

Once you've presented your value proposition and obtained valuable customer feedback, it's time to inject a call to action to measure behavior to confirm enthusiasm and whether what they have told you in answer to your questions is what they will actually do in practice. You want to get customers to perform an action that you can learn from—such as register for e-mail updates, participate in a survey, registration for notice when the product is available to purchase, pre-order the product, and/or make a referral to other persons.

Finally, it's important to point out once again how your customer segment and value propositions work hand in hand every step of the way. When planning your market research strategy, the persons you identified in your customer segments offer your best guide about the type of person you should approach in gathering feedback for your value proposition. And their problems and needs and characteristics should guide you in what you need to know to validate and finalize your value proposition.

Assessing, Revising and Iterating Your Value Proposition

Once you have collected and assembled all of the feedback, first list and rank the pain relievers and gain creators that the persons you have interviewed in your target customer segment said that they valued the most. Afterwards, see if you can match them to the pain relievers and gain creators you listed in your most recent customer profile and whether you can identify the specific gains and pains that they solve. If you can match a pain reliever or gain creator and are comfortable that the data you received is reliable and sufficient, then you can mark that aspect of your value proposition as validated.

On the other hand, if customers told you that pain relievers and gain creators that you had not included in your value proposition were very important to them, or if they listed any of those you had included as unimportant, you need to understand why they gave these responses and use those insights to revise your value proposition. For example, had determined that 60 percent of customers must be highly enthusiastic about a feature in order to retain it, but only 50 percent gave this answer, then you have a choice to make. You can either discard the feature, or attempt to improve it in a manner that would increase the level of enthusiasm. You will have similar choices to make after reviewing the number and percentage of people who positively accepted the call to action you included in your test.

Adding and deleting product features or other aspects of your value proposition will not always be as straightforward as it seems. Some features that customers highly value may not be viable from either a technological or cost standpoint. Others they valued less highly may have value to another customer segment. In these cases, you will have to assess exactly how to modify your value proposition based on all relevant factors—and almost surely retest the modified version to confirm a product with new desired features and/or without undesired features actually leads to the enthusiasm you need to validate your value proposition.

When analyzing what features to keep, add or discard, it's time to think about a topic we have withheld up until now because we didn't want you to limit your creative thinking in any way: the concept of a "minimum viable product," or MVP.

If you try to be all things to all people, especially at the start, then your business will take too long to get off the ground, and probably fail. So at the beginning, you should select a manageable target customer segment and create an offering that includes the minimum feature set necessary to solve their biggest problems/ meet their most important needs so that they purchase your product, have a positive experience, and become repeat customers and "word-of-mouth" references. That may mean delaying some of the features and services you ultimately want to provide, and not being able to service some groups of potential customers at the start. But it will also give you the ultimate test of your product and customer feedback—meaning actually selling your product in the market— before your business gets in too deep to easily pivot and adapt as necessary.

Therefore, the goal of all these pre-launch iterations should be to discover and confirm the best value proposition to be offered in connection with your MVP, which will be what you offer your customers at launch. It's important to emphasize that the MVP is not a beta version whose development is not yet complete. And it does not simply mean cutting features to launch quickly. It is a real product that has been streamlined to the features most valued by the target customer segment because they solve their core problems and satisfy their core needs, with the goal of continuing to iterate and improve the offering based on post-launch feedback.

Validating Your Value Proposition

When all of the hypothesis contained in your value proposition have been confirmed—when the pain relievers and gain creators have been validated as important by a sufficient number of target segment customers and match up with important pains and gains also validated by customers—then you have evidence of a product/solution fit and are close to validating your value proposition. But you also need evidence of product/market fit, so you need to make sure you have evidence that enough of those customers are enthusiastic about your product, and believe it will create enough value for them, to buy it and then become loyal customers and good references. Finding product/solution/market fit is what searching for the best value proposition is all about. So in validating your value proposition, the key is to make an honest assessment as to whether you have achieved this fit based on the evidence you've obtained in testing.

So what does the evidence of your latest round of testing show? What percentage of your customers that confirmed a product/solution fit said they were highly enthusiastic about your value proposition, said they would purchase it immediately when it becomes available, and have demonstrated this by a call to action? What percentage said your value proposition solved their important problem and said they were likely to purchase, but weren't rabid about obtaining your product? What percentage thought you had a good idea but weren't sure if they would spend money to have it? What percentage weren't interested at all?

If you have met your threshold percentage of highly enthusiastic customers who can't wait to have your product, then it is time to move on to validating your business model that surrounds your value proposition and customer profile. If you have a significant percentage in this category, as well as a significant percentage who said you have solved an important problem but couldn't absolutely commit to buying just yet, then you probably need to assess, revise, and iterate your value proposition once again. But if a significant percentage of customers are either lukewarm or uninterested, you need to take a hard look in the mirror and potentially pivot to another product idea altogether—which often can be done successfully based on all of the feedback received in testing.

LinksBuddy Case Study

Chapter 5
Value Proposition

Now it's time for Steven and Martin to get down to what, for most entrepreneurs, is the most exciting part of creating a new business enterprise: deciding exactly what value they want to offer their customers. They soon discover, however, that it's also the most difficult aspect. Because it quickly becomes apparent that the customers aren't interested in everything they wanted to offer, and have other problems and needs they had never thought about. It is through this process, however, that Steven and Martin discover just how important it is to create, test and verify their business model at the beginning of the process, and just how valuable the Business Model Canvas is in doing so.

Initially, Steven and Martin created an extremely long list of products and services, gain creators and pain relievers to offer their customers, both the golf travelers and the accommodation providers. This list was cut in half following their testing and iteration in the customer segment section once they acquired input directly from customers about the jobs they wanted most to perform, the pains they wanted to avoid and the gains they wanted to achieve. It was further reduced once they had settled on their real target audience, because the realized that some aspects of what they initially thought they needed to offer their customers was not important to their target segment.

So after finishing their sister cities field test and the follow-up interviews, Steven and Martin revised and refined their value proposition first using the Value Proposition Canvas, and then transferring those results to the Business Model Canvas.

Their final value proposition hypothesis for golf travelers focused on several key categories that directly addressed the jobs, pains and desired gains their customers had reported back to them after the field test: reliable information on the website regarding golf travel destinations; a solid network of reliable accommodation providers who matched their ability and interests; efficient and low-friction logistics of golf travel; a cost-effective method of golf-travel; a unique and hospitable golf-travel experience; and participation in a virtual golf community.

Regarding the network of accommodation providers, the LinksBuddy value proposition needed to include an extensive list of accommodation providers, reliable and complete information on the providers and the accommodation, review and curation of the accommodation providers so that no unsatisfactory providers were included, the ability to search accommodation providers by stated preferences, and the ability to communicate directly with accommodation providers. With respect to logistics, they would offer through their website the ability to book and pay for their accommodation and tee times, as well as transportation if they desired. And all of this would be provided on a basis that allowed for a golf travel experience that was just as cost-effective, if not more, than booking through a tour operator.

That took care of the more nuts and bolts aspects of their value proposition. But they found through their customer segment testing that the sizzle had to be in the experience, not in the logistics. What their customers really desired were two things: a *unique* golf travel experience that could not be obtained by booking through a tour operator, and a chance to become a member of a golf *community* that could not only share experiences online, but in person as well. This meant that their value proposition had to offer accommodation and accommodation providers that could provide the type of hospitality and friendship, reliability and safety, local experience and knowledge, and golf buddy camaraderie that their golf travel customers were in search of. This was their competitive advantage over the tour operators—the question was how to ensure quality control in this area since in many aspects it was beyond their control.

Steven and Martin's value proposition hypothesis for the accommodation providers is to some extent the other side of the coin of what was offered to golf travelers; and to some extent the same. The principal aspects of the value proposition for accommodation providers is: a critical mass of reliable golf travelers on the platform who met their preference requirements and are subject to peer reviews; the ability to build a listing on the platform, curate golf travelers who could contact them, and communicate with golf travelers where a mutual interest exists; low-friction logistics of renting their accommodation to golf travelers, including initial booking and payment, schedules and tee times; the ability to make a sufficient financial return for their efforts; a safe and satisfying interpersonal experience with their golf travelers; participation in an extended golf community.

With these value propositions written into their parallel business model canvases for their golf traveler and accommodation provider customer segments, Steven and Martin devise a manner of testing, iterating and validating those value propositions, as well as further testing, iterating and validating their customer segment, and customer problems and needs hypothesis. Their first step is to create a higher-tech homepage and several linked pages that are more realistic and functional than the low-tech version they used in their previous field test. Then they invite all of their previous contacts to visit the site, and ask them to invite friends to do so as well. Finally, they post the site online so that random golfers can also find and test the site. The high-tech site makes clear that it is a prototype being used for testing purposes, and the site includes a call to action where viewers can provide demographic information and sign up for e-mail notification once the site became operational. As part of this process, Steven and Martin make sure that as many web-site metrics as possible can be collected for review.

Steven and Martin then take all of the information they receive from their website test and used it to further refine their value proposition, their target segment and message, their calls to action and their website functionality and contents. This enables them to build their MVP website that can be used in an expanded field test that they hope will validate their value proposition hypothesis and customer segment hypothesis.

For their expanded field test, Steven and Martin build upon their sister cities test by choosing three more locations outside of California to match with the three original locations. Once again they chose one private golf club, one semi-private club and one public course located in Scottsdale, Arizona; Palm Beach, Florida; and Atlanta, Georgia, respectively. Even though they had previous contacts in Florida and Georgia, Steven and Martin found it much more difficult to enlist accommodation providers to participate in the test. In the end, they had to rent several houses themselves and have local golf pros round up friends to stay in the houses and golf with the guests. In addition, all of the required features and functionality could not be programmed into the MVP website in short order, so Steven and Martin handled requirements such as booking transportation and tee times themselves by telephone and e-mail. All other functions they attempted to push the golf travelers and accommodation providers to handle among themselves.

Steven and Martin went into their value proposition tests thinking they had pretty much nailed it already and just needed confirmation. They were blown away by how much they learned and how many adjustments they still needed to make. They learned that their target segment for cross-country travel shifted about ten years to the younger. They learned how important assurances of safety and reliability would be for strangers. They learned that a key strategic decision that had to be made was how much to centralize operations and provide many services as part of their value proposition, and how much to decentralize and push into the hands of their accommodation providers and golf travelers. If they had never run these tests and just ramped up and launched their operations based on their hypothesis, they would have fallen flat on their faces. Now they have the chance to revise, iterate, and test once more before spending big money on marketing and an official launch. Steven made a special call of thanks to Peter, and took the opportunity to ask for some more advice.

CHAPTER 6:
CHANNELS

Chapter Overview

Types of Channels 122
Making Your Channel Hypothesis 123
      Promotion of Your Product/Value Proposition 123
      Sale and Distribution of Your Product 124
      Customer Service and Support 129
Which Channels Should I Choose? 129
Gathering Customer Feedback on Your Proposed Channels 131
Revising, Iterating and Validating Your Channels 132
LinksBuddy Case Study 133

CHAPTER 6

CHANNELS

Once you have your value proposition and have identified a specific segment of potential customers who desire what you have to offer, the question now is: how do you quickly, efficiently and cost-effectively get your value proposition into the hands of those target customers, provide them with its full benefits, and keep them coming back for more?

In order to answer that question, you need to ask yourself several other questions:

- How will I communicate my value proposition to attract a target customer's attention and convince them to buy my product?

- How will I actually sell my product?

- How will I distribute my product?

- How will I provide customer support?

- How will I retain my customers and convince them to buy multiple times in the future?

The answer to each of these questions will require some form of interaction with your customers. And the vehicles you will use to interact with your customers at different stages of what some refer to as the *"customer journey"* are called *"channels"* of communication, sales and distribution.

The stages of the customer journey are as follows:

- **Attention:** making the customer aware of your product offering/value proposition

- **Evaluation:** providing the customer with the information necessary to generate interest, compare your product offering favorably with the competition, and consider making a purchase decision

- **Desire:** convincing the customer to select your product offering and commit to the purchase

- **Action:** transacting the actual sale

- **Delivery:** providing your product and the benefits of your value proposition to the customer

- **Satisfaction:** providing customer support that keeps the customer satisfied and loyal

- **Retention:** convincing the customer to purchase again and again

- **Growth:** persuading the customer to buy more of your product and also purchase other products you have for sale

Your choice of channels at each stage of the customer journey is extremely important, to the degree that it can actually become part of your value proposition. Your channels of communication will clearly have a large impact on whether you are able to translate your value proposition into a successful sale, and your channels of sales, distribution and customer support, retention and growth will affect whether you end up with a satisfied customer who will make repeat purchases.

This second point is critical, because what is called your *"cost of acquisition"* (discussed in greater detail in Chapter 10) in securing the first purchase is almost always much higher than for follow-on purchases. So the more times a customer purchases your product, the higher profit percentage you will make off that particular customer. What you are shooting for is a high *"lifetime value"* of purchases relative to your customer's cost of acquisition.

In addition, your choice of channels will have a large impact on the economic viability of your business model. Every interaction with a customer requires an expenditure of time, resources and money. So you need to choose channels that perform the task well and achieve the results you require, while not costing so much that the business model collapses under their weight and you can't turn a profit no matter how many customers buy your product. In other words, you need a good return on your investment of time, resources and money in each channel you choose.

It may be an effective product awareness method to go door to door to every house in your town and tell them that you have just opened a new computer repair shop, but it certainly wouldn't be efficient or cost-effective to do so. Neither would spending thousands of dollars on television advertising broadcast in areas well beyond your reach. You need to find a channel that most effectively and efficiently reaches your target customer segment during the relevant stage of the customer journey, and allows you to develop the relationship with your customer that you desire, which we will discuss in the next chapter.

At each stage, therefore, you will need to evaluate what type of channel best performs its individual function and best integrates with the rest of your business model. You also need to examine which works best for your particular product—meaning you have a good *"product/channel fit."* Finally, you need to decide at each stage whether to interact with different customer segments through the same or different channels.

Types of Channels

Channels at every stage can be physical or virtual, direct or indirect.

Physical channels are the traditional forms of communication, sales and distribution, such as the use of salespeople to meet with customers, the physical shipping of products to stores, and the use of cash and a cash register to transact a sale. Physical channels are often high cost in terms of both time and money, but effective in terms of personal service.

Virtual channels have revolutionized the customer journey and how business is transacted. No human involvement is required, with advertising, sales and even distribution of many products all possible over the Internet, on mobile devices, etc. Most companies use both physical and virtual channels today. For example, although it offers its products online, Amazon.com still must physically distribute its products to customers. And although it has dealerships nationwide, General Motors still promotes its products and offers customer service and retention programs online.

Direct channels are where your business or its representatives interact directly with the customers. For example, you communicate with customers through your own website, sell to customers through your own retail shop, and/or deliver your product to your customer directly. Indirect channels are where you use a third party to perform one of these functions. For example, you sell to a wholesaler, who in turn sells and distributes to retailers, who then advertise, sell and distribute directly to the customers.

Making Your Channel Hypothesis

You will need to select a vehicle or vehicles for interacting with your customers in each of the following stages:

- Promotion of your product (attention, evaluation, desire)
- Sale of your product
- Distribution of your product
- Customer support both before and after the sale
- Customer retention to ensure additional purchases
- Customer growth

Promotion of Your Product/Value Proposition

Promotion is one of the 4 Ps of traditional marketing, and is what most people typically think of when they hear the term "marketing." It is the communication of information to your target market in an attempt to get their attention, educate them and convince them to buy your product both now and in the future. Promotion can be earned (free but requiring the use of human resources) or paid for. The four major types of promotion typically integrated into a marketing strategy are advertising, publicity, sales promotions and personal selling. Your promotional mix should be designed to reach as much of the target audience as possible in a manner that gives you a good return on your investment of money, time and other resources—i.e. best achieves your marketing and business goals of acquiring, retaining and growing customers.

Communication channels for product promotion include:

- Owned website
- Third party websites
- Mobile applications
- E-mail
- Traditional media such as television, radio and print
- Direct sales staff
- Sales agents
- Direct mail advertising
- Signage

The communication channels you choose will be directly related to the nature of your product, the promotional mix you choose, the type of customer relationship you wish to develop, the cost of using the channel, and the return on channel investment you will receive.

Sale and Distribution of Your Product

Another of the 4 Ps is "place," which involves where, when and how your customer will actually purchase your product, as well as where, when and how you will deliver it to the customer. In filling out your Business Model Canvas, create initial hypotheses about whether your customers wish to purchase directly from you or from wholesalers or retailers, whether they will place orders online or otherwise and have them shipped, or take possession of the product at its point of sale. The first key is to determine where your potential buyers will expect to purchase your product, and make the purchase available to them in that location. The second is to determine how, when and in what quantity your customers will expect to have the product delivered to them, and devise an efficient and cost-effective manner of doing so. Of course all of these hypotheses will be subject to testing and validation—you may think your customers wish to purchase your product in a certain place and have it delivered in a certain manner, but you may find out in testing they have other preferences.

The ultimate goal of all your product development, marketing and sales efforts will be to get your product into the hands of the end user, because it is the end user who will drive product demand. You can have the best product in the world and thousands of eager buyers, but if you can't get your product to your customers where and when they want to buy, none of it has any meaning.

While direct sales are one way to accomplish this goal, it is not the only or necessarily the best way to do so. Your strategy should be to sell to the person or organization in the distribution channel that will best deliver your product to the end user.

A distribution channel is the chain of individuals and organizations involved in getting a product or service from the producer to the consumer. There are many factors to consider when selecting the appropriate distribution channel for a given product. You need to fully understand who it is you are planning to market to and select distribution routes that will make the most sense for those targets.

Depending on the type of product your business offers, the best distribution channel may be obvious, or you may have multiple viable routes to choose from. Keep in mind, however, that while increasing the number of ways in which a consumer can find your product has the potential to increase sales, it also creates complexities that can make distribution management difficult and costly. In addition, the longer the distribution channel, the less profit you might get from the sale.

The basic physical distribution alternatives are:

- Direct Sales

- Independent Sales Agents

- Distributors
- Dealers
- Retailers
- Wholesalers
- Mass Merchandisers
- Original Equipment Manufacturer (OEM)
- Systems Integrators/Value Added Resellers (VARs)

Direct sales: direct salespersons are employees who promote and sell your product to the end user or an intermediary. While you have the ability to directly manage their efforts and require that they sell only your products, this is a very expensive method of sales.

Independent sales agents: to avoid many of the fixed costs involved in maintaining a direct sales staff, and to have access to good salespersons across a broad geographic territory, many businesses use independent sales agents who work on a commission basis. The downside is that there is less control over independent agents, and the agents will most often represent more than one product line so their focus and loyalty will be diluted.

Distributor: a distributor is an independent agent who offers and sells the product of another business but does not use the product manufacturer's name as part of its own business name. As opposed to a sales agent, a distributor buys products from the manufacturer, stores them, and resells them to dealers, retailers or customers. Most distributors also provide some marketing, technical support, and other services that benefit the supplier.

Dealer: a dealer is similar to a distributor, but is not an agent of the producer. A dealer normally buys from the producer or a distributer and then sells only to retailers and customers. Some of them might actually add some service or support but they're essentially an extension of the distribution channel.

Retailers: retailers are small and large businesses that sell products directly to consumers, whether individuals or businesses. To realize a profit, retailers search for products that coincide with their business objectives and find suppliers with the most competitive pricing. Generally, a retailer can buy small quantities of an item from a distributor, dealer or wholesaler.

Wholesalers: Wholesalers buy one or more products in bulk from one or more manufacturers and sell them at prices that are typically lower than those available from retailers. They often sell in bulk to businesses or large institutions who use the products in their business operations.

Mass merchandisers: mass merchandisers are national chains such as Wal-Mart and Costco.

Original Equipment Manufacturers: OEMs buy a product and then integrate it into their own product. For example, a PC maker buys hard drives, semiconductors, circuit boards and keyboards from scores of manufacturers and assembles those products into a computer for sale to end users.

Systems integrators/VARs: systems integrators/VARs add value to the products they sell by providing services such as consulting, or by including additional products from other manufacturers.

The basic virtual distribution alternatives are:

- Owned website
- Independent e-distributors
- Dedicated e-commerce
- Aggregators
- Mobile applications
- Social commerce
- Free to paid channels

Owned website: you offer your products for sale and provide information about your products directly on your own website.

Independent e-distributors: these are e-commerce sites that help generate awareness and demand such as Amazon.com and Apple and Android app stores. This channel maintains inventory, packs and ships the goods, and collects payment.

Aggregators: The online equivalent of a physical shopping mall, usually in a single category of products. They aggregate consumers with common areas of interest and direct them through a virtual supermarket of products.

Mobile-app commerce: Apple and Google's Android offer app stores that allow mobile users to buy everything from games to expense-account software for their iPhone or Android phones.

Social commerce: social networks like Facebook and Twitter have moved quickly to turn their platforms into commerce to monetize their vast audiences.

Flash sales: Flash sales offer a list of consumers deep discounts on branded merchandise with offers expiring in 24 or 48 hours. These social-commerce sites deliver the revenue and a volume of customers.

Free-to-paid channel: A few fast-growing companies such as Zynga have used social networking to create vast audiences of free users of games. They provide a certain amount of game play for free—sometimes even all of it— but sell lots of web/ mobile goods for real cash as they "hook" their users on the game.

The strength of your distribution network can make or break your business, and if physical distribution of your product is required, it is often more effective and efficient to have distribution performed by third parties that are familiar with the local market and close to the customers. This will especially be the case when you are selling products outside of your home state, or the United States for that matter.

It also makes sense to hire businesses that specialize in distribution because they will have the infrastructure and systems in place to most efficiently get your product in the hands of your customers, and will often be responsible for marketing in their assigned region as well. In addition, distributors will be responsible for warehousing and shipping and will take on credit risk for uncollectible accounts receivable.

Distribution intermediaries need to make a profit as well, however, so in return for shouldering these responsibilities the distributor may request preferable terms for the purchase of your product. In addition, the distributor might demand exclusive rights to the territory they cover, which will add a whole new level of negotiation when it comes to the distribution agreement.

A mistake many new businesses make is to use too many sales and distribution channels. At the outset, you should select a sales and distribution channel that best meets your needs and focus on it to the exclusion of all others. You can add additional channels as you scale and grow.

Customer Service and Support

Exceptional customer service is one of a business's primary means of attracting new customers and ensuring repeat customers. Customers will take their business elsewhere if they are not completely satisfied with the way a company treats them before, during and after the sale. Channels for customer service and support include the following:

- Telephone
- E-mail
- Chat via website or social media
- FAQs
- Direct service calls
- In-shop service

Which Channels Should I Choose?

The bottom line for channels at each stage of the customer journey is that every channel will have its own economic model, and there will be a cost-benefit tradeoff to each choice that you need to understand thoroughly when creating your business model.

One of the best ways to do this is to make a flow-chart showing the channels used throughout the customer journey, how the product moves from your business into the hands of the customer, and the costs involved at each stage. In general, you will find that partner/indirect channels have lower margins but allow your organization to expand its reach and benefit from the strengths of your partner, and owned/direct channels have higher margins but can be expensive to put in place and operate.

Keep in mind that you almost surely will not be able to afford all of the channels possible, at least not when you first start your business. Most successful new enterprises choose a limited number of channels that will best accomplish their purposes in a cost-effective manner, and then expand into others as the business matures and the business model is more fully validated.

So now it's time to get down to business and make your initial channel hypothesis. Start by asking yourself these questions:

- Where and when can you best get across your marketing messages to your target market?

- Through which channels do our customers want to be reached at each stage?

- How will these channels be integrated?

- Which channels do you have access to?

- Which ones are the most cost efficient?

- What channels will make you most visible to customers?

You will have to assume certain things in order to make these propositions. Document your assumptions and see if they hold true once you receive some feedback from customers. And experiment with new possibilities. You've got a new business idea; look for new channel opportunities as well.

Gathering Customer Feedback on Your Proposed Channels

In order to efficiently and cost-effectively communicate with your key customer segments and convince them to buy, make your product available where, when and how they want to purchase it, and deliver it to them where, when and how they want it delivered, you need to understand in detail everything your customers do on a daily basis—i.e. where you can reach them, and more importantly where they want to be reached, every step of the way on the customer journey. So you need to perform interviews and get detailed answers to questions that will allow you to create a profile journey for your profile customers.

For example, you will want to collect the following information from your target customers:

- Do they use the Internet and how often?
- Where else can you reach them to make them aware of your product?
- Where do they shop for products?
- How do they pay?
- Where do they take possession?
- Do they buy often?

With respect to each channel proposition you have made, you can also ask questions similar to those you asked about your value proposition. For example: Does this channel meet their needs? Does it solve their problems? Does it reduce or eliminate pain points? "Why" and "what if" questions are also helpful.

You will also need to test both the cost-effectiveness and volume potential of several channels to determine where to put your energy, focus, and marketing dollars. Design the test to see which channel delivers customers at the lowest cost per customer, and which delivers the greatest absolute number of customers.

Revising, Iterating and Validating Your Channels

As much as anything in your business model, settling on the right channels to use, and how to efficiently and effectively use them, is going to require a lot of trial and error and a lot of difficult decision making. You need to choose the appropriate channel in all five different stages of the customer journey, with the added possibility that these channels will be different for different customer segments. Then you need to integrate these channels with each other and the rest of your business model.

To do all of this, try and break it down into simple steps. First sift through the data you have received from your testing, and determine whether you need to add to, subtract from, or revise your initial channel propositions. Then analyze the strengths and weaknesses of each channel you have selected, as well as your channel proposition as a whole.

Focus on these key areas:

- How effective will this channel be in reaching my customers and satisfying their expectations?

- How cost-efficient will this channel be—i.e. how will it impact the overall economics of my business model?

- How well can I integrate this channel with the other channels, customer relationships, key partners and the rest of my business model?

- What channels need to be different for different customer segments, and where they might overlap?

In the end, you want to choose the channels for each stage of the customer journey that your testing has validated will be the most effective and cost efficient, and best fits your product and the other aspects of your business model.

> **LinksBuddy Case Study**
>
> # Chapter 6
> # Channels
>
> Once Steven and Martin feel like they are approaching validation of their customer segment and value proposition, it's time for them to look seriously at the vehicles and methods they will use to acquire, retain and grow their customer base. And in doing so, they are now squarely confronted with the P2P chicken-and-egg problem that they identified at the start of the process. How do they acquire, retain and grow accommodation providers when the best, and maybe only, way to do so is to have on board a strong network of golf travelers looking for accommodation and golf partners, and vice versa?
>
> Upon Peter's advice, Steven and Dan agree to trust the iterative business modeling process they are engaged in to provide the answers. Starting at the beginning, they work step-by-step through the entire customer journey for both their accommodation providers and golf travelers, identifying what they think will be the best channels and customer relationship approaches at each step: attention; evaluation; desire; action; delivery; satisfaction; retention; and growth. Their initial channel and customer relationship hypothesis include mostly virtual channels and automated service through the website. But during the customer segment and value proposition testing process, they experience a seismic shift in their view of the best approach for their business model.
>
> In particular, the initial difficulties that Steven and Martin experienced in recruiting accommodation providers to participate in their second sister city field test, when they attempted to recruit only through invitations to view their higher-tech homepage, and their subsequent success when they enlisted local golf pros to help them recruit, led to a virtual epiphany: they could go a long way towards solving their chicken-and-egg problem if they could first recruit a network of local golf professionals (and/or local club members) to act as their representatives in each destination. These local representatives could recruit members or frequent golfers at their club to form a network of accommodation providers who, as a community, could market themselves and their home course as a golf destination. In doing so,

they could all make extra money by renting out available space, and form an extended, potentially worldwide community of golfers to enrich their golfing and social lives. Once a community of accommodation providers was formed in several locations, a range of internet marketing methods could be used to draw golf travelers to the website to get them to evaluate the possibility of traveling to one of those destinations and staying with a member of the local golf community.

In addition, the direct experience that Steven and Martin gain in answering phone calls and making transportation and tee time bookings for golf travelers, and helping with listings for accommodation providers, make them realize they will convert and acquire a much higher percentage of customers on both sides of their P2P platform if they have live customer support personnel who could interact with the customer. These two revelations, each acquired through the testing and iteration process, lead to dramatic changes in the channel and customer relationship pieces of their Business Model Canvas.

Following these revisions, Steven and Martin's channel and customer relationship hypothesis, broken down by step in the customer journey, looks like this for the accommodation provider side of the equation:

In order to attract the accommodation provider's *attention* and make them aware of the LinksBuddy value proposition, Steven and Martin will use a combination of physical and virtual, direct and indirect channels. Of course their website will be a primary channel throughout the customer journey. In order to make potential accommodation providers aware of their website and the value proposition it offers, however, they will need to use SEO and other internet marketing techniques that involve indirect channels, including public relations efforts, links from other websites and some traditional advertising (if cost effective), to drive viewers to the LinksBuddy homepage. But their discovery during testing has convinced Steven and Martin that at the outset of their business, the best way to acquire a critical mass of accommodation providers will be through the channel of local representatives who make golfers in their communities aware of what LinksBuddy has to offer. And once an accommodation provider community is established, then members of that community can become an additional channel to recruit more accommodation providers to list on LinksBuddy.

Once they have a potential accommodation provider's attention, Steven and Martin will use some of these same channels to provide them with the information necessary to *evaluate* the offer and instill the *desire* to list their accommodation and become a links buddy. The website will contain all of the necessary information and calls to action. But it will be reinforced by local representatives meeting with potential accommodation providers, and once the business is up and running, by the community of accommodation providers themselves. In addition, as Steven and Martin discovered during the testing process, in order to close the sale and turn a potential accommodation provider into one who actually lists, there will be customer service representatives available through chat, e-mail and telephone support.

With respect to *action* and *delivery*, there are two aspects to the equation. The first is getting the accommodation provider to take action and list the accommodation on the website, as well as make the offer to become a links buddy with a golf traveler. The second aspect is actually transacting the sale with the golf traveler. Each of these will take place through the website channel. But once again, a customer support channel will be available for assistance, particularly with respect to getting the listing up and running, and with respect to transaction logistics. The local sales representative will also assist in these matters.

Retention of accommodation providers, Steven and Martin realize, will be a key to their business. Until they obtain a critical mass of accommodation providers, the cost of acquisition will be high due to the need for customer support and recruitment by local representatives. And because of the vital importance of obtaining that critical mass, retaining a high percentage of accommodation providers that list will also be a key to the success of the business. Therefore, Steven and Martin will use all available channels to ensure customer satisfaction and retention. In particular, their local representatives will be vital in making sure their accommodation providers have a satisfactory experience. Customer support will follow up with every accommodation provider. Loyalty and recruitment programs and awards will be put in place. In addition, the website will also be a key to customer retention. The more accommodation providers participate in the online community of golf travelers and accommodation providers, the more likely they will remain customers of LinksBuddy.

Finally, Steven and Martin also want to *grow* the business of their accommodation providers. How do they do this? In two ways: first, they want to provide their accommodation providers with incentives to recruit other accommodation providers to LinksBuddy; in addition, they want to motivate their accommodation providers to become golf travelers as well. One of the best ways for Steven and Martin to grow their business, and solve the chicken-and-egg problem at the same time, is to have many customers sitting on both sides of the platform as accommodation providers who are also golf travelers.

CHAPTER 7:
CUSTOMER RELATIONSHIPS

Chapter Overview

Creating Your Customer Relationship Proposition 139
Keep Your Focus on Acquiring, Retaining and Growing Customers 142
      Acquiring Customers 142
      Retaining Customers...144
      Growing Customers..145
Gathering Customer Feedback on Your Customer Relationship
Proposition..146
Revising, Iterating, and Validating Your Customer Relationship
Proposition..148
LinksBuddy Case Study...149

CHAPTER 7

CUSTOMER RELATIONSHIPS

Now that you've identified the customer segments you want to target, and the channels you want to use to reach those customers, you need to consider a block of the business model canvas that many entrepreneurs do not focus on nearly or clearly enough—the type of relationship they will have with their customers.

A *relationship* with customers does not mean your business simply promoting and selling a product and the customer buying that product. In fact, if that is the only relationship you have with your customers, then your business will surely fail. We are talking about a conscious decision regarding how and why you will interact with your customers at every stage of the customer journey. You need to choose and develop the best type of relationship to develop with your customers while getting your customers' attention, educating them about your value proposition, and convincing them to buy your product or service; all while making a concerted effort to retain them as loyal customers who come back to buy more and more in the future.

That sounds like the same thing as a channel, but it's a bit different. Channels and customer relationships are closely interlinked, but they are not the same thing. The channel is the vehicle you will use to interact with your customers, while a customer relationship is the method of interaction over that channel. For obvious reasons, they need to be completely integrated, as do the strategy and tactics involved in achieving your goals at each stage of the customer journey.

The spectrum of possible customer relationships ranges from direct person-to-person service, such as the salesman at your local auto dealer provides, to an automated service where the customer never interacts with a human being, such as ordering books from Amazon.com. Much will depend on the type of product you are selling, the depth, breadth and location of the customer segment you are targeting, and the types of channels you will use to interact with your customers.

Creating Your Customer Relationship Proposition

So how do you choose what type of customer relationship to develop? And what options do you have to choose from?

The first thing to keep firmly in mind, as always, is that you are selling more than just a product—you are selling an entire range of need-fulfilling, problem-solving solutions. So in order to attract customers and convince them to buy, you will need to create a relationship with them that best allows you to educate them about your value proposition and create a desire to purchase your product. In addition, since one of your key business goals is to develop customer loyalty and garner repeat purchases of greater and greater value, you will need to create a relationship with your customers which best allows you to accomplish this objective as well.

So to begin with, go back to the same type of question you have asked yourself several times already during the Business Model Canvas process:

- What kind of relationship do my customers want and need?

- What kind of relationship will best solve their relevant problems, i.e. eliminate pains and create gains?

You need to answer these questions for every stage of the customer journey, because you may need to develop a different kind of relationship at different stages. For example, very often a different type of customer relationship must be established to grow a customer than was used to acquire them in the first place.

Similarly, you should also answer these questions separately for each of your different customer segments. In order to do so, you need to expand the customer profiles you created for each segment to include as much detail as possible regarding their wants, needs and problems in this area. Think once again about: Who are the actual buyers? Who are the purchase decision makers? Who are the users? What kind of relationship do they want and need with my business? What kind of relationship and tactics would be most efficient and effective? How can I best develop that relationship to get them to buy and then keep them as a highly satisfied repeat buyer?

This last question is incredibly important. As we said in the last chapter, one of the keys to making a business model work is ensuring that the *"lifetime value"* of your customers is an adequate multiple of your *"cost of customer acquisition."* In general, the lifetime value is the amount of money a customer spends over the course of his or her relationship with your company. The cost of customer acquisition is how much you spend on acquiring and retaining that customer. It is almost always more expensive to acquire a customer than to retain one and get him or her to purchase additional products.

The better the relationship you have with your customers, the better you will be able to retain them and get them to buy more following the original purchase. This will raise the lifetime value of the customer and lower the relative cost of customer acquisition. You can clearly see that the relationship you have with your customers will have a direct affect on your profitability and sustainability.

So what are your choices? The basic categories include:

- Personal assistance

- Dedicated personal assistance

- Self-service

- Automated service

- Customer communities

Personal Assistance means direct interaction between a representative of your business and the customer. During the promotion and sales process, as well as following the purchase, this could mean personal, telephone, or Internet contact (by email, chat, etc.) with a sales, customer service, or technical representative. For example, if you buy a Whirlpool washing machine you can speak directly to a sales agent in person at the dealership when buying the appliance, to a customer support representative by telephone if you have questions after purchasing the appliance, and to a service technician at your home if you have a problem covered by warranty.

Dedicated Personal Assistance takes direct contact with the customer to a much higher level. In this case, a specific person (or persons) is tasked with taking care of all the needs of a particular customer during a particular stage—or every stage—of the customer journey. In the case of a product that is expensive and highly technical, a knowledgeable sales rep may be dedicated to the customer until the purchase is finalized, but a technical customer support specialist may be dedicated to help with questions and issues that arise afterward.

Self Service allows the customers to act on their own without any direct interaction with a business representative. Everything is laid out for the customer, so they can get the information they need to understand the product and make a purchase decision, as well as actually conduct the transaction. While this may not seem like an actual "relationship" with a customer, it is just that. And to work properly, the relationship should be a conscious one. Many people do not want to be bothered with personal interactions with real people in buying many items. So if done properly, providing a self-service option is actually giving them the type of customer relationship they need and desire.

Automated Services expands the concept of self-service, most often using information technology to personalize the customer's self-service experience by giving them information and options based on the personal preferences they demonstrate over time. An example of this would be Amazon.com making a book suggestion based on the characteristics of the previous book(s) purchased.

Customer Communities, particularly online communities, have become a cost-effective and popular method of having business representatives and customers interact, answer questions, and problem-solve together. These forums not only keep current customers informed and give them a vehicle for handling any issues they might have, they also help create customer loyalty and provide useful information to potential customers.

In selecting one or more of these options for each stage of the customer journey, keep in mind that the chosen relationship must match the type of channel and the business objective. For example, the approach you will use to developing your customer relationship and acquiring, retaining, and growing your customers will be different in some respects depending on whether you are using a physical channel or a web-based or mobile channel.

A cost/benefit or return on investment analysis is also extremely important in selecting the type of customer relationship you will develop. While this area may appear straightforward, the costs of developing different types of relationships could actually sink your business model, and therefore your business, if not properly considered and controlled. An extreme example would be assigning a personal sales rep to every customer. Clearly these costs would almost always be prohibitive. The cost of software development for self-service and automated self-service must also be considered, or the cost of purchasing out of the box solutions. Remember what we said about customer acquisition costs—the higher they are, the higher the lifetime value of your customers must be for your business to be profitable and sustainable.

The bottom line is that for every profile customer in every customer segment at every stage of the customer journey, you need to choose the type of customer relationship you want to develop, and then decide on the details of how you will develop that relationship to achieve the desired ends in cost-efficient manner.

Keep Your Focus on Acquiring, Retaining and Growing Customers

The goal in selecting the type of customer relationships you will develop, and channels you will use to do so, is to acquire customers, retain them and grow their business. These goals should constantly be at the forefront when making your choices. Always ask whether this type of relationship or channel will be the best method for you to get, keep and grow customers. Often, the best type of customer relationship to adopt will be driven in large part by the optimal tactics to accomplish these goals.

Acquiring Customers

Customer acquisition encompasses the first four phases of the customer journey that we discussed in Chapter 6:

- **Attention:** making the customer aware of your product offering/value proposition

- **Evaluation:** providing the customer with the information necessary to generate interest and consider make a purchase decision

- **Desire:** convincing the customer to and buy your product

- **Action:** transacting the actual sale

Therefore the channel and customer relationship strategy and tactics you choose must accomplish each objective in order to effectuate the sale in a cost-effective manner—they must work in tandem to make potential customers aware of your product and then drive them towards an actual purchase. This may sound straightforward, but it requires the consideration and integration of many factors, including the needs of your customer segment, where and how you can best communicate with them, the cost of finding and communicating with them, the most-effective tactics to achieve the goals of each phase and the best channel and relationship for adopting those tactics, the nature of your product offering, your marketing budget, the acquisition strategy and tactics used by your competition, scalability using these channels and customer relationships, etc. All of these factors must be considered when deciding which channel and relationship will allow you to acquire the most customers in the most efficient manner.

You will most likely need to choose a combination of communication channels that include both paid and earned promotions, physical and virtual channels, to promote your product. This could range from public relations in the form of trade press interviews to a sophisticated online marketing strategy meant to drive customers to your e-commerce website, followed up by direct contact with customers who visit your retail store. Even if you are doing most of your marketing online, you may choose to participate in community conversations, conduct one-on-one chat interviews or sales calls, etc. From a strategic standpoint, however, you should minimize costs until you test each channel, relationship and tactic to make sure it will produce the return on investment you are looking for. In addition, as we said earlier when it comes time to the actual sale and distribution of your products, you should not spread yourself to thin— it is best to choose one channel to begin with, and expand from there.

Also, keep in mind that if your product is a web or mobile product, then your customer acquisition tactics will be different from those used for traditional physical products. For web and mobile products, the customer acquisition phase focuses on bringing as many customers as possible to the company's landing page where they can learn about the product. In order for a website to be successful, this could mean drawing a huge number of people to the site, sometimes millions. And because of the vast number of products available, it is a daunting task to get customers to find your mobile application or website. For this reason, the tactical aspects of "acquiring" customers for a web or mobile product, which in this space means getting them to the site or to view the application, has developed a set of tactics unique to the web and mobile world.

After getting a customer to the site, the next step for web and mobile businesses is customer "activation." This means getting the customer to show interest through a free download or trial, a request for more information, or a purchase. A customer is considered activated by many web-based businesses even if they don't buy anything, as long as the company has enough information to re-contact him or her with explicit permission to do so.

Retaining Customers

Because acquiring customers is such a difficult and expensive process, it's important to develop a clear strategy for how you will retain those customers. This requires providing great customer service and support, collecting as much information as possible about your customers, and proactively interacting with customers after they have made their initial purchase.

One of the most important steps is learning who your individual customers are and how to contact them, and then observing how they behave after purchase. For example, if possible you want to collect information regarding purchase patterns, calls to customer service, participation in loyalty programs, etc. For web based products, you want to track start dates, activity level, onsite behavior, etc. From a channel and customer relationship perspective, customer retention often becomes much more direct than customer acquisition. The more data you have about your customers, the easier it is to develop tactics to retain them. Therefore, any way you have of collecting this type of information about your customers' behavior patterns should be used and incorporated into your retention strategy. Most importantly, consider the type of relationship and channel that will allow you to best collect relevant information and then communicate with your customers.

Also consider specific customer retention tactics, including loyalty programs, customer follow-up calls or e-mails, customer satisfaction surveys, product updates, customer service options, social network and other online communities, etc. Each one of these programs will lend itself to a certain type of channel and customer relationship.

Growing Customers

Some of the basic approaches to growing customers by getting them to buy more product include:

- **Cross-sell programs** that encourage buyers of a product to buy adjacent products.

- **Up-selling programs** that promote the purchase of "more" of higher-end products.

Some simple "grow" programs to consider include suggesting other items the customer might be interested in, communicating special offers and discounts for larger orders, introducing add-on features, etc. Again, you need to choose the best type of relationship for communicating these offers effectively and turning them into sales, as well as the best channel to use in doing so. The relationship and/or channel for customer growth is often not the same as you used for customer acquisition. For example, once a customer has purchased once and you have their contact information, a direct sales call may be much more effective than it would be to someone who has never purchased your product.

Customer referrals are probably the best and most common way to grow the business you obtain by landing one initial customer. You want to get happy customers to generate attention, interest and consideration among the largest audience possible. Find as many ways as possible to encourage current customers to invite their friends to learn more about your product offering. What you are shooting for is a viral word-of-mouth effect, which is the cheapest and most effective marketing program you can have. This type of viral effect also boosts purchases of your product by current customers, as it acts as a self-validating mechanism and in many cases they use your product together with other new customers they bring in.

There are lots of different viral marketing tools and tactics that help you get customers to refer other customers to the company. Tactics to consider in order to grow customers through referrals include offering discounts for sharing with friends or bringing friends in as new customers, encouraging Facebook likes, highlighting social networking action buttons on your websites, getting outside bloggers to write about your product, etc. Again, determining which of these tactics would be most effective will also help you determine which channel and customer relationship would be most effective.

Gathering Customer Feedback on Your Customer Relationship Proposition

As discussed above, the process of gathering customer feedback in order to either confirm or correct your initial customer relationship hypothesis will be focused on expanding your customer profiles to incorporate their wants and needs in this area, as well as the particular problems that must be solved. So both open-ended and pass-fail questions should be asked in order to get suggestions from your customers in the first instance, and then get their feedback on whether specific methods would be acceptable in the second.

The types of questions you want answered include:

- What type of relationship do our profile customers expect us to develop with them at each stage?

- What is the minimum relationship they would accept and still do business with our company?

- What problems do they have that a certain type of customer relationship would solve for them?

- What type of relationship do they currently have with similar businesses?

- What are they currently satisfied or unsatisfied with in their current customer relationships with similar businesses?

In this area in particular, some additional market research and analysis might be necessary as well. You definitely need to understand the cost structure of each type of relationship and the added value it would produce in order to estimate your overall costs, the cost of customer acquisition under a given relationship type, and the lifetime value each relationship type would produce. Of course at this stage these estimates would remain hypotheses, but these guesses can become closer to fact the more you know about your customers and costs—so it is important to turn these hypotheses into as many facts as possible.

In addition, however, because the type of customer relationship you will choose will be interdependent on the tactics you will use to acquire, retain and grow customers, it makes sense to also test the effectiveness of the tactics you believe will work best in each of these areas. One obvious caveat, however, is that initially this will be focused on customer acquisition tactics, because you will not yet have customers to retain and grow.

Create a series of small-scale, inexpensive customer acquisition tests to determine the tactics that move customers from awareness to evaluation to interest to desire to purchase in a scalable and cost-effective manner. Once again, create a pass/fail test for each channel/customer relationship/tactic hypothesis you test. For example: will we get one sales call for every 30 phone calls made to prospects? And test many different combinations to see what works best. Direct sales cold calls may be ineffective, but calls to customers who have signed up to e-mail lists may work well. Create objective metrics for measuring customer acquisition cost—chart the costs and projected results in terms of sales of each channel/relationship/tactic combination. Try and find ways to communicate in person with customers and using web and mobile marketing tactics—in today's world both are important for different reasons we have discussed.

You can integrate testing customer acquisition tactics with your testing of the customer problem and value proposition. For example, you will want to attract as many customers as possible to participate in those tests, so you can use various acquisition channel/relationship/tactic combinations to find those customers and measure the results. Then when customers respond to your call to action in a problem or value proposition test, you can further test various other follow-up acquisition tactics.

Revising, Iterating, and Validating Your Customer Relationship Proposition

Once you've collected as much customer feedback as possible, you'll have a good idea of what your customers expect as far as relationships at each stage of your journey go. But be careful. In some blocks of the Business Model Canvas, you can basically take this information, plug it in as "this is what my customer needs, so I will give it to them," and move forward. In the case of customer relationships, however, it is not that easy.

You have to closely analyze any proposed customer relationship and answer the following questions—even if this is the type of relationship your customer wants, or even demands:

- Is it possible to deliver my value proposition using that type of relationship at all?

- Is it possible to develop that relationship on a cost-effective basis so that my business model still works?

- Can this type of relationship be effectively integrated with the rest of my business model, particularly the channels I feel are the optimum to use?

The answer to one or more of these questions may well be no. And in that case, you'll have to make a cost/benefit tradeoff—calculating not only monetary costs, but other costs as well—and settle for a customer relationship that best balances customer wants and needs, the costs involved, and integration with the rest of your business model.

After making that tradeoff decision, it is critical that you iterate and test your new customer relationship proposition out with real customers. You need to know for certain whether you have met your customers' minimum requirements at least. Otherwise, you may find your business either doing a gigantic belly flop on day one, or seeing very few repeat customers to drive the business forward.

> **LinksBuddy Case Study**
>
> ## Chapter 7
> ## Customer Relationships
>
> Steven and Martin quickly grasp that for their business model to work, the channels and channel relationships must be intimately linked together at every stage of the customer journey. Turning to the golf traveler side of their platform, they list the following channel/customer relationship hypothesis:
>
> The primary channels that Steven and Martin propose to use in order to get the *attention* of golf travelers will include the use of a variety of internet marketing techniques to pull golf travelers to their website. They will also use cost-effective traditional advertising, but their non-internet methods will focus on public relations in as many golf-related channels as possible in order to minimize costs. They will also use their local representatives to spread the word to all golfers in their area of responsibility. The key to the customer relationships in both the PR push and with the local representatives will be the message of "golf community", which is the ultimate customer relationship they want to establish.
>
> Once they have a golf traveler's attention, this is when the relationship that LinksBuddy will have with its customers will become vital, and Steven and Martin will have critical choices to make. Again, the website should provide all of the information necessary for a golf traveler to *evaluate* the offering and make a decision about whether to use the LinksBuddy platform and services for his golf holiday, as well as establish a *desire* to become a LinksBuddy customer. In an ideal and most cost-efficient world, this would be all that the company would have to do to acquire a critical mass of golf traveler customers. However, while they may not need to establish quite as much of a direct personal customer relationship as with accommodation providers, Steven and Martin do believe that in order to launch and grow the golf traveler side of their platform, they will need to give golf travelers a live person to communicate with. They will therefore provide three contact options: customer support personnel available by telephone, chat and e-mail; the local representative at the

golf traveler's desired destination; and of course the golf traveler's preferred accommodation provider. Each one of these contacts should be able to supplement the website in helping the customer understand the LinksBuddy offering and its value, and go beyond the website in instilling a desire in the golf traveler to try LinksBuddy for their golf trip—i.e. convert the customer and close the sale.

The transaction in terms of payment will occur through the website directly with LinksBuddy, rather than between the golf traveler and accommodation provider. This will be easier in terms of efficiency, and will save LinksBuddy the difficulty of collecting accounts receivables from the accommodation providers. Once again, the customer relationship in this area will be reinforced by customer support staff.

Steven and Martin can see that with the addition of local representatives and customer support staff, the cost of acquisition of both golf traveler and accommodation provider customers is likely to be quite high. It will be critical for them to test and validate their customer relationship and verify that these costs can be incurred and absorbed until they reach break-even and beyond, and that they can still run a profitable and sustainable business going forward with this type of expensive customer relationships. They also need to test and validate their hypothesis that adding local representatives and/or customer support staff will achieve the desired results, and that doing so will give them a sufficient return on their investment in this area. In order to do this, they conduct an A/B test in their next field test, with one sample recruiting golf travelers using only the website, one sample recruiting using the website and customer support, one sample using the website and the local representative, and one sample using all of the above.

The two entrepreneurs also realize that the high initial cost of customer acquisition will make it even more critical that they retain and grow their golf traveler customers in order to increase the lifetime value of these customers as much as possible. In order to do so, they will use a combination of channels and customer relationships in order to encourage their golf travelers to become active members of their virtual golf community, travel to play golf frequently within that network, and recruit more golf travelers and accommodation providers to try the LinksBuddy experience. This will involve customer support and local representative follow-ups with golf travelers after each golf trip, as well as e-mail promotions and recruiting incentives, participation in online community discussions, etc. The key will be to create a virtual club atmosphere that becomes organic and begins to recruit its own members without the costly intervention of LinksBuddy itself. What they are looking to achieve is the network effect. And if they get there, their business will go into orbit like a Rory McIlroy drive.

CHAPTER 8:
REVENUE STREAMS

Chapter Overview

How to Create a Revenue Stream Hypothesis 156
Pricing Your Product Offering 157
        Single-sided versus Multi-sided Markets 160
        Integrated Revenue Streams 161
Generating Customer Feedback and Revising Your Revenue Stream Proposition 162
Revising, Iterating, and Validating Your Revenue Stream Proposition 163
LinksBuddy Case Study 165

CHAPTER 8

REVENUE STREAMS

Now that you have identified your customer segment, the value proposition you want to offer them, and the vehicle and method you will use for interacting with them, it's time to figure out how, how much, for how many, and for what your customers will pay you. This used to be a fairly straightforward proposition. But in today's modern economy there are many revenue generating options to choose from, and the goal is to optimize your income so you want to consider them all—and even create new ones if possible.

Broadly, a revenue stream is the manner in which you receive income in exchange for the product or service you offer. Hopefully your business will have multiple ways of making money, and each one is considered a separate revenue stream. The key is to find as many cost-efficient ways possible to exploit the value proposition that you have created for your customers.

Examples of potential revenue streams include:

- Asset sale
- Service fee
- Usage fee
- Subscription fees
- Rental or leasing fees
- Licensing
- Brokerage fees
- Advertising

Asset sale is the transfer of ownership of a product or other asset. This is what happens every time you buy groceries from the supermarket, buy a car from the auto dealership, buy plants from the nursery, etc.

Service fees are what you receive for providing a third-party service to your customer. Everything from attorney's fees to dog walking charges would fall into the category of service fees. Service fees can also come in combination with assets sales, rentals, etc. For example, a hotel may charge a service fee to cover part or all of the cost of cleaning, booking, etc.

Usage fees are what you receive for allowing your customer to use an asset that you own for a period of time or on a per use basis. While similar to a rental fee, it's normally used in different contexts. Train tickets and usage charges for mobile network coverage are examples of usage fees.

Subscription fees are generated by providing access to a continuous service, such as an online magazine, a television on-demand sports network, a wine-of-the-month club (in which you would also sell assets—i.e. the wine), etc.

Lending/leasing/rental fees means giving a customer the right to use an asset for a designated amount of time. Apartments, copy machines, office furniture, ski equipment, e-mail lists—anything can be rented out for a fee.

Licensing fees are received in exchange for the exclusive or non-exclusive use of intellectual property such as copyrights, patents and trademarks. They can take many forms, including a one-time fee, annual fees, and royalties.

Brokerage fees are generated in exchange for facilitating a transaction or relationship between other parties. Stock and real estate are the most recognizable forms. But there are many creative ways of assisting transactions and getting paid in exchange.

Advertising fees are fees paid in exchange for providing a space for advertising, which can be anywhere from a billboard on your property, the side of your car, or a website.

Referral fees are payments for referring or directing traffic or customers, such as referring customers to web sites or products.

These categories are not all-inclusive and are only there to give you some reference points to get you started thinking about revenue streams. Don't limit yourself by thinking only inside these revenue stream boxes.

In fact, of all the building blocks, it is in the area of revenue streams that you want to be extremely creative and think outside the box about all of the potential ways that you can capture the value of—i.e. get customers to pay for—your product offering/value proposition. You want to maximize this captured value, and often the best way to do that is to develop multiple revenue streams flowing from multiple customer segments. Web and mobile products have a wide variety of potential revenue sources, and while product sales are most often the prime revenue source for physical products, if you look hard enough you will likely find additional revenue sources.

How to Create a Revenue Stream Hypothesis

Determining the universe of potential revenue streams, and then choosing the best ones to pursue in creating a revenue model, requires a combination of market research, brainstorming and analysis, and then of course testing and iteration. First, review your market research and identify all of the types of revenue streams that are currently being used in your market or similar markets. Then, go back to your customer profiles and your value proposition and ask some questions that will lead you to possible revenue streams (remember to ask these questions separately with respect to each customer segment):

- What are the different components of my value proposition that my customers are willing to pay for?

- How are they willing to pay?

- How much are they willing to pay?

- Do they require permanent ownership of the product?

- Am I offering both a product and a service and can I charge for both?

- Would it be best to receive revenues per transaction, on a recurring basis, or both?

- Does my product need to be sold all at once, or can it be broken down and its components sold separately?

- What are the cost benefits of one type of revenue stream versus another (i.e. licensing or renting versus selling ownership)?

At the end of the process, you should be able to identify what value the person meeting a particular customer profile is paying for, and the revenue stream you are receiving as a result.

The next question is whether you are capturing the optimum amount of value in each revenue stream in exchange for what the customer is receiving. This comes down to pricing strategy and tactics, which go hand in hand with choosing and implementing a particular revenue stream. Because in order to determine what revenue streams will work the best, you need to simultaneously determine how much you can charge your customer and how they will pay you using that approach. And each revenue stream will require its own pricing strategy and tactics.

Pricing Your Product Offering

Pricing is a complex subject, but in creating your business model you should consider the two basic types of pricing—fixed and dynamic.

Fixed pricing means a price that is set and does not change (at least not often). The question is how do you set a fixed price for your product or service? There are a few basic methods of doing so (which like everything else in this area are a starting point for creative thinking):

- Cost plus markup

- Customer's perceived value

- Volume oriented

- Product feature dependent

- Return on investment

- Portfolio pricing

- Freemium model

- Competitive pricing

- Customer lifetime value

Cost plus markup and volume-based pricing are traditional forms of pricing. Cost-plus markup is where you determine your cost of goods sold and then add on an amount sufficient to give you the gross and net margins you desire for your business. They key issue here will be how you determine cost for pricing purposes, whether by a standard cost of goods sold definition or some other method—for example taking into account the total cost of ownership of the product for the customer, including training time, cost of adoption, etc. In volume-base pricing, the per item cost is reduced based on the quantity purchased.

Charging based on perceived value means not limiting yourself to a standard markup over cost, but rather looking at what part of your value proposition a particular customer segment is paying for and determining how much they are willing to pay to receive that value. In this manner, a good marketing program promoting a good value proposition can convince customers to pay a higher price because they perceive that your company is providing more value than lower priced competitors.

Product feature dependent pricing means the overall price of a product is based on what features are included in that product. So a laptop computer that includes one set of performance features would be one price, and each added feature would mean an additional charge. This type of pricing can be based on cost plus markup, customer's perceived value, or both.

In business to business sales, some customers care less about initial price than they do about their total return on their investment. Therefore, in some circumstances you may want to price your product based on a demonstrable return on investment for your customers.

Portfolio pricing can be used when you have multiple products and services. You will still use one or more of the other pricing methods, but then you can adjust the prices on particular products or services with an eye toward optimizing the revenue of your product portfolio as a whole.

In the "freemium" pricing model, you provide basic products, or more often services, free of charge and premium products or services for a fee. This works when there is a low marginal cost to adding additional free users, so you can have many free users subsidized by those paying for the premium services.

Competitive pricing is based solely on positioning your product against direct competitors, or adjusting prices determined by other methods to position your prices as desired with respect to competitors.

Customer lifetime value is often directly related to pricing. In setting a pricing strategy based on lifetime value, you determine how much your customers will spend not just in the first purchase but over the life of their relationship with the company.

Each of these types of pricing is more flexible than they appear and you should analyze all factors in order to determine a price. In most cases, a good fixed pricing model takes into account the factors underlying many or all of the above options, including manufacturing costs, the value received by customers, the competition, and volume—as well as the overall economy and micro-economy in your location, and whether different pricing is appropriate for different customer segments.

Dynamic Pricing means a pricing structure that determines the price of a particular sale based on certain guidelines, or based on negotiation or bidding.

Categories of dynamic pricing include:

- Auctions or real-time markets
- Yield-based pricing
- Negotiated pricing

Auctions are real-time markets such as E-Bay, where customers bid on a product or even service and the sale goes to the highest bidder at the price they offered. "Yield-based" pricing means the price fluctuates based on certain factors—for example occupancy rates in the hotel and transportation business. Negotiated pricing means that you bargain with your customer with respect to every transaction. This often is the case in businesses such as construction contracting or consulting services agreements.

New vs. Existing Markets

As we mentioned above, revenue stream and pricing strategy is not done in a vacuum. If you're entering a market that already exists, you need to consider how the competition prices its value proposition and how their customers respond. In addition, you must take into account how your value proposition compares to your competitors', what your competitive advantages are, and how you will differentiate yourself. This will help you determine whether you need to develop similar revenue streams at similar prices, need to price lower or can afford to price higher, or whether you can have alternative revenue stream options, etc.

If you are attempting to create a new market then this equation changes. You will still need to select the right revenue stream options, and may be able to be more creative in breaking new ground. But both your value proposition and your chosen revenue stream options may take time to be accepted by the market. So you need to factor that in when estimating the quantity you will be able to sell and price you will be able to sell at for a significant period of time until you gain market awareness and acceptance. Not building in a cash flow buffer for this period and/or spending too much at this time can be disastrous.

Single-sided versus Multi-sided Markets

You also need to take into account whether you have a single-sided or a multi-sided market, and adjust your revenue stream and pricing strategies accordingly. For single-sided markets, you simply look to each of your customer segments and decide if they need different strategic revenue stream and pricing approaches. But multi-sided markets are where things get really interesting.

A multi-sided market brings together two or more customer segments with very different problems and needs—and therefore most often requires a different value proposition, channel, etc. for each segment. The market provides a platform for interaction between the different customer segments, and is valuable to the paying customer segment on one side because that segment's own customers, the platforms "users" on the other side, are drawn to the platform in large numbers.

Web/ mobile markets are often multi-sided, and the simplest example is that of an informational website. You have a multi-sided market with users coming to your website to get information on the one side, and advertisers placing ads, links, and banners on your site on the other. Here you may have several different types of revenue streams coming from the advertisers, such as direct payments for ad placements and other payments for Google AdSense links, etc.

Some very familiar and successful examples of multi-sided markets include:

- Visa credit card, which links merchants with cardholders

- Microsoft Windows operating system, which links hardware manufacturers, application developers, and users

- Facebook, which links advertisers with users

- Financial Times, which links advertisers with readers, and

- Wii game console, which links game developers with players

- And then of course there's Google . . .

Multi-sided markets must attract a sufficient numbers of customers for each side of the platform, and that often creates their biggest challenge. The business owners must determine the best way to attract enough users, and often that is by offering a value proposition they are interested either for free or for a subsidized amount. The problem is that they then have to attract enough paying customers on the other side quickly enough to cover the cost of those subsidies. Many businesses have tried and failed in this "chicken and egg" endeavor.

Integrated Revenue Streams

In many cases, it makes sense to take one product that would produce a single revenue stream and break it down into component parts, or multiple products, to produce several revenue streams which in combination would produce higher profits than a single stream. One way to do this is by creating a range of similar products that differ slightly in the number of features and/or quality, obviously charging more for the higher quality products. When a customer is attracted to the lower-priced products, you find ways to "up-sell" the premium product.

Or you can also up-sell additional products and accessories that complement the main product or service you are offering. For example, a spa may up-sell massage oils and body lotions in connection with its primary services. With respect to Internet businesses revolving around websites, you can consider what is called a "freemium strategy," where you allow free access to the basic version of your website, but charge for access to premium content, services, etc.

Generating Customer Feedback and Revising Your Revenue Stream Proposition

When developing a strategy to obtain customer feedback on your revenue stream proposition and pricing strategy, keep in mind that the market research you will perform for each block of the business model canvas when carrying out interviews, surveys, etc. is not mutually exclusive, but interrelated and overlapping.

For example, the questions you ask regarding what portions of your value proposition will create the most value for each customer segment will be crucial in determining which types of revenue streams to focus on for each segment, as well as to what pricing strategy and tactics you should use. Just as valuable will be all of the information you gathered for your customer profiles regarding buying habits, daily routines, demographics and geographic and virtual locations.

In addition, you now want to both test your revenue stream and pricing propositions, asking the proper questions to get direct feedback. This is especially true if you have gotten creative and intend to propose a new form of revenue stream. While you may have the best idea since credit card purchase over the Internet, you need to remember that every new revenue stream proposition will take time to gain market acceptance—just as online credit card purchasing had to gain acceptance and still needs to do so with many people.

Ask your customers in each segment:

- If they bought your product or service, what would they be primarily buying?

- Would they accept your revenue stream proposition as a means of payment?

- How would they otherwise prefer to pay?

- Do they consider different payment options important?

- How much would they be willing to pay?

- Would they be willing to pay more or less than for a competing product?

- Which type of revenue stream would they prefer?

If you have a multi-sided market, you need to get specific feedback on whether users would be willing to pay for what you offer, or expect it for free. You also need to speak with the payers, for example advertisers, and determine on what terms (including the critical mass of users you must have) they would be willing to pay for advertising—because what they are paying for is access to your user base. Make sure that whatever deal you strike up with advertisers complies with data protection rules.

As much as any other section of the business model canvas, validating your revenue streams and pricing strategy will be a continuous trial and error process. Propose—test—iterate—revise—test—validate, etc.

Revising, Iterating, and Validating Your Revenue Stream Proposition

You may not have any more difficult choices in starting your business than deciding which revenue streams to pursue, and more importantly which not to pursue. The key to this decision is often integration.

The best revenue streams and pricing mechanisms will not only produce the expected revenue, they will integrate well with all other aspects of your business model. For example, they must capture the most value from your value proposition, contribute towards developing the desired customer relationship, be cost effective to produce, be feasible over the channels you have available, and most importantly be acceptable to your key customer segment. Your revenue streams and pricing strategy must also be integrated.

So hard choices need to be made. Some potential revenue streams, while generating some additional income, may not integrate well with your overall business model. Others may not be cost-effective to implement and therefore not generate a sufficient return on investment. And others may get lukewarm responses from your target customers. Your initial tests should have given you most of the information needed to make these decisions, and you should now be able to identify the revenue streams that will work with particular customer segments. But now comes the hard part: you have to choose—and then test your choices once again to validate them.

Of course you also need to choose a pricing strategy with respect to each revenue stream. Will it be cost plus markup, perceived value, etc.? These choices must also be tested and validated.

Finally, you will need to develop a strategy on how to implement your chosen revenue streams. Once again, it would be tempting to choose an "all at once" solution. But just as it may make sense to initially launch a minimum viable product, it may also make sense to launch a minimum viable selection of revenue streams. Importantly, these revenue streams must match the minimum viable product you intend to launch.

When it comes time to validating your revenue streams, you will in part be validating your entire business model because you need to determine whether the roughly anticipated revenues from your chosen revenue model—based on anticipated unit sales and pricing—leads to a profitable business if all other factors in your business model pan out as expected. In answering this question, you first want to make sure your anticipated revenues will cover costs, next whether you can expect revenues to grow over time, and finally whether you expect your profit margins to increase as your revenue increases. If you have evidence to answer all of these questions in the affirmative, then you have validated a viable revenue model. The only question left to validate is whether this viable revenue model is the optimal revenue model for your business.

LinksBuddy Case Study

Chapter 8
Revenue Streams

When Steven and Martin sit down to brainstorm potential revenue streams to list on their Business Model Canvas, they spit out a slew of alternative ways to generate income. Of course they can charge their business travelers and accommodation providers for their services. But they could also recruit advertisers to their website and charge them fees; charge users subscription or membership fees for use of their website; collect commissions for booking green fees, transportation, club rentals, etc.; collect referral fees from golf pros, golf courses, local tours and restaurants, etc. As they list all of these money making options, Steven and Martin see dollar signs dancing before their eyes. But when they meet with Peter and excitedly tell him all of these ways to make "found money" with their new business, he has two cautionary words for them: focus and integration.

For example, Peter says, look at allowing advertisers on your website. If Steven and Martin decide to recruit advertisers to their website in order to generate additional revenues, they will in effect be opening a third separate side of their platform to go along with the golf traveler and accommodation provider sides. The sale of advertising space on the website will be its own separate business requiring its own business model: different customer segments, value propositions, channels and customer relationships, revenue streams, costs, etc. This will not only add to the complexity of an already complex P2P business, it may have unintended side effects on their core business. Steven and Martin are trying to build a virtual golf community. Will the members of that community want to be inundated with paid advertising in the comforts of their virtual clubhouse? Can that sense of community be incubated in that type of online environment?

The use of a subscription fee also provides an interesting question. Steven believes that a fee to become a LinksBuddy member would drive away many potential customers. So many sites want me to pay a subscription now, he says. I'll only do that for a select few. Martin, on the other hand, argues that charging a fee would add a sense of exclusivity to the site that many golf club members would appreciate, and may help to attract the type of customers who would best help build the business as a virtual golf community. It would also be a built-in method of curation, weeding out customers who would not contribute much to either side of the business.

The other tangential types of revenue streams, while they may not be businesses in themselves, will also require tradeoffs in terms of costs of acquiring the additional revenue versus the amount of actual revenue that would be generated.

With respect to revenues generated from the two core sides of their business, golf travelers and accommodation providers, Steven and Martin have key decisions to make in terms of how to charge, and what to charge, their customers. On each side of the platform, their options on how to charge include flat fees and percentage of accommodation charges. What to charge for their P2P business becomes an even trickier question than normal, because it could have a significant impact first on how they solve, and whether they solve, their chicken-and-egg problem, and second on whether their business model will be profitable.

At the beginning of the business modeling process, Steven and Martin are inclined to go with the approach used by golf tour operators and simply charge a flat fee to both golf travelers and accommodation providers. When they test this concept in interviews, they receive positive responses from customers on both sides of the equation, although they hear from some accommodation providers that they wouldn't be expected to be charged much of any fee, or they wouldn't participate. However, Steven and Martin discovered in their sister city and extended field tests that charging a flat fee was very difficult to implement, resulted in less revenues than a percentage charge, and was resisted by customers who were aware of the Airbnb business model.

Aifbnb charges both their renters and accommodation providers a percentage of the renter's bill, with the renter paying a higher percentage. Steven and Martin tested and verified this approach as the best for their business as well. Because the transaction really takes place between the accommodation provider, who sets the per-day price for his accommodation and companionship, and the golf traveler, it was unworkable for LinksBuddy to "bake in" its fee to the overall cost to the golf traveler. In addition, that embedded fee would stand out to the customer much more than a percentage-to-be-calculated. Finally, since Airbnb was becoming the standard for P2P travel, its pricing mechanism was also becoming the accepted standard. Steven and Martin decided it would be best to piggyback on all of Airbnb's prior research and experience rather than recreate the wheel, and their tests confirmed that their customers would prefer this approach also.

That begged the question of whether they should also charge the same, or similar percentages to Airbnb. Steven and Martin's hypothesis was that for their business model, they could charge golf travelers a higher percentage because they were receiving much more than just simple accommodation: they were also receiving a links buddy to golf and hang out with, etc. In other words, they could charge an additional percentage for the unique golf travel experience that accommodation providers would provide. In testing this concept, they validated their hypothesis, but not to the extent they had hoped. They found that their customers were willing to pay a higher percentage for the LinksBuddy experience, but there was a limit to the price elasticity in this area. Many golf travelers actually mentioned the Airbnb percentage when the test went beyond more than three percent above what Airbnb charged.

The other area of price sensitivity for golf travelers came with respect to a comparison to a golf tour package to the same destination. Some golf travelers came in anticipating a cost savings if they used LinksBuddy versus a golf tour package, the same way many people try to save money with Airbnb versus hotels. Other golf travelers were more focused on the quality of the accommodation and experience, and were happy to pay more than for a golf travel package for this type of "exclusive" experience. In addition to helping them revise and iterate their revenue stream/pricing hypothesis, all of this sent Steven and Martin back to retest and validate their customer segment proposition as well!

On the accommodation provider side, testing revealed that Steven and Martin faced an even bigger dilemma. Should they charge the accommodation providers at all? In analyzing their chicken-and-egg problem, Steven and Martin decide that the best way to solve this problem for their business is to make a big push through their local representatives and other marketing initiatives to create pods of accommodation providers in selected locations. Once they obtain a critical mass in these locations, they can work to replicate this model in other locations. And once the business hits critical mass, their hope is that potential accommodation providers in other locations will be knocking on the LinksBuddy door to list their own pod. However, Steven and Martin ran into some headwinds when they discovered through testing their hypothesis that accommodation providers felt that they would not recoup the value of the time, effort and experience they contributed to acting as a local links buddy, and therefore they were reluctant to pay a percentage, or at least a high percentage, of the accommodation cost as a fee to LinksBuddy. So Steven and Martin were receiving pressure on both sides of the platform to minimize, or even eliminate, the percentage fees charged. The problem is that Steven and Martin need revenues from both sides for a viable business.

Steven and Martin know that without a critical mass of accommodation providers in their initial locations, they will have no business to grow. In testing, they discover that accommodation providers are even more eager to sign up when they feel they are getting a "freemium" or at least a discount price, as opposed to if they are charged a low percentage to begin with. So Steven and Martin tested three different pricing concepts for accommodation providers: a five percent price; a two percent price; and a five percent price "discounted" to two percent for those early adopter accommodation providers who list within the first three months of launch in their location. Because the tests revealed and validated that the "discounted" price motivated a significantly larger number of accommodation providers to list, this was the pricing mechanism that Steven and Martin chose.

CHAPTER 9:
KEY RESOURCES, ACTIVITIES AND PARTNERS

Chapter Overview

Key Activities 170
Key Resources 173
Key Partnerships 175
LinksBuddy Case Study..177

CHAPTER 9

KEY RESOURCES, ACTIVITIES AND PARTNERS

What you've been focused on so far is the fun part. Fleshing out your value proposition, identifying your true customer base, and of course discovering potential revenue streams—this is all exciting stuff. Now comes the hard part. Because now you need to figure out exactly what needs to be done to make all of this work on a profitable basis.

"What do you mean by make it work?" you might ask. "If I have a good value proposition and a willing customer base, shouldn't the rest be easy?"

The answer is: Not at all. In fact, you may actually discover that parts of your value proposition, proposed channels, and the like cannot be created at all, or at least not on a cost effective basis. So what you need to do now is to look at the next three building blocks on the Business Model Canvas—key activities, key resources, and key partners. You should first identify all of the key activities you need to successfully perform and key resources you need to obtain in order to make your business work. Then you can look at what activities you can or should outsource or share with partners, and what partners will be required in order to obtain your key resources.

Key Activities

Let's start with key activities, because the primary activities you will have to engage in will drive what resources your business will require and what partners you will need to engage. Remember that at the business model level, we're trying to identify only the "key" activities—the critical tasks you will need to perform for your business model to work. We don't want to get bogged down in day-to-day tactics right now. This will help you focus on what is really important, and separate out what is not—a good practice that will make you more efficient and profitable going forward as well.

To begin the process, walk through the entire right side of the business model canvas and think about what has to be done to make the propositions contained in each building block work. For example: What are the key activities required to create, offer and maintain your value proposition? What will be required to effectively implement your proposed customer channels and customer relationships? What will you have to do to optimally capture value from the revenue streams you have identified?

General categories of key activities include the following:

- Product research, design and development
- Raw materials sourcing and purchasing
- Manufacturing
- Platform creation
- Platform management
- Marketing
    - ☐ Traditional
    - ☐ Internet
- Sales
- Distribution and logistics
- Customer service and support
- Information technology
    - ☐ Internal

☐ External

- Human resources and recruiting

- Financing

- Intellectual property protection

- Legal

Within these general areas, however, you need to identify with more specificity exactly what *your* business will need to do to implement your business model. The key activities for every business will be different, even for very similar businesses. This is because each will depend on the nature of the value proposition, composition of the customer segments, selection of channels, customer relationships, revenue streams, competitive environment, access to key resources, etc. It will also depend on what you consider to be your critical success factors, as well as what you need to do to create and take advantage of core competencies and competitive advantages, which we will discuss in more detail in Part III.

For example, if your value proposition requires complex software development, then your key activities will certainly include the design and programming of this software to meet your specifications and your customers' needs, as well as the retention of talented programmers to do the work. If the software will be difficult for some customers to use, then a key activity will be to develop a good customer support solution using the right type of customer relationship and channel.

If your value proposition incorporates new technology that you have developed that will give you a key competitive advantage, then a key activity will be protecting your intellectual property, perhaps in the form of a patent application. If your product will be distributed in distant locations, then a key activity will be to put in place an efficient and cost-effective manufacturing, sales and distribution system.

On a more local level, if you're opening up a new restaurant, then your first key activity will be to find a desirable location, followed by creating and implementing a marketing plan that will make people aware of your new restaurant and convincing them to visit. And of course a key activity will be to develop and refine your value proposition by creating a menu that satisfies your target customers' desires and hiring a chef with the qualifications to deliver the quality of food they will expect, as well as hiring and training a professional service staff.

Remember also, determining what is *not* a key activity is almost as important as identifying what is a key activity. Once you've brainstormed and listed all of the tasks you think you need to perform to make your business model work, step back and take a closer look at each activity and rate just how important it really is. Is this something that should be a top priority? Is it even necessary at all? If you removed it, would your business model suffer? Especially as a start-up company, you will have limited resources and should focus on the essential in creating and implementing your business model.

Key Resources

As we said previously, the key resources your business model requires will be driven in large part by your key activities. So get started by identifying all of the resources you will need to have in order to perform each of these activities. Then go back and take a look once again at your value proposition, channels, customer relationships, and revenue streams, and make sure you have identified all of the primary resources you will need to make your propositions in each of these building blocks happen.

There are four main categories of key resources, and walking through each category for each key activity/building block will help you brainstorm about what is required:

- Physical Assets
- Intellectual Property Assets
- Human Resources
- Financial Resources

Key physical assets include raw materials to manufacture a product, real property and buildings, machinery and equipment, computer hardware and software, vehicles, etc. You need to identify what type of facilities your business will require such as office space, retail space, or a manufacturing plant. In addition, what technological infrastructure will need to be in place to develop, manufacture, offer, and sell your product to your customers? For example, will you require high capacity servers? Also, will you need to own or lease any vehicles for distribution or other purposes? One of the most important activities you may engage in is creating and operating a website—what physical assets will you need to obtain in order to so do?

Key intellectual property assets are the copyrights, trademarks, patents and trade secrets that will be required to operate your business model. If you own these assets because you have developed the technology or written the code yourself, then they may provide one of your main competitive advantages—but only if you protect them properly. The licensing of intellectual property may even provide an important revenue stream for your business, in which case a key activity may be to find companies or individuals who want to pay for a license. And if you do not own the necessary intellectual property to operate your business model, then a key activity may be to obtain the appropriate licenses yourself.

Key human resources include your management team, key employees, key groups of employees and key independent contractors. This is one area where you really want to focus on who is "key" to your business model, and begin planning and recruiting for that position—or finding a reliable third party to perform the role—at the appropriate time. Most businesses are driven by a few key individuals, and having the right people on your team can be the difference between a good business model succeeding or failing. This is why it is important at the business model stage to determine who those key employees will be.

Key financial resources include not only the amount of cash you will need to run your business, but available bank lines of credit, guarantees, lease-lines and other financial resources that will be required. At this stage, you should identify your main sources of cash, either from personal savings, investors, lenders or projected cash flow from your revenue streams. But once you have completed the final step of the Business Model Canvas and identified your key uses of cash, i.e. costs, then you will want to circle back and make an estimate of your projected cash flow and identify how much outside financial resources you will require, and of what type. For example, if you will not generate positive cash flow until one year after you launch your product, how will you fund your business in the interim?

Key Partnerships

In today's economy, no business is an island unto itself. Inevitably, you will have to enlist some third party help in delivering your value proposition to your target customers. So as part of creating your business model, you should identify the third-parties that you will need to make your business model work. You should also identify what resources you will acquire from them and/or the activities they will perform.

These days it's possible to outsource almost anything. This means that with respect to each of your key activities, you can first ask yourself whether you *need* to outsource that activity, such as when a third party can provide services that you cannot perform yourself or hire somebody to perform, or has resources that you are incapable of creating yourself. But you also should determine whether it simply makes more sense to have an external partner perform, or help perform, some or all of the functions you require. The same goes for each of your key resources—you can ask whether they can be obtained from an outside source on a more cost-effective and profitable basis than producing them yourself.

For example, it would make sense to enlist the services and/or resources of a third party if doing so would:

- Create economies of scale
- Create economies of scope
- Reduce risk and uncertainty through shared economics
- Give you access to specialists who would not be efficient to hire
- Give you broader and/or deeper access to customers
- Give you a competitive advantage

In order to determine what key partners your business model will require, look once more at all of your key activities and key resources with respect to your value proposition, customer channels and relationships, and revenue streams, and ask whether your business model would work best by partnering with a third party in any particular area.

For example, you may need or want to consider the following types of partners:

- Software development firms
- Website designers and developers
- Suppliers
- Manufacturing partners
- Outside sales agents
- Distribution partners
- Investment partners
- Function outsourcing such as human resources or accounting
- Industry consultants
- Independent contractor specialists
- Joint ventures
- Strategic alliances
- Virtual channels

With respect to each potential partner, you will need to assess and then test whether they will create the benefits and efficiencies you desire, as well as assess and test the viability of performing an activity or obtaining a resource on your own. You will also need to assess and test the working relationship, work flow, synergies, etc. you may or may not have with outside partners. Most importantly, you will need to obtain evidence of the cost of partnering with a third party versus keeping the task in house. And that brings us to the final building block of the Business Model Canvas—determining the cost of implementing and running your proposed business in the manner you've decided in the other eight blocks.

> **LinksBuddy Case Study**
>
> ## Chapter 9
> ## Key Activities, Key Resources and Key Partners
>
> At the beginning of the business modeling process, Steven and Martin thought they had a pretty good handle on what key activities they would need to engage in, resources they would need to acquire, and partners that would be useful in launching, growing and operating their LinksBuddy business. As the testing, iteration and validation process for their customer segments, value proposition, channels and customer relationships, and revenue streams progresses, however, they find themselves continuously revising the key activities, partners and resources section of their Business Model Canvas.
>
> With respect to *key resources*, they sit down after the extended field test to once again revise their canvas. The key physical asset is of course their platform, and the key to their platform is the platform software. On the face of it, this seems like a straightforward proposition. But once Steven and Martin scratched below the surface, they realized that the term "platform software" may include a vast array of different features and functions, and must include some level of informational content provision, listing, matching, curation, LinksBuddy-customer communication, golf traveler-accommodation provider communication, and e-commerce logistics. These features and functions will be driven by the value proposition that LinksBuddy will offer, and also by the customer relationships they want to develop and revenue streams they choose. The bottom line is that all of the desired features and functions need to be designed and programmed into the software, as well as all of the back office functions that need to be performed. The entire business is dependent on the website. It must be designed and work as planned.
>
> Because the platform software will be the key resource of the business, the key *human resource* will be software designers and programmers who can create and maintain that resource. Close behind will be internet marketing specialists who can make the best use of that software and deliver viewers to the platform who can be converted to customers. In addition, Steven and Martin's decision to use local representatives to recruit and attend to their

pods of accommodation providers make these local representatives a key human resource as well.

Once the platform software is developed, it will become a key competitive advantage for LinksBuddy. Therefore, the copyright on that software will become a key *intellectual property resource* that needs to be protected. This is particularly true since Steven and Martin are beginning to see how their business model could be replicated and reproduced in other areas of sport and adventure travel. Once the software for LinksBuddy is programmed, tested, and validated, the cost of that process could be much lower for other related businesses they choose to launch in the future.

One thing that has become crystal clear to Steven and Martin during the initial stages of their hypothesis testing: they are going to need outside *financial resources* to launch their business. Peter provides them with enough seed capital to complete the business modeling process, but to launch their business and obtain a critical mass that gets them beyond the chicken-and-egg problem, Steven and Martin will need to raise additional funds to cover platform development, marketing, launch of new locations, previously unexpected expenses such as customer support and local representatives, and initial discounts and promotions given to accommodation providers.

One final key resource for LinksBuddy will be access, through accommodation providers or otherwise, to tee times on great golf courses. An inventory of attractive golf course destinations will be the resource the company will build its accommodation provider network around, and use to attract golf travelers.

Steven and Martin's *key activities* will track fairly closely with their key resources. The first primary key activities will be the design, development, testing and validation of the software, including all of the key features and functions, for their platform. The second primary key activity will be recruiting a critical mass of accommodation providers to list and participate as links buddies for golf travelers. This will include the key activity of finding, training and supporting local representatives in their efforts to recruit and enlist a pod of accommodation providers in their location. The third key activity will be the internet marketing and public relations effort aimed at making golf travelers aware of LinksBuddy and getting them to view the website and try the service. The fourth key activity will be building trust on both sides of the platform. This will include efforts to create a reliable peer review system, customer curation efforts, and the provision of insurance to accommodation providers (and possibly travel insurance to golf travelers as well). The fifth key activity will be the selection and roll out of Links Buddy in chosen destinations. And the final key activity will be building the virtual community of golfers, both golf travelers and accommodation providers, which the Links Buddy value proposition will be centered on.

The testing and validation process has also revealed the need for *key partners* in the Links Buddy business. One key decision that Steven and Martin will have to make is whether to hire a software designer and/or developer to create and then maintain the platform software, or whether to either enlist a software development partner to do the same, or potentially to buy a pre-developed P2P software package and services from one of several companies now offering this type of product. The second key partner will be the necessary investors. This will mean additional decisions about how much ownership and decision making in their company that Steven and Martin want to allow any outside investors. Golf courses themselves may also become key partners, as Steven and Martin will need to develop relationships with the golf courses their business is centered around. Other key partners will include golf websites where they wish to embed their public relations content and links, insurance companies who will insure the accommodation providers, transportation providers with whom Steve and Martin can seek mutually beneficial deals, and golf associations and golf travel associations.

CHAPTER 10:
HOW MUCH WILL ALL THIS COST?

Chapter Overview

Identifying Costs 182
Fixed Versus Variable Costs 184
Cost Driven Versus Values-Driven Business 185
Economies of Scale and Economies of Scope 185
Cash Flow and Costs 186
LinksBuddy Case Study 187

CHAPTER 10

HOW MUCH WILL ALL THIS COST?

Now it's time to circle all the way back to square one. Let's remind ourselves once again of the ultimate purpose of the business model: to create a sustainably profitable business. This means that while all of the work we've done so far on the business model canvas is nice, if we can't perform all of the activities and acquire all of the necessary resources on a cost efficient basis, then it all means nothing. You can have the best value proposition and customer base in the world, but if you can't deliver your proposition to your customers at a profit, then you don't have a business model that works.

This means that now you need to sit down and figure out what everything you've listed in the last eight blocks of the Business Model Canvas will cost, including the cost of creating and delivering your value proposition, generating revenue streams, maintaining channels and developing customer relationships. compare that to your projected revenue, and then look to see whether this leaves you with a sustainable profit.

Like with the other items, we don't want to get bogged down at this point with specifying every cost that will be incurred in running the business—only the major ones. While we want to be as detailed as possible in assigning costs to specific items, we are still at the hypothesis stage. So to help, we can identify the major cost items, and then assign estimated costs to major areas of operation.

Identifying Costs

First look at the costs associated with performing your key activities and acquiring your key resources. That way you can not only assess your estimated costs and potential profitability, but also the cost-efficiency of all of your business activities and where you can either become more efficient or eliminate extraneous activities to become more profitable. You also want to assess whether your key costs are contributing directly to creating and delivering your value proposition to your target customer segment. If they are not, then you may be seriously misallocating your resources. In other words, if you have a major cost allocation which is not associated with a key activity, you should scrutinize those costs to determine whether they are really necessary. If they are, then your key activities block probably needs an additional item. If they are not, then you may have just found your first way to cut costs.

So the starting point is to look at each key activity and key resource and identify the associated costs. Then next look at major areas of operation and assess any further major costs. For example, you need to determine key costs with respect to:

- Product research, design and development
- Materials necessary to produce your product
- Labor necessary to product your product
- Manufacturing
- Website Design and Development
- Website Management
- Website Hosting
- Sales and Marketing
- Customer Channels
- Customer Relationships
- Creation of Revenue Streams
- Distribution
- Salaries, Commissions, Bonuses and Benefits
- Legal Fees

- Licensing Fees

- Rent

- Finance such as interest expense

Fixed Versus Variable Costs

In looking at each of your cost items, keep in mind that there are two kinds of costs.

- Fixed Costs

- Variable Costs

Fixed costs, as the name implies, do not change regardless of the volume produced by the business. A fixed monthly rent would be an example of a fixed cost. Too many fixed costs can drag a business down in times of slow sales. Keep in mind that fixed costs will not remain the same forever—for example rents and salaries will likely increase.

Variable costs do change based on certain factors, mainly the volume of product offering a company produces, and cannot always be easily predicted. For example, your monthly electricity bill would be a variable cost as would raw materials to produce a product. Sometimes these variable costs can swing wildly based on factors such as seasonality—this becomes important when it comes time to analyze your cash flow.

As we said above, it's important to attach key costs to specific activities and resources, and key activities and resources to your value proposition, to determine whether they are effective and necessary in implementing your business model. Also with respect to each key activity and resource, you should assess whether it costs more to perform the activity or produce the resource yourself, or to outsource all or part to a key partner.

You also should analyze whether specific costs will stay the same, increase, or decrease over time. You may be able to get by with a handful of employees at the outset, but to scale your business you may also need to scale your staff. And the relative variable costs of some items may go down, do to economies of scale (as output expands cost advantages arrive) and economies of scope (costs go down due to incorporating other businesses which have a direct relation to the original product).

Cost Driven Versus Values-Driven Business

It is also important to assess whether your want your business to be cost-driven or value-driven. While cost control is important to any business, some businesses are cost-driven and built around the minimization of costs at all levels in order to deliver a low-cost product to their customers. Adopting this strategy would obviously have an impact on the choices you make in the other building blocks of your Business Model Canvas.

Other businesses take the opposite, values-driven approach. These businesses are willing to spend more than competing businesses on producing their product, customer relationships, etc. in order to deliver a high-value product and experience to their customers, and one which is customized to their preferences.

If you have a cost-driven business with value-driven costs, then you will not be profitable. If you have a value-driven business with cost-driven mentality, you may not deliver on the value proposition your customers expect.

That being said, most businesses fall somewhere in the middle, trying to find a balance between minimizing costs and maximizing value.

Economies of Scale and Economies of Scope

In analyzing potential cost structures for your business and whether your business model will be sustainably profitable, you should look at whether it will create economies of scale and/or economies of scope.

Economies of scale are achieved when higher volume of output results in lower overall costs per unit produced. This can take place when your fixed costs stay costs stay relatively stable while volumes increase. Bulk buying is a related way to achieve economies of scale, as with volume purchases you often get discounts that also lower costs per unit produced.

Economies of scope occur when a business with an infrastructure in place for one line of business or market can be expanded into new lines of business or markets without duplicating the infrastructure. For example, a company with an accounting, human resources and marketing infrastructure may use those departments for two lines of business. Or a company with excess manufacturing capacity on one product line may launch a new product line that utilizes that capacity.

Cash Flow and Costs

It is very important that you assess not only what costs your business will incur, but when you will incur them in relation to the timing of revenues and financing you will receive. You need to determine how much cash you will burn before reaching break-even, and then whether you will continue to have enough cash when cost factors such as seasonality decrease revenues for certain periods of time, or one-time costs such as capital expenditures increase costs in a given period without a concurrent increase in revenues.

LinksBuddy Case Study

Chapter 10
How Much Will All This Cost?

As Steven and Martin progress through the business modeling process, one of the things that worry them most is keeping costs under control. The projected expenses keep adding up and adding up, and threaten to sink their business model. This, Peter tells them, is the reason why it's so important to break out your key costs as part of the business modeling process and test to make sure your estimates are accurate: so you validate the profitability and sustainability of your business model, rather than just guess as to their accuracy.

Looking at their key activities first, and then breaking down each function of their business by key costs, Steven and Martin identify the following items that will make up the brunt of the costs for their business.

Development of the platform software will be their key expense prior to launch of the website. Exactly how much software development will cost depends on whether they develop the software themselves internally, contract it out to a third party, or purchase a P2P white label software package. Steven and Martin estimate the costs of each option, but then test those estimates by speaking with software developers and white label vendors. They decide to hire a third party to design and develop the software. This will add a substantial upfront cost to their operation. They also decide that they need an experienced programmer in-house that understands the software inside and out, and who will be responsible for the program going forward. So platform maintenance and management will also be a significant cost going forward.

Marketing and sales expenses will be the largest ongoing cost of operations for LinksBuddy. This is where expenses could really get out of hand if not managed properly. But it will also drive the business, and significant costs will be necessary to push each side of the platform to critical mass as quickly as possible. Internet marketing expenses, both internal and external, will be a large piece of these costs. And one of the most significant expenses in this area will now be the amount paid to the local representatives. Both of these items will be variable, as Steven and Martin decided, after testing and validation with many potential local representatives, that they will pay their local representatives primarily on a commission basis. Destination launch expenses will also be significant as they roll-out each new location.

Another major expense that Steven and Martin had not anticipated when they launched their business the cost of training and supporting accommodation providers. Their accommodation providers will provide much more than just living space, they will be the front line face of LinksBuddy with their customers, both before the transaction with their website listing and communication, during the transaction as they provide their links buddy service, and after the transaction as a primary contact in the virtual golf network. Therefore, the testing process has revealed to Steven and Martin how vital it will be to help their accommodation providers prepare listings that can actually attract golf travelers, and to train their accommodation providers in order to have them provide a unique and hospitable experience that will cement the golf traveler as a repeat customer. Last but not least, the provision of insurance for accommodation providers will be a major expense.

Finally, while they intend to start lean, management and key employee salaries will also constitute a significant general and administrative expense once marketing, customer support and IT personnel are added. And unfortunately, Steven and Martin have realized by following Airbnb that legal fees may become a major expense as well. Airbnb has sensitized many locations to the absence of regulations covering accommodation rental businesses, and LinksBuddy is likely to get caught up in that wave and find legal compliance a significant expense.

Running the numbers and making initial financial projections, Steven and Martin see that they have several options on how to proceed. One option is to start very small, lean and low-tech. They could basically launch their business the way they launched their business model tests—by choosing just four or five destinations where they personally know golf pros or club members willing to act as local representatives to recruit a dozen accommodation providers or so, and then handle most of the other marketing and support tasks themselves. Once the business catches on through word of mouth and they increase their numbers on each side of the platform, they could slowly expand one destination at a time. On the other end of the spectrum, they could take their validated business model and shop it to venture capitalists in hopes of raising several million dollars and rolling out their business nationwide, or even worldwide, right from the start. The middle path would be to raise a modest amount of money that would fund a high-tech MVP website upon which additional features and functions could be added in the future, choose enough initial destinations to provide their golf traveler customers with options across the country, and put enough marketing spend behind their launch to gain critical mass liquidity within a year.

After consulting with Peter, the last option is Steven and Martin's choice. So now it is time to write a business plan to flesh out how they will execute their business model, and to use as a marketing document to sell potential investors on their exciting new business.

PART III

WRITING YOUR BUSINESS PLAN

CHAPTER 11:
GETTING STARTED ON YOUR BUSINESS PLAN

Chapter Overview

Strategy and Goals 195
SWOT Analysis 196
Operational Planning 200
The Audience..201
Length of Your Business Plan 203
LinksBuddy Case Study..205

CHAPTER 11

GETTING STARTED ON YOUR BUSINESS PLAN

At this point you should be feeling pretty good about yourself. Using the Business Model Canvas technique, you've created and validated a business model that on its face will give you a good chance of launching a profitable business. Congratulations!

It may now seem like you're ready to get started with that enterprise. After all, you've spent the last few weeks learning everything you can about the most important aspects of your business, and your customers and partners have told you that they can't wait to see your product out there in the market. So it would be natural to believe that you should focus on getting your business up and running and putting your product in the hands of your customers.

You could conceivably do just that. And in fact many start-up business owners focus on launching their products at this point—especially tech start-ups or others working in a rapidly changing environment. But as we discussed back in Chapter 1, we wouldn't recommend entering the market without first creating a business plan to state your goals and objectives, and to determine your strategy and tactics for executing your business model and meeting those goals and objectives.

In essence, a business plan is just an expanded business model—fleshing out some areas and addressing others that were implicit rather than explicit in your Business Model Canvas process. Likewise, a business model is a business plan synthesized to its essential elements. It didn't make sense to write a business plan until you had verified your business model, because much of it may end up on the cutting room floor. But now that you have verified your business model to the appropriate extent to launch your business, then it does make sense to write a business plan that details how you intend to execute your business model.

Remember that planning isn't just about creating a written document. Planning is about setting goals and objectives, and creating a strategy and formulating tactics to achieve them. And while everyone understands that business is a constantly evolving process and much of what is in the business plan will need to change over time, how you prepare and present the plan will be a strong indication of your passion for your idea and competence to realize it successfully.

So where do you start? The good news is that as you work through your business plan, you will find that much of the research, analysis, testing and verifying has already been done in connection with your Business Model Canvas. But the first action item is to once again take a step back, look at the big picture, and think strategically.

Strategy and Goals

To develop a business plan that best executes your business model, you first need to think strategically, and then operationally. Strategic thinking is broader-based and longer-termed. You already began this process when you created your vision, mission and values statements. Now would be a good time to revisit each of those statements, reevaluate them based on what you learned during the Business Model Canvass process, and make any revisions you think are appropriate.

In combination, your mission, vision and values statements constitute a concise strategic picture of where you want to take your business for the foreseeable future (which is normally about 3 years in traditional businesses, shorter in faster moving technology related businesses), what are the principal goals you want to achieve, and how you want to realize that vision and achieve those goals.

Again, this does not mean that you'll never change course. In fact, you probably will. But your vision, mission and values statements give you a solid foundation for setting goals and making operational planning decisions—they are a prism through which every strategic and operational decision should be viewed.

Once you have your top-level strategy in place, you need to engage in strategic thinking with respect to each block of your business model canvas, and each functional area of your business. For example, how do you see your value proposition evolving in the foreseeable future to further meet your customers' needs? Remember you are most likely starting with your MVP (minimum viable product), rather than your ideal product—do you have a strategy for introducing additional product features going forward? In addition, what is your strategy for reproducing and scaling your business model for future growth?

Also keep in mind that all of the areas of your business plan must be integrated in the same manner as the blocks of your business model. This integration must occur both vertically and horizontally. Vertical integration is from your vision, mission and values statements down to your organizational goals and objectives, and then further down to the strategy, goals, objectives and action plans of each functional area of your business. Horizontal integration is between the strategy, goals, objectives, and operational tactics of each functional area—i.e. product development, marketing and sales, operations, human resources, and finance—to ensure that they are all in sync.

In order to help answer these and other strategic questions, and to help set goals and objectives for your business to achieve by executing on your business model, now would be a good time to conduct what is called a SWOT analysis, which stands for "strengths, weaknesses, opportunities and threats."

SWOT Analysis

In order to write a good business plan, you need to take a brutally honest look at the strengths and weaknesses of your business model, yourself and your organization. While doing so, keep in mind that business planning is an iterative process just like creating a business model was. During the business planning process, you will inevitably discover flaws in your business model, strategy, goals and action plans that need to be addressed, as well as outside threats that need to be protected against.

Identifying weaknesses and threats at this early stage allows you to make required changes before they become problematic. You'll also uncover opportunities that may otherwise have been overlooked, providing you the chance to take advantage of unfilled gaps in the market that may prove to be the difference between success and failure. Finally, you will hone in on the strengths of your business model and organization and find the best ways to exploit them to your competitive advantage.

A SWOT analysis allows you to begin this process right up front. In conducting this analysis, you will identify your organization's most important internal strengths and weaknesses along with the most important opportunities and threats presented by the external environment. Then you will analyze these strengths, weaknesses, opportunities and threats in relation to each other and use this analysis in setting the strategy, goals and objectives, and operational plans of your organization.

The SWOT acronym can be fleshed out as follows:

- **Strengths** are the internal capabilities and resources of your business and organization that best allow you to successfully execute your business model and achieve your goals—your most important strengths will give you a clear competitive advantage

- **Weaknesses** are a deficiency in your internal capabilities or resources that will hinder your ability to successfully execute your business model and achieve your goals—the most critical weaknesses are those that allow your competitors to have a competitive advantage over your business or prevent you from attaining your own competitive advantage

- **Opportunities** are favorable external factors that if taken advantage of will strengthen your business model and operating results—the most important opportunities are those, if seized upon, would allow you to develop a new strength and give you a competitive advantage

- **Threats** are unfavorable external factors which could negatively impact your business model and/or affect your operating results and capabilities—the most important would dilute your competitive advantage and/or provide such an advantage to a competitor

As stated above, strengths and weaknesses are internal and within the management control of your business. When identifying strengths and weaknesses, it is important do so in relation to your competitors. What do you do better or worse than they do? What strengths do you have that give you a competitive advantage? What weaknesses do you have that give your competitors an advantage?

When conducting your SWOT analysis, look for strengths and weaknesses in the following areas:

- Each block of your business model canvas; and the integration of your business model as a whole

- Each functional area of your business—including product development; marketing, sales and distribution; customer service; operations; technology; intellectual property; finance; and management and key employees

- Each step of the "value chain", which is the process by which value is added to your product at each phase until it reaches the customer, and even afterwards.

- Specific metrics such as the cost of customer acquisition and customer lifetime value

- Resources such as property and location, equipment, knowledge, brand equity, intellectual property, etc.

- Distinguishing skills and capabilities—i.e. core competencies

Opportunities and threats are external to the business and not within its control. However, once they are identified you can anticipate, plan and take proactive steps to take advantage of opportunities and defend against threats.

When conducting your SWOT analysis, look for opportunities and threats in the following areas:

- Your competitors' strategies, business models, value propositions, strengths and competitive advantages, weaknesses, etc.

- Changes and trends in your industry, market and target customer segment—including the emergence of new problems and needs, new uses for products, availability of new geographical markets, etc.

- Changes and trends in the political, economic, social, technological, environmental and legal arenas (sometimes collectively referred to as "PESTEL") that could positively or negatively affect your business

The process of performing a successful SWOT analysis is similar to that of creating a business model canvas. Begin by brainstorming—get creative and generate as many ideas as possible without self-editing. Then separate the wheat from the chafe and narrow your lists down to 3-5 items per category, defining each item as clearly and specifically as possible. Finally, test your items to make sure they are based on facts rather than opinions.

You should also prioritize each of the items in your lists so that you identify the most significant factors for your business. In the case of strengths and weaknesses, prioritize based on importance. And in the case of opportunities and threats, prioritize based on both importance and probability.

Once you've created your four prioritized lists, you can begin using your SWOT analysis in strategic planning and goal-setting. For example, by asking the following questions:

- How can we use our strengths to take advantage of the opportunities we have identified?

- How can we use our strengths to defend against and overcome the threats we have identified?

- How can we best use our strengths to execute our business model and achieve our goals and objectives?

With respect to weaknesses, you will want to focus on how you can improve or minimize your weaknesses so that they do not impede your ability to execute your business model.

Having answered these questions and finalized your lists, you can now use the SWOT analysis to set your business goals and develop strategies to execute your business model and achieve those goals. In doing so, you will want to develop goals and strategies that utilize your strengths, take advantage of your opportunities, improve and minimize your weaknesses, and defend against threats. You may also find that there are areas of your Business Model Canvas that may need to be revised based on your SWAT analysis.

Operational Planning

Now it's time to get down to brass tacks. Once you've identified your business model and set your strategic goals and objectives, you need to develop a shorter term action plan for executing your business model and achieving your goals and objectives.

Operational planning is more detailed than strategic planning, but for purposes of your business plan we don't mean deciding on or describing the minute details of managing each functional area. We are still talking about setting goals and objectives, just more short-term and with top-level action plans attached. For example, your marketing plan, human resource hiring plan, product development milestones and annual budget are part of your operational planning.

In order to begin thinking on an operational level, brainstorm about what concrete steps you will need to take in order to effectively and efficiently launch and execute your business model. For example, you will need to set goals and objectives for each functional area of your business that you can measure progress against and which align with your overall goals and objectives; develop a strategy and action plan for meeting those goals and objectives that aligns with your overall strategy and action plan; and identify the key activities for each functional area the same as you did for your overall business model. In addition, you need to make sure that all or this is both horizontally and vertically integrated and consistent. Simple, right?

It's actually not as complicated as it sounds. As an initial step, you can break your business down into functions, and then create specific strategic and action plans for each function, such as:

- Marketing and Sales Plan
- Web Site Design and Development Plan
- E-Commerce Plan
- Technology Plan
- Human Resources Hiring and Compensation Plan
- Operations Plan

- Financial Plan and Projections

- Funding Plan

Many people would just go and do each of these things separately, or assign a team member to perform the task separately for each business function. But if you look at the list of functions you need to perform, it will collectively makes up what a good business plan should consist of. So doesn't it then make sense for you and your management team to sit down together and pool your efforts into one coherent business plan, rather than creating half a dozen separate non-integrated plans? An overall plan that everybody buys into and you can present to potential partners and investors?

Some entrepreneurs object that time is of the essence, and everything is going to change anyways. While they are absolutely correct, nobody said you have to take months to put your business plan ideas together, that it will be set and stone, or that you necessarily have to formally write them up in a detailed manner. But regardless of whether you intentionally create a business plan and document it, you clearly have to have one. So it's better to quickly and efficiently do it in a focused and coherent manner. And in many cases you have to write a business plan anyways, because you need to raise money from angel or seed capital investors, and probably later VCs. Most will require you to have a business plan, and they'll use it to see whether you know what you're talking about and have the level of competence they require.

As such, one of the most critical aspects of writing a good business plan is to keep the audience in mind.

The Audience

When writing a business plan, you need to always remember your audience, because the tone and content will change depending on who will be reading the plan and for what purpose. The primary initial audience should always be yourself and your management team. Even if you're preparing the plan to show to potential investors, you should go through the process of writing the business plan for your own team as well. Not to do so would be a wasted opportunity.

However, if your business plan will be read by potential capital investors, lenders, key employees, and partners, you need to tailor your business plan to your intended audience and make sure that it clearly and compellingly sells them on your business and answers all their key questions in a manner that convinces them to jump on board. This means that while you need to *create* your business plan with the motivation of better executing your business model and successfully operating and growing your business, you will likely need to *write* your business plan in a way that sells your intended audience on your business model, business plan, and ability to execute them to the benefit of that audience.

Depending on the type of new business you are starting and the point at which you need to raise money, your audience could include:

- Angel Investors
- Venture Capital Investors
- Crowdfunding Sources
- Banks and other Lending Institutions
- Strategic Partners
- Key Management or Employee Recruits

Angel and Venture capital investors will want to see a significant return on their investment as well as a clear "exit strategy," or manner in which they will be able to realize and pocket that return. As such, they will be looking for you to demonstrate a clear need in a market that represents a significant opportunity and a value proposition that fits that need and that market. They will then be looking for a business model that if executed would generate the desired return a management team capable of executing the business model. And finally they will be looking for a financial plan and projections that credibly demonstrate the desired return on investment if all of this takes place.

Traditional lenders don't care about a return on their investment, as there is most often not any upside for them other than interest on the loan. They will be primarily focused on the company's ability to generate enough cash flow to make the principal and interest payments on loans when due. Of course this means that they will also want to see a credible market and business model, as well as a competent management team.

In addition to the above, strategic partners will want to see whether there is a strategic and visionary fit that will lead to the desired synergies, return on investment, and competitive advantages.

If the business plan will be purely for internal consumption, then the tone may be less marketing-oriented. In addition, you will not *necessarily* have to address such matters as potential rates of return on investment dollars, exit strategies, etc. However, keep in mind that you as founder are the primary investor in your business. Therefore, even if no outside investors or lenders are involved, you should put on your own investor hat and think through these issues for yourself. In addition, do not discount the benefits of using this document as an internal marketing document as well. If your passion along with your clear and concise vision is reflected in the plan, then key employees who read the plan will share your passion and vision. If you cannot communicate such passion and vision in your business plan, then you need to look at what might be wrong with both.

Length of Your Business Plan

How long does my business plan need to be? That depends on who will be reading it and why. The times are changing with respect to business plans. As an outside parameter, your plan shouldn't be more than 25-30 pages. Anything longer than that means you haven't taken the time to properly think through and synthesize your business model, goals, strategy and action plans. But within that range, the length of your plan will literally depend on the audience and the circumstances and what works best.

For example, your business plan could consist only of a well-conceived power point presentation covering each area of the plan. This should not mean that any less thought went into developing the plan, just that a targeted presentation is the most effective way to communicate with your intended audience, and a manner which they welcome. This may be all you need for a plan that has only an internal audience. And it may all some outside investors want to see as well.

The benefits of a synthesized business plan are that you are more focused on ideas rather than words, and it helps you communicate as clearly and concisely as possible. The danger is that you will truncate the planning process as well, and in fact not think through all of the important issues that need to be addressed. Remember, the process of fleshing out these bullet point ideas can be very valuable and have many internal benefits including synergistic strategic thinking and buy-in. In addition, if you are soliciting investors, lenders or key partners, it is likely that some potential candidates will want a fully written business plan in text form (along with charts and tables, etc.).

Therefore, a good way to create your business plan would be to follow a similar pattern to creating a business model canvas. First create your business plan bullet points for each section and put it in power point format. Then flesh out your plans, test them where appropriate, and document them for each functional area of your business. And finally go back and revise your bullet points based on what you've learned throughout the business planning process—which will likely be a considerable amount.

LinksBuddy Case Study

Chapter 11
Getting Started on Your Business Plan

With a tested and verified business model in hand, Steven and Martin felt like writing a business plan to present to investors was mostly a formality … and the told this to Peter. Their mentor, however, urged them to hold off on making that judgment until after performing a SWOT analysis.

"Go back to brainstorming," Peter says. "Tell me your strengths. What are the capabilities you possess that will best help you execute your business model and give you a clear competitive advantage?"

It didn't take long for Steven and Martin to realize that, despite the fact that they had a validated business model in hand, they still had a long way to go towards establishing a business with the kinds of core competencies and competitive advantages it would take to win in the Golf Travel marketplace. They believe that their unique value proposition, which is unlike any other in the industry, provides them with a competitive advantage right from the start. And Steven's long-term experience with almost every aspect of the golf industry, and Martin's long-term experience in the golf travel and hospitality industry, as well as internet marketing, provided them with a solid foundation of relevant experience. And the fact that they have a verified, repeatable and scalable business model will give their overall operations a significant competitive advantage in the future. But beyond that, all of the strengths they can list for their business are strengths they have yet to develop. For example, their proprietary software containing all the key features of their MVP, and the website it supports, will be one of their strengths and competitive advantages. As will their brand, which will signify and instantly evoke the worldwide golf community they plan to build. Their network of dedicated local representatives, and the flights of accommodation providers that those representatives build, will be a strength and competitive advantage once in place, as will the community of accommodation providers and golf travelers who communicate online and off. Finally, the holy grail of liquidity and the network effect, once achieved, will be the supreme strength and competitive advantage they will enjoy.

When Steven and Martin present their list to Peter, they expect him to be unimpressed.

"That's great," Peter says after reviewing their perceived strengths. "And now you can see why it's so important to develop a business plan to execute your business model. As part of your business planning process, you need to develop a strategy that turns all of those potential strengths and competitive advantages into a reality. Every aspect of your business plan should be geared towards making sure that happens, along with making sure you realize your corporate vision, mission and values."

Next Steven and Martin take a look at their weaknesses, and find out that this category is the inverse of what they found in analyzing strengths: most of their weaknesses exist right now. The primary weakness is that they need to overcome the chicken and egg problem in order for their business to be viable. In addition, they are attempting to re-segment the golf travel market and doing so will require them to convince existing golf travelers to change their consumer habits, or convince new golf travelers to enter the market. While Steven and Martin have certain types of valuable experience, they do not have start-up entrepreneurial experience, particularly in the challenging P2P environment. And until they raise money from investors, they do not have the financial resources to launch their business. Finally, once they launch their business, there will be few barriers to an Airbnb or larger golf tour operator piggybacking on their groundbreaking efforts and entering the new market they have created.

"Once again," Peter says, "that is why you're sitting here today writing a business plan rather than immediately launching your business. You've now identified weaknesses and challenges that need to be overcome, and you need a specific strategy to do so."

Not to mention a strategy to overcome or minimize the future operational weaknesses that they've identified, such as the need to grow and manage many diverse locations; the potential for a few "bad apples" to create bad publicity as Airbnb has experienced; the requirement that their accommodation providers perform a personal service, acting as active hosts, rather than simply renting out space; seasonality of different preferred golf destinations; the intangible difficulty in creating and maintaining the "community" of golfers they envision driving their business, etc. They will also need a strategy and tactics to minimize or overcome these weaknesses in their business model.

On the flipside, they see several great opportunities that they can take advantage of in the future. These include expansion into the European market and other international markets, the addition of new revenue streams, a focus on additional customer segments such as female golf travelers, senior golf travelers, etc.; the chance to enter into strategic partnerships with larger organizations in the golf travel and/or hospitality industry, etc.

"In order to really take advantage of these opportunities," Peter says. "You need to prepare for them, lay a foundation for them, in your business plan and operations, so your company can jump on the opportunities when the time is ripe."

Finally, Steven and Martin take a hard look at some of the most significant threats they will face and have to plan for; some of which are related to the weaknesses they identified. The entrance of Airbnb or a large golf tour operator into their space would pose a significant threat, so they need to think about differentiating their business from such a competitor now, before one even exists. In addition, they look at the battle Airbnb has engaged in with respect to laws and regulations regarding private accommodation providers, and realize they need to be prepared for resistance from local authorities, spurred on by hotels and others in the hospitality and golf travel industries which stand to lose market share to the new disruptive entrant. Finally, they need to take a hard look at the golfing economy and its trends. While golf travel has stayed relatively solid, the overall golf economy has been shaky. Steven and Martin need to strategize as to how to insulate their business as much as possible from future downturns—hopefully even finding ways to take advantage of such dips through cost-effective offerings, more local golf travel options, etc.

With all that in mind, and using their SWOT analysis as a platform to identify their top-level strategic goals, Steven and Martin begin work on writing a business plan that will both be their own blueprint for operating their business and executing their business model, as well as convincing investors to put their faith and money in their business model and plan.

CHAPTER 12:
THE EXECUTIVE SUMMARY

Chapter Overview

Contents of the Executive Summary..211
Length and Style of the Executive Summary 215
When to Write the Executive Summary 216
LinksBuddy Case Study..218

CHAPTER 12

THE EXECUTIVE SUMMARY

The executive summary is the most important section of the business plan. It is not a "summary" as the subheading suggests—at least not in the classic sense of the word. The executive summary is a concise and compelling description of the business opportunity you have identified; the value proposition and business model you have created; the goals, strategy and means you will use to execute your business model and capitalize on the opportunity; the resources you will require; and the potential payoff for everyone involved.

In other words, the executive summary is the most important aspects of your business plan condensed into two pages, and whoever reads it should come away with a very good understanding of exactly what your business is all about and feel realistically excited about its prospects. The executive summary will force you to prioritize, and will reveal to the reader how you do so. It will also require you to be able to communicate clearly and concisely the strategy you will pursue with respect to those priorities.

This is where you make your pitch. If you don't hook the readers with the executive summary, then you've lost them already. The rest of your plan will never get read. If you sell them here, then the rest of the plan should just confirm what they've already come to believe.

Therefore, you must convey your enthusiasm and get the reader to share it, leaving him or her chomping at the bit to read the rest of your business plan. If you do not achieve this in the executive summary, your business plan is destined to be tossed in the financier's "slush pile" where unfunded businesses go to die. On the other hand, a well-written and well-thought-out executive summary can be the seed from which your company springs to life.

Contents of the Executive Summary

There are two schools of thought on how to organize and write your executive summary. They may sound mutually exclusive, but they aren't.

The first school follows the guiding principal that the purpose of the executive summary is to act as a sales pitch that gets the reader excited about the business idea and wanting to read more. They argue that only the essence of the business plan should be included in the executive summary, and it is not necessary to provide a synthesis of everything that is to follow. Therefore, the format should be that of a power point pitch rather than a summary of each section of the document.

The second school of thought is that the executive summary should in fact follow the same format as the rest of the document, with a concise presentation of the most important points of each section forming the contents of this initial section of the business plan. That way, someone reading the executive summary could in theory not read any further and still understand enough about the all-around nature of your business and the investment opportunity being offered to decide whether to move forward.

You absolutely should convey the essence of your distinctive business opportunity and the business model you have created to take advantage of it in a way primarily designed to sell the reader. But it is possible to do so while including the most important points from each section of your business plan, so the reader comes away with a big-picture sense of your entire business and your competence to run it as well.

So don't feel you have to be tied to a particular format, but don't leave anything essential to your business out as well. Anticipate the most important questions, and if you haven't provided the answers in the executive summary, then go back and revise.

Because the executive summary will describe the factors that are most critical to your business, in many respects it is a description of the business model you just created using the Business Model Canvas. So use that as your guiding principal, and convey your passion, excitement and commitment to your business model along with your strategy for making it work.

Whatever format and style you choose, make sure you clearly and concisely discuss all of the following:

- The important problem/need of your target customer segment
- Your solution/value proposition and how it directly addresses the problem/need
- The opportunity—the size and shape of the market and your target customer segment
- The competitive environment
- Your core competencies, competitive advantages and product differentiation strategy
- How you will identify, attract, convert, retain and grow customers
- Your expected revenue streams
- Your financial model for profitability
- Your projected financial results
- Critical success factors and key milestones
- Your management team
- Your funding requirements
- The expected return on investment

The Problem: The point from which your entire business model flows is the problem that your target customers need solved (which could be a need or desire that they want satisfied). Without such a problem, you have no business model and no business. So this is the starting point of your pitch. Go back and review the "customer segments" block of your Business Model Canvas, and clearly describe the problem that you identified and why it is so important that your customers must find a solution to that problem. Make your audience understand that a solution to this problem is something a large number of people *have to have* and will spend good money to buy.

Your Solution: Solving the important problem of your customer is the reason for your business's existence—and your value proposition is that solution. Remember, your value proposition is more than just your product and its features. It includes all of the ways your business model will work to provide the best overall solution for your customers. Present your value proposition in compelling terms and make sure to link it specifically with the problem to which it is addressed, and explain exactly how it will solve that problem.

The Opportunity: This is where you make your reader understand that you will be providing a solution to the problems of a significant number of people who will be highly motivated to pay for your product/value proposition. You need to communicate that the size of your target market and the portion of that market you can capture is big enough to provide the financial returns your readers will expect (or you will expect if your business plan is for internal consumption only). Again go back to the "customer segments" portion of your business model canvas and use your findings to describe your target customer segment. Then provide the highlights of your market research findings about the size and shape of your market and target customer segment.

The Competitive Environment: Your business does not exist in a vacuum. If you have identified a significant problem experienced by a large number of people, then it is likely other businesses have as well and they will be competing either directly or indirectly for your customers' dollars and loyalty. Later in your business plan you will go into some detail about those competitors, their attributes and what threats they pose. But the purpose of discussing the competitive environment in the executive summary is to set up a discussion of your competitive advantages, as well as to demonstrate your appreciation for the challenges you face in the market. So briefly describe what competing products are currently on offer and how they succeed or fail to meet your target customers' needs.

Your Competitive Advantages, Product Differentiation and Core Competencies: Once you have succinctly stated what the competition is doing to solve the problem faced by customers in your target market, you can tell the reader how you will do it better and why customers will prefer your value proposition over that of another business. Communicate clearly the unique benefits that your product and overall offering will provide customers and how you will differentiate yourself from the competition. Also describe any core competencies, key resources or key partnerships that your business has that give rise to a competitive advantage. Finally, state how and why you will be able to sustain your competitive advantages going forward.

Your Strategy to Identify, Attract, Convert, Retain and Grow Customers: This time go to the "channels" and "customer relationships" sections of your business model canvas and describe the vehicles and methods you will use to communicate with your customers and sell and distribute your products. Also go to your marketing plan, discussed in Chapter 15, and pull out the key messages you will convey and strategies and methods you will use to do so. Remember, this executive summary is your sales pitch, so this should not be a bland description. Convince your readers! They must be sold on how you will attract customers and get them to buy—and buy more and more, again and again.

Expected Revenue Streams and Financial Business Model: The previous points you have made about the problem, solution, opportunity, competitive advantages, marketing strategy, etc. should have already convinced the reader that you will generate revenues, but if you can't do so at a profit then once again you have no business. First tell the reader about the revenue streams you identified in your Business Model Canvas; then explain how they will generate a sustainable profit, acceptable profit margins, positive cash flows, and the desired return on investment for your audience. In doing so, summarize your financial projections for the next 3 years, as well as your historical financial results for the previous three years if you have an existing business.

Management Team: You need to convince the reader that not only do you have a great opportunity and business model to capitalize on that opportunity, but you and your team are highly capable of bringing it to successful fruition. Hit the highlights of who you all are and why the reader should invest in you and your team—because that is exactly what they will be doing. This is not the place to summarize resumes. It is the place to communicate capabilities, both on an individual and integrated group basis. If there are hiring gaps, which there likely will be, state what they are and how you will fill your management and key employee needs.

Key Milestones and Critical Success Factors: A description of key milestones serves several purposes. The milestones show that you have specific target dates for achieving your goals; they can be matched to cash flow projections to see when additional rounds of funding may be required; and they can demonstrate a credible understanding of how your product launch will take place and business model will be executed. A description of those factors that are the most critical to capitalizing on your business model both demonstrates your appreciation for, and gives the reader an understanding of, what the most essential elements will be in your achievement of your business goals and their achievement of the desired returns.

Funding Needs: Present clearly how much capital you are looking to raise or borrow at this juncture, and how long you expect it to last before another round of funding takes place, which is commonly a future key milestone.

Expected Return on Investment: If your audience is potential investors, you need to understand exactly what return on investment they will be looking for and provide a summary of your projected financial results that credibly demonstrates how and when they will receive their desired return. If your investors don't see this return in a timeframe that meets their investment requirements, or if they don't believe it will be achievable, then your business model and plan will have no meaning to them.

Length and Style of the Executive Summary

As discussed above, the executive summary should clearly, concisely, and compellingly present your business idea, business opportunity, and business model so a reader can fully understand what you intend to offer and be quickly convinced of its potential. You should be able to make each point described above in a few sentences at most. The entire executive summary should comprise two, or at most three, pages. Some believe one page is enough, but most investors find that there is not enough information in one page to understand and evaluate a company.

In doing so, keep the following style points in mind:

- Understand that your reader is extremely busy: focus on and hit only the highlights; the detail comes later

- Every sentence should be clear, concise and compelling: use simple direct sentences rather than long compound sentences; use nouns and verbs; use very few adjectives and avoid jargon

- Be strong and positive with your language: do not be passive, uncertain or use weak words

- Be visual, but only if it achieves the desired purpose: you can use charts and graphs, but make sure they help to present a clear and compelling picture of revenue, profits and/or customer growth

- Be original: Don't just cut and paste from the rest of your document

Remember that the outline provided in this chapter should not be applied rigidly. There is no template that fits all companies. You need to think through what points are most important in your particular case, what points are irrelevant, what points need emphasis, and what points require no elaboration. Go with a format and contents that match your business and circumstances, but make sure you touch on each key issue for your business.

The best business plans tell a compelling story about an opportunity and how the founder of a business intends to take advantage of that opportunity. They provide a credible and interesting narrative of how that will happen: how the business plans to create and deliver value to its target customer segments, compete and convince them to buy, and create value for the business that can be returned to its investors. This is the spine of the story, and it should be evident and consistent throughout the business plan. If the story isn't consistent, or the plan is a hodgepodge of loosely related material, it will be ineffective.

When to Write the Executive Summary

There are also two schools of thought on when to write your executive summary. A majority of those in the know would say to write it last, after you have fleshed out the plans for each business function that will comprise each section of your business plan, e.g. marketing plan, operations plan, financial plan and projections. Their argument is that you don't want to try and make the rest of the plan fit the executive summary—and if you do in fact write your executive summary first and cast it in stone, they have a valid point.

But if you treat the creation and documentation of your business plan as an iterative process the same way you did the creation of your business model, then you can write your executive summary at the beginning, as your initial proposition, and then revise and rewrite it at the end of the process.

As you can see from the information above, much of what you will include in your executive summary comes directly from your business model itself—which has already been subject to testing and validation to a significant extent. Therefore you should be able to create an initial executive summary using only your business model canvas and the supporting information you have collected. But even a validated business model is still a running hypothesis that will continue to be tested and revised, both during the business planning process and after the launch of your product. In addition, writing an initial draft of the executive summary at the beginning allows you to focus on the most important items and not get bogged down in too many distracting details.

So one way to approach the executive summary is to write it at the beginning and treat it as a working hypothesis. Then go through the process of creating your separate marketing, operations and financial plans, etc. which should include testing and validation of your strategy and means for accomplishing the goals of each function. This process will no doubt result in some tweaking of your business model as well.

After these strategies, goals and top-level action items for the overall business and each functional area have been determined and validated, you can use them to go back and rewrite your executive summary into its final form as the last step in documenting your business plan.

> ## LinksBuddy Case Study
>
> # Chapter 12
> # The Executive Summary
>
> Steven and Martin decide to draft their Business Plan in two phases. The first phase will consist of a power point presentation hitting the highlights of each section, and allowing for an easy overview of the entire plan. This will allow them to integrate the different parts of their business plan, iterate and revise where necessary, without getting bogged down in details which may change before the finished product is produced. Once they have the power point outline in place, then they will flesh out their business plan into paragraph form, incorporating all of the details. Their power point plan will also allow them to make sure they have a focused message to excite their audience of investors to fund their start-up.
>
> The Executive Summary portion of their business plan will consist of the following points:
>
> **What is LinksBuddy?:** LinksBuddy is an online peer-to-peer marketplace where golfer travelers can meet and match with fellow golfers from around the world who are willing to provide accommodation, golf comradery and local knowledge to a visiting golfer.
>
> **What Our Customers Desperately Want and Need:** There are millions of golf enthusiasts who fantasize about having a buddy who has access to a great golf course in an interesting location who they could conveniently stay and play golf with ... And there are millions of other golf fanatics who own a home with extra space near a great golf course in an interesting location, and would love to make friends from around the world who could come stay with them and play their home course together.
>
> **Our Customers' Problems:** There is no golf travel option that allows golf enthusiasts from around the world to meet each other and conveniently make arrangements to share their love of golf. Most golf travel tour operators offer a golfer only one type of experience: traveling with a group of friends from their hometown and staying in an impersonal hotel or resort with no local host who knows the course or the area. There is

no more interesting, more fulfilling, more personal option available. In addition, golf course memberships and unused living space are expensive underutilized assets that could be converted into supplemental income by avid golfers. However, there is currently no way for golfers who own these assets to meet and offer their extra living space and golf course access to people who share their love of golf.

The LinksBuddy Solution: LinksBuddy will provide a convenient trusted online location where golf enthusiasts can meet new golfing friends with similar interests and characteristics who live near great courses in attractive locations around the world, and arrange to stay in their homes and golf their home course together. LinksBuddy will also provide an online platform for those golfers who wish to rent out space in their homes to persons from around the world who they are interested in meeting and playing golf together with on their home course.

The Large and Growing Market Opportunity: The Total Available Market (TAM) for LinksBuddy golf travelers includes every person who travels and plays golf as part of their trip. The golf travel market is estimated at over $$$ worldwide and $$$ in the United States. The Serviceable Available Market (SAM), consisting of golf destinations in the United States where residential accommodation is available and a flight of LinksBuddy accommodation providers could be established is present, is $$$, of which the Serviceable Obtainable Market (SOM) is estimated to be $$$. The SAM for future expansion into Europe is $$$, of which the SOM is $$$. The SAM for future expansion worldwide is $$$, of which the SOM is $$$. In addition, there would be numerous additional large market opportunities to use the LinksBuddy business model in other sports travel segments.

Our Target Customer Profile: For both golf travelers and accommodation providers, the Links Buddy target customer is a male between 35-55 years old; has a middle-high income; is a serious or serious-social golfer with a low or medium handicap who plays golf at least once a week; spends free time not only playing golf, but also following, learning about and discussing the game of golf (i.e. a golf enthusiast); and enjoys meeting, golfing, and discussing golf with new people. For golf travelers, our target customer travels to play golf at least once a year, but enjoys cultural and educational travel as well. They desire a golf destination that has more to offer than simply a resort relaxation experience. They are willing to use Airbnb type accommodation in private homes and are willing to travel and golf without friends from home. For accommodation providers, they have mid-to-high end space available for rent; are either members of a club with guest access or play frequently at a top-tier public course near their home; are primarily motivated to rent space for the purpose of meeting fellow golfers; and have sufficient free time to golf with guest golf travelers.

The Chicken and Egg Challenge: The primary challenge to a successful launch and growth of the LinksBuddy business will be overcoming the "chicken and egg" challenge of a P2P marketplace. As a multi-sided marketplace, the company will be required to grow its customer base both on the golf traveler side and the accommodation provider side in order to have a viable business. The chicken and egg challenge arises because in order to attract one side, it is necessary to have the other side already in place.

Our Chicken and Egg Strategy: We intend to initially focus on the accommodation provider side of the market, using local representatives in ten different destinations to recruit and list an initial flight of 10-20 accommodation providers in each destination. We believe this will be possible by ensuring that the initial flights of 100 plus accommodation providers will not be out-of-pocket any expenses, and by using our local representatives to instill a sense of community among each flight or providers. With this number of accommodation providers, we believe we can use an intensive internet and public relations marketing campaign to attract a sufficient number of golf traveler customers to our website who will meet accommodation providers online and choose to try our service as early evangelists. This will allow us to successfully launch our business. Over the following nine month period we will systematically add new destinations and flights of accommodation providers while attracting large numbers of curious golf travelers to our website. We believe that we will hit critical mass of both accommodation providers and golf travelers by the end of this period, at which time we will be on our way towards organic growth (where new flights of accommodation providers request to organize themselves in new destinations), and the holy grail of the network effect (where the value of our platform catapults because customers on both sides of the platform believe they will find and obtain what they are looking for from our service).

Finding and Converting Target Customers: Our strategy for recruiting our initial flights of accommodation providers will be to retain a local representative in each destination who is either in the golf industry, such as a local teaching golf professional, or someone who wants to be an accommodation provider. This person will be responsible for recruiting and listing the initial flight or accommodation providers. Our strategy for recruiting and converting golf travelers is to use a wide range of internet marketing techniques and public relations methods to drive golf travelers to our website, where we will convert them into traveling customers. Once we have obtained our initial flights of accommodation providers, we will also use these marketing and public relations approaches to recruiting and listing new accommodation providers. However, we still intend to have a local representative in each destination.

Revenue Streams: Golf travelers will generate our primary revenue stream. They will pay LinksBuddy a fee equal to 15% of their total accommodation and green fee price. Accommodation providers will pay a fee of 5% of that price. However, because recruiting our initial flights of accommodation providers will be a key the successful launch of our business, we anticipate offering discounts on this fee, or waiving it altogether, for our initial flights of accommodation providers.

Key Milestones: Our first two key milestones will be the final development and implementation of our platform software and website, including all or our key initial features and functions. The target date for completion of this milestone is three months following receipt of funding. In that same time period, we will recruit our initial flight of 100 accommodation providers in 10 destinations. During the following three months we will list and train our accommodation providers, while at the same time driving golf traveler traffic to our website. The website will officially launch six months after funding. At this time, golf travelers will be able to communicate directly with accommodation providers and make bookings. Nine months after funding we will have 10 additional destinations online with flights of 10-20 accommodation providers listed and trained in each destination. We will target destinations in the northern half of the United States for these flights. Our strategy will be to have destinations in both the northern and southern half of the USA so that our business as a whole does not experience significant seasonality. Twelve months after funding we will have 10 more southern half destinations and reach both break-even and positive cash flow. Three months later we will have 10 more northern half destinations. At this point, 15 months after funding, we will reach critical mass and will begin promoting organic destination growth. Our goal is to launch our first destinations in Europe 18 months after funding.

Critical Success Factors: In order for our business to succeed and thrive as we know it can, we will need to make sure that several things happen. First, we must design and develop a user friendly, captivating website containing all of the key features required, and the smoothly functioning software to run those features and functions. This must be done on time and on budget. Second, we must recruit a lineup of personable and motivated local representatives capable of recruiting a lineup or local accommodation providers. This is the key to overcoming the chicken and egg problem, because this will stock one side of our platform which will attract the other. Third, we must create a golfers online community with a keen sense of comradery and strong participation, and a unique, cost effective and convenient golf travel experience based on hospitality, friendship, and a shared love of the game of golf—then build our brand around that strong sense of golfing community. This will attract the target customer we most desire, and differentiate us from any future entrants into the market. Fourth, we must control costs while at the same time expanding destinations on schedule. Fifth, we must gain critical mass/liquidity where each person who visits our site from either side is able to obtain what they desire from our platform. And finally, we must retain and grow a high percentage of our customers in order to reduce our customer acquisition costs and increase our lifetime value per customer.

Competitive Environment: While we will become the first P2P golf travel platform, our business will sit at the crossroads of the hospitality and golf travel business, and our competitors will be on either side. Our principal competitors will be the golf tour companies who book golf travel packages for golf destinations around the world. But we will also compete with the likes of Airbnb for the business of golf travelers who may want to rent their own accommodation.

Core Competencies and Competitive Advantages: We intend to develop core competencies in the following areas, each of which will become a competitive advantage. First, our business model, which can then be replicated in other sports travel segments. Second, our platform software, which can also be replicated, and which will be a key to developing our golfers community as well as providing a low friction golf travel-links buddy experience. Third in our model and performance for solving the chicken and egg problem in our P2P space, i.e. in our local representative model for recruiting and servicing flights of accommodation providers. Fourth, in community building, creating an organic experience that lies on top of and renders invisible the actual business. Our other competitive advantages will include being first to market in the P2P golf travel space, having a tested and validated business model and platform, and having a critical mass of customers on both sides of our platform.

Management Team: Our founders, Steven and Martin, have a combined decades of experience in the golf travel business. Steven is a teaching golf professional at Silverado Country Club in Napa, California. His role will be to recruit and manage the local representatives and accommodation providers, ensuring that the company builds a critical mass of quality accommodation providers and that every golf traveler has a unique and satisfying experience. Martin, a former Silverado resort marketing executive and internet marketing specialist, will be in charge of platform software and website development, marketing and public relations, and generating and acquiring a critical mass of golf travelers.

Financial Model: Our path to profitability and beyond is based on our chicken and egg problem solving model. We will have a substantial upfront research and development cost in completing our platform software and website. In addition, we will have significant pre-launch costs in building our flights of accommodation providers at each location. Once those two assets are in place, assuming we launch new destinations on schedule as described above, our operating expenses as a percentage of revenues will decrease over time, as will our cost of customer acquisition, while at the same time our revenues are rising dramatically as each quarter we are operating a substantially greater number of locations. We expect to achieve both break even cash flow positive after one year of operation. Shortly thereafter, however, we expect to expend a significant amount of cash and see profitability temporarily dip as we launch our European operations. Once our transnational operations are in place, however, we believe the skies the limit in terms of revenues and net profits. For the first fiscal year, we expect to generate $$$ in total revenue with a net profit margin of %%%. By then end of the second fiscal year of operations, we expect to generate $$$ in total revenues with a net profit margin of %%%, and for the third fiscal year $$$ in total net revenues with a net profit margin of %%%.

Funding Requirements: We intend to raise $1 million to fund our platform software and website development, destination development, and operations for the first fiscal year. We will raise an initial $1 million to expand our operations into Europe and increase our marketing activities to achieve network effect.

CHAPTER 13:
DESCRIPTION OF THE BUSINESS

Chapter Overview

Company Background 226
Vision, Mission and Values Statements 227
Nature of the Business 228
Core Competencies and Competitive Advantages 230
Description of the Value Chain 231
Financial Business Model 232
Strategic Goals and Objectives 233
Critical Success Factors 234
Funding Requirements 234
Business Ownership 235
LinksBuddy Case Study 236

CHAPTER 13

DESCRIPTION OF THE BUSINESS

Now that you've hooked the readers with your executive summary and given them a targeted understanding of your business—including your business model—you can walk them through a more detailed description of each component of your business plan and model.

Begin with an overall description of your business and business model. This may sound repetitive to what is included in your executive summary. But remember in the summary you only include several sentences at most on each point. Here you will flesh out the customers' problem, your solution, the market opportunity you are addressing, anticipated revenue streams, etc. in greater detail, and provide facts to support your statements and assumptions.

Company Background

Start by providing some basic background on your organization, including:

- The name of your business

- Your website domain name

- Who are the founders

- When and why they founded the business

- Location of the business headquarters and state of incorporation (if any)

- Legal structure of the business

This may not be the most exciting portion of your business plan, but don't give it short shrift, because it involves issues with tremendous implications.

For example, the name of your business will likely be its most important brand. So you need to put a lot of thought into choosing a name that you can build into a brand that can be used to successfully market your products. The people reading your business plan will be experienced business persons, and they will recognize both a well-chosen and a poorly-chosen name. In addition, taking the proper steps to ensure you have the exclusive right to use your business name everywhere you intend to do business is critical. For similar reasons, a website domain name has become very important to the success of a business, and should also be chosen and protected with care.

The legal structure you choose can also have significant financial and operational consequences to your business and its owners. There are many important differences between operating as a sole proprietorship, a Subchapter C corporation, a Subchapter S corporation, a limited liability company, and a general or limited partnership. Your investors, partners, management team and key employees will very much care about the structure you choose, as well as whether you have taken the time and effort to understand, think through and implement the best legal structure for your business. Similarly, your state of incorporation (if any) will be important to investors, as well as members of your board of directors and management team, as it may affect the level of legal protection they will receive as owners and managers of the business.

Finally, if you have other investment or operational partners already, then everyone reading this document will want to know who they are and what role they will play in the business.

Vision, Mission and Values Statements

Now that you've described some of the nuts and bolts of your business, it's time to get back to the compelling story you have to tell about your business prospects. A good way to re-excite the reader at this point, and lay the foundation for the rest of your business plan, is to introduce your vision, mission and values statements.

Remember from Chapter 2 that your "vision statement" communicates the type of business you intend to create—what you want your business to become. This statement will tell the reader directly and concisely the reasons you are going into your particular business and the primary goals you want to achieve. The "mission statement" conveys the benefits you will provide to your customers and the manner in which you will satisfy their needs. And your "values statement" identifies your organization's core set of beliefs and the qualities that it prioritizes over all others—it clearly states the manner in which you want to realize your vision and accomplish your mission.

In combination, these statements establish right away your top level strategy and goals. And once your vision, mission and values are understood, as your audience reads the rest of your business plan they should be able to see clearly how every aspect of your plan is consistent with and geared towards the implementation of this strategy and realization of these goals.

Nature of the Business

You offered up concise assertions in your executive summary, and now it's time to elaborate on the important problem that you've identified and the solution that you will offer your customers who have that problem. The goal is to develop a compelling narrative about the line of business that you're entering, your reasons for choosing that particular business, and the product and other benefits that you will offer to your customers as your value proposition.

There are many ways to do this, but you may want to begin by describing your profile customer from the "customer segments" block of your Business Model Canvas and the problem that person (or business) needs solved. What exactly are your profile customer's jobs, pains and gains? What are the customer's needs that you can satisfy? What does your profile customer want made easier, faster, cheaper, better, etc.? What can your product offering do that your customer cannot do for himself or herself?

You need to communicate why your customers have a problem important enough for you to start a new business to solve. All of this information should be at your fingertips since you have already created your business model based entirely on this customer problem that you have identified. Now you just need to communicate what you know in a compelling fashion that provides the background facts necessary for audience buy-in.

With the "important problem" firmly established, you can now describe in detail how your business will solve this problem. This is the place where you can provide a more detailed description of the products or services that you will offer. Give the reader enough information to understand how the product works, how it will be used, its features, the technology involved, etc. You want the audience to have a sufficient understanding to be able to compare your product with others on the market. But focus on those aspects of your product that directly contribute to your value proposition. For example, describe how certain features of your product directly solve your profile customer's problem—what features provide the tangible and intangible benefits the customer is really buying.

Keep in mind, however, that your product and its features are only part of the value proposition that you offer to your customers. So in addition to describing your product and how it helps solve your profile customer's problem, you should also describe in some detail the other benefits your business provides—other portions of the value chain that are part of your value proposition. For example, customer service, location, delivery time, warranties, etc. may be just as important in your customer's mind as the actual product.

You may also want to perform a targeted SWOT analysis focused solely on your product/value proposition. What are the strengths and weaknesses of your product offering? What opportunities does it provide? What threats are present to your ability to successfully sell your product?

In analyzing the strengths of your product, you want to determine what it is about your product, as well as other aspects of your value proposition, that customers value the most and make you distinctive from the competition. Conversely, understanding the weakness of your product and other aspects of your value proposition, especially vis-a-vis the competition, can help you either improve what you have to offer or develop a marketing strategy that convinces customers to buy regardless.

You should also delineate how your product will be differentiated from others in the marketplace and what attributes of your value proposition are unique and will cause customers to choose your offerings over those of the competition.

As such, this would be a good time to introduce a discussion of your "core competencies" and "competitive advantages."

Core Competencies and Competitive Advantages

Core competencies are those skills and tasks which your business does exceptionally well and are highly valued by your customer. Hopefully your business may have many areas where you excel, but your core competencies are the ones that you do better than the rest; the ones that make you stand out from the competition. As such, a core competency should contribute significantly to your value proposition and should help your business achieve a competitive advantage.

A competitive advantage is an aspect of your organization or product offering that makes your value proposition more attractive to customers than that of the competition and/or makes your business more efficient, effective and profitable than the competition. Competitive advantages are those critical things that you have that your competition does not, or that you do much better than your competition.

You should either be able to link a core competency directly to a competitive advantage, or be able to chart how you can use a core competency to create a competitive advantage. And this core competency and resulting competitive advantage should be difficult for competitors to replicate or it may be illusory and short-lived. In contrast, it should be easy for you to replicate your core competencies in order to open up new markets, or introduce new products or lines of business—remember that one of the keys to a successful business model is how easily it can be replicated. In addition, you should harness your core competencies and competitive advantages to generate the maximum amount of revenue at the highest possible margins, as well as to maximize market share.

In other words, core competencies are both an opportunity in themselves and a strength that will allow you to take advantage of your greatest opportunities. Developing, using and leveraging core competencies usually provide the best chance for a company's continued growth and survival. For your business to succeed over the long term, you must identify, develop, exploit and maintain your core competencies and competitive advantages, and you need to have a strategy to do so.

One specific area that is worth mentioning with respect to your core competencies and competitive advantages is intellectual property. If you have proprietary technology (whether patented or not), copyrighted material or trade secrets that are protectable and provide you with a competitive advantage, then those items should be highlighted in your business plan.

Description of the Value Chain

At this point, you can describe in sequence how you will produce, market, sell and deliver your product/value proposition to the customer. Focus on what is sometimes called the "value chain"—the steps in the business process where value is created in the eyes of the customer relative to the competition. The total value delivered by a business to a customer is the sum of the value added at each step. As part of this description, go back to your Business Model Canvas and use it to indentify your key activities and key resources, key partners, channels and customer relationships that are part of your value chain. If appropriate, you can also speak about where you stand in the product development process.

Focusing on the value chain demonstrates your sense of business priorities, as you will receive a greater return on any investment of resources into an activity that adds value as opposed to one that does not.

Your description of the value chain in this section should include, as appropriate:

- Product research and development

- Purchasing and procurement of supplies and resources

- Manufacturing and Operations

- Marketing and sales

    - Channels of communication

    - Customer relationships

- Channels of distribution and logistics

- Customer service
- Management
- Organization
- Finance
- Financial controls
- Location(s)
- Technology
- Intellectual property
- Contribution of key partners

You will go into more detail regarding the goals and strategy for most of these areas in later sections of the business plan, so focus on providing the reader with an overview of how your business process will function as a whole, and the contribution to your value proposition by each step in that process. Highlight the strengths and any core competencies and competitive advantages you have in these areas. In addition, address any weaknesses you have identified and what you intend to do to strengthen your business.

Financial Business Model

As we discussed throughout Parts I and II, the goal of the Business Model Canvas was to create a business model that if properly executed would generate a sustainable profit and cash flows. If that is not the end result of your business model, then you can have all the customers you can manage but your business will still not succeed. So here you need to demonstrate the manner in which you will generate sufficient revenues at a low enough cost to make a sustainable profit and produce positive cash flow. Your financial business model identifies all of your sources of revenue—i.e. revenue streams from your business model canvas—as well as how you will get paid, how much, by whom, and when. Most importantly, it demonstrates that the revenue can be generated at a low enough cost to produce a sufficient net profit and the required return for you and your investors. When you get paid is important also, so the description of your financial business model should also include a description of how you will manage cash flow, including covering start-up costs, seasonality, etc. Again, this is only an overview of the financial business model—you will go into much more detail in the financial projections discussed in Chapter 20.

Strategic Goals and Objectives

Your vision and mission statements will contain the ultimate goals of your business—what type of organization you want to become and how you want to benefit your target customers. But in order to operate your business successfully, you need to drill down further and develop a more comprehensive set of goals, strategies, objectives and tactics that will allow you to realize your vision and accomplish your mission. So what is the difference between a goal and an objective? A strategy and a tactic?

- A goal is a broad primary outcome that you intend to achieve

- A strategy is the approach you take to achieving a goal

- An objective is a measurable step within a specific time frame that you take to achieve a goal

- A tactic is a method you use in pursuing an objective in order to achieve a goal

Both your goals and objectives should be verifiable and achievable and tied directly to your vision and mission statements, as well as to your business model. Goals, however, are your destination and they are usually not described in terms of financial results. Once you know your goal, you can break it down into quantifiable objectives and determine action plans for reaching those objectives, and ultimately your goal, in a set timeframe.

Critical Success Factors

Finally, you should identify and focus on the "critical success factors," which are those essential things that must be achieved in an optimum manner for your vision, mission, and other goals and objectives to be achieved.

To determine what your critical success factors are, go back to the strategic statements, goals and objectives you have established, and ask what is absolutely critical to making those things happen. First do this at the top level, and then for each individual goal and objective, keeping in mind that there will be certain critical success factors that are specific to your industry and target market. Afterwards, evaluate the list of critical success factors to find the essential elements for success in your overall business.

By identifying and communicating your critical success factors, you will have a common point of reference that will help ensure your team understands and is focused on the most important aspects of achieving success, and are all pulling in the same direction. In addition, you can track your progress against these factors and measure the success of your business.

They also serve as a constant reminder of those areas of your business that should always be monitored, and around which strategy and goals should be developed.

Funding Requirements

If your business will not generate sufficient funds to cover its initial cash requirements, then you need to identify:

- How you have been funded to date
- What is your current financial status
- What outside funds will be required
- How you intend to raise those outside funds
- How you intend to use the funds you raise

- How and when the investors and/or lenders will be repaid.

In this final respect, investors will be particularly interested in the growth potential of your business, the exit possibilities, and the return on investment they can realistically expect. Part of that calculation is whether additional outside funding will be required in the future, and if so how much and on what timeframe. This will all be fleshed out in your "financial projections" section, but an overview should be provided here.

Business Ownership

Here you should provide a detailed description of who owns your business, including what type of ownership interests and what percentage each person or entity holds. If there are founders or shareholders agreements in place regarding the ownership and/or operation of the business, then they should be described as well. In addition, you should include the proposed ownership structure after the desired investment.

LinksBuddy Case Study

Chapter 13
Description of the Business

"Remember," Peter says to Steven and Martin, "You need to tell a story. This is your narrative of how you intend to execute your business model. The reader should be able to visualize that narrative. To see how your business plan will come together to execute your business model and grow a successful enterprise that generates substantial and sustainable profits."

Taking Peter's advice, Steven and Martin organize their "description of the business" section in a manner that best communicates how they see LinksBuddy launching and growing into the company they envision. Then they summarize the principle components of this part of their business plan as follows:

Company Background

LinksBuddy, Inc. is a Delaware corporation formed in 2016, with its company headquarters in San Francisco, California. It is currently owned by its founders, Steven Duffer and Martin Marketer, each of whom own 40% of the company. The company's seed capital investor, Peter Programmer, owns 20% of the company. These three men also comprise the current Board of Directors.

Vision, Mission and Values Statements

Our *vision* is to create a worldwide network of golf enthusiasts who can first meet and get to know each other on our website, and then use our platform to arrange for one golfer to travel and stay as a guest in the other's home, where they can play golf together on the host's local course and share comradery, experiences, information and knowledge. Developing a worldwide golfing "community" is the key to our vision, and our *mission* will be to create an online platform which provides our golfing customers with the most efficient and cost effective way to discover fellow golfers living in a top-tier golf destination who would be willing to host them for a unique golf travel experience. The LinksBuddy platform will allow our customers to match, communicate, socialize and share the game of golf in the comforts of their living rooms, club houses, and home golf courses.

We intend to bring the *values* inherent in the game of golf to our business operations. Golf is a game where players pride themselves on knowing both the written rules of golf and unwritten rules of golf etiquette, and conduct themselves within both the letter and the spirit of those rules with the utmost integrity. We intend to operate our business with this same code of ethics. While from time to time this may rule out certain "stroke-saving" strategic options that other companies might pursue, we believe that our values will attract fellow golfers who respect the fact that we are running our business for their benefit in the same way as they would expect us to conduct ourselves on the course.

The LinksBuddy P2P Platform

LinksBuddy will create a multi-sided online market platform that will optimally facilitate a peer-to-peer ("P2P") golf travel marketplace. In doing so, we will tap into the rapidly growing "sharing economy" best exemplified by the highly successful Airbnb. Our multi-sided market will provide value to two separate but interrelated customer segments—"golf travelers" and "golf hosts," and our company will generate revenue from each segment. Our P2P platform will bring together golf enthusiasts who wish to travel to play top-tier golf courses with those who wish to host such travelers in their home. We will then facilitate their ability to directly interact, create and exchange value, and participate in a community of golfers through our online platform. In many cases, we believe that persons utilizing our platform will become both golf travelers and golf hosts.

The LinksBuddy P2P Platform will combine four basic functions: 1) a value proposition that attracts a critical mass of golf travelers and golf hosts to our website, provides them with all relevant information, and convinces them to use our platform services; 2) a "curation and matching" function that collects relevant information from golf travelers and golf hosts and then matches those with similar criteria; 3) an online infrastructure that allows golf travelers and golf hosts to meet, directly interact, and transact their exchange of value; 4) a community building function that encourages and allows our network of golf travelers and golf hosts to form their own organic community of golf enthusiasts. The goal of each of these layers is to encourage and incentivize participants to interact and interact often, both online and in-person, as part of a unique golf travel/hosting and community building experience.

What our Customers Crave

The millions of golf enthusiasts in the United States and around the world are a unique obsessive breed. They forever dream about playing the best courses around the world. They constantly think about the game and talk rounds, courses, equipment and techniques. And they would love the convenient ability to grab their clubs, travel to a top-tier golf course outside their home area, and play the game they are passionate about with a local golf enthusiast who both shares their passion and has local course and area knowledge. Most have the money to do this if they only could. On the flip side, there are millions of other golf fanatics who own a home with underutilized living space near a great golf course in an interesting location, and would enjoy having friends from around the world come stay with them and play their home course together—while at the same time earning additional income.

Our Customers' Primary Problems

There is currently no golf travel option that allows golf enthusiasts from around the world to conveniently meet each other and make all arrangements necessary to share their love of golf. Most golf travel tour operators offer a golf traveler only one type of experience: traveling either alone or with a group of friends from their hometown, and staying in an impersonal hotel or resort with no local host who knows the course or the area. The more interesting, more fulfilling, more personal option that our customer's crave is simply not provided by any business in the golf travel industry. In other words, there is no way for our golf traveler customers to have what they crave unless they go out and do it all by themselves. It would be a vast understatement to say this would be a difficult task for individual golf travelers to perform.

The pains in doing so would include somehow finding a golf host who would be willing to provide accommodation and who matched their criteria with respect to level of play, motivations, age, income, personality, background, club memberships, etc. They would also include all aspects of planning and booking the trip that a golf tour operator would normally deal with, such as finding acceptable transportation to and around the desired location, booking tee times, etc. Finally, they would have to find some way of ensuring the safety and quality of their accommodation, not to mention their host.

For the golf host who desires to make additional income and form additional golf friendships, the pain points would be equally daunting. They would have to find or develop a platform where they could list their offering, pull a large number of golf travelers in to view their offering, curate those golf travelers to find only those who they would be interested in hosting, develop some convenient way to communicate and transact business with those golf travelers, insure the safety of their person and property, etc. This would involve a tremendous amount of time, money and energy, and it's safe to say that for most potential golf hosts it would not be worth the effort.

How LinksBuddy Will Solve Our Customers' Problems and Satisfy Their Cravings

LinksBuddy will provide a convenient, efficient and trustworthy online location where golf travelers and golf hosts with similar criteria can meet and make all necessary arrangements for the golf traveler to visit the golf host and share their love of the game on the host's home course.

For golf travelers, our value proposition will offer extensive information on our website regarding some of the top golf travel destinations in the world; a network of vetted and personable golf hosts who provide the type of hospitality and friendship, reliability and safety, local experience and knowledge, and golf buddy camaraderie that our golf travel customers are in search of; the ability to search and match with hoses with similar golfing ability, interests and other desired criteria; peer reviews of both the golf destinations and golf hosts; the ability to communicate directly with golf hosts through our online platform; the provision of efficient and low-friction golf travel logistics; a cost-effective method of golf-travel; a unique, personal and hospitable golf-travel experience that cannot be obtained anywhere else; and continued participation in a worldwide community of golfers.

Our value proposition for golf hosts will include a critical mass of reliable golf travelers on the platform who met their preference requirements and are subject to peer reviews; the ability to build a listing on the platform, curate and filter golf travelers who are able to contact them, and communicate with golf travelers where a mutual interest exists; low-friction logistics of renting their accommodation to golf travelers, including initial booking and payment, schedules and tee times; the ability to make a sufficient financial return for their efforts; a safe and satisfying interpersonal experience with their golf travelers; and participation in an extended golf community.

The Links Buddy Value Chain

This is how LinksBuddy will work, and how we will create value for our golf traveler and golf host customers by facilitating their ability to create and exchange value with each other:

Platform Software and Website: we will design and develop proprietary software and a website which will allow the following primary functions to be performed in an efficient, user-friendly manner: creation of golf host listings; content generation and regeneration; curation of golf host and golf traveler information; golf traveler and golf host search function; direct communication between golf hosts, golf travelers and local representatives; peer reviews of golf hosts and golf travelers and golf destinations; contact us and customer support including live chat; creation of golf traveler account; search and book transportation options; e-commerce transaction including payment options; creation of golfers' community including forums.

Golf Travel Destinations: we will select golf travel destinations that meet the following primary criteria: a top-tier private, semi-private or public golf course in a non-resort location; a sizeable residential population in the near vicinity from which to recruit golf hosts; an interesting travel destination in terms of culture, sights, business, etc.; a sizeable number of golfers who have access to the chosen golf course (or courses) through membership and guest membership privileges, or otherwise. We will initially select a proportionate mix if destinations in the northern and southern half of the United States in order to smooth out the seasonality of our business and open up non-traditional destinations in the northern half to golf travelers.

Local Representatives: We will recruit and retain a local representative in each destination who is active in the golf community of the course we have selected, with our initial targets being teaching golf professionals and club members. This person will be responsible for recruiting, training and assisting golf hosts; making local bookings including tee times and playing partners; acting as a customer service representative and liaison for golf hosts and golf travelers; retaining and growing the flight of golf hosts. Local representatives will be paid a flat monthly fee plus a bonus for each new golf host and a commission on the gross amount LinksBuddy earns on each golf traveler customer.

Golf Hosts: together with our local representatives, we will recruit flights of golf hosts for each destination (a minimum of 10 hosts per destination) and help them list on the LinksBuddy website, then train them to be hospitable hosts who provide an enjoyable and unique golf travel experience to our golf travelers customers. We will curate the golf hosts to make sure they will provide a good match with a large number of golf travel customers. They will be required to provide a minimum standard of accommodation.

Online Content: we will create interesting and informative content for our website that will pull golf travelers to the site and convince them to use the LinksBuddy platform for their golf travel journeys, as well as pull golf hosts to the site and convince them to join our local flight of golf hosts. In addition, we will use the website to pull and recruit local representative who wish to form a new flight of golf hosts in a new location. Finally, website will include peer reviews of all listed golf hosts as well as golf travelers who have used our service.

Golf Traveler and Golf Host Interaction: Both golf hosts and golf travelers will enter a set of criteria for their LinksBuddy experience, such as age, golf handicap, frequency of play, etc. The golf traveler will then search by his preferences in a desired location to see if he finds a match.

If a match is found, the golf traveler can contact the golf host directly by private message chat function, and the traveler and host can get to know each other. If they choose to do so, they can then work out the details of a trip by the golf traveler to visit the golf host. The details of the trip in terms of date, price, tee times requested, etc. will then be forwarded to LinksBuddy customer support.

Golf Traveler and LinksBuddy Customer Support Interaction: LinksBuddy customer support will contact the golf traveler to arrange and book the details of the trip, including transportation if they desire, as well as to answer any questions the golf traveler may have. The golf traveler will pay for the accommodation and green fees directly to LinksBuddy, plus a facilitation fee of 15% of the total and any damage deposit required by the host.

The Golf Travel Experience: our golf travelers will stay in the homes or other approved living space of our golf hosts. Our golf travelers and golf hosts will play at least one round of golf together on the host's home course, and if the host is not available for additional rounds desired by the golf traveler, then the host and/or the local representative will arrange for additional playing partners. We will encourage our golf hosts to interact with their visiting golf travelers as much as possible, hosting meals and/or showing them and advising on local dining options, sightseeing and cultural opportunities, chances to meet other members of the local golf community, etc.

Post Travel Follow-up: once the golf traveler has departed, LinksBuddy will transfer the accommodation fee less a 5% fee to the golf host. LinksBuddy customer support, the local representative, and the golf host will all follow-up with the golf traveler for feedback and to welcome him or her as a valued new member of the LinksBuddy community.

The LinksBuddy Community: all of our golf travelers and golf hosts will be encouraged and motivated to become active members of our LinksBuddy international community of golfers. There will be online forums, local community events, travel events and much more to build an esprit de golf among our participants. This will be one of the keys to the successfully achieving our vision for our enterprise.

Our Key Challenges

Many of the primary challenges we will face in launching LinksBuddy relate to the challenges all P2P multi-sided marketplaces face at inception. Those challenges, along with others we will face include:

New/Re-Segmented Market: While there is currently a very large and growing market for golf travel, there is virtually no current market for golf travelers staying in private accommodation with the renters as active hosts. We are therefore attempting to re-segment the golf travel market and convince golf travelers to change their behavior and adapt a new form of golf travel.

The Double Company Problem: the "double company problem" means that in creating a P2P marketplace, we will in essence have to build two different companies at the same time—a golf travel company offering accommodation, golf playing partners and other services to traveling golfers, and a second company offering a customer discovery and matching service to persons wishing to rent accommodation to traveling golfers. Each side of the platform therefore requires a different business model, including different value propositions, customer relationships, revenue streams, etc. And each side's business model must succeed or the entire platform will collapse.

Chicken and the Egg Problem: the "chicken and egg problem" means that for our P2P marketplace to work, it needs both golf travelers and golf hosts on the platform—which means that our double companies must both be created and be successful in a relatively simultaneous timeframe. The problem is that many golf hosts won't be interested in listing what they have to offer unless there is a sufficient golf traveler user base, and golf travelers won't be interested in coming to the website platform unless there are a sufficient number of golf hosts to find what they are looking for.

Need for Critical Mass: it will not be enough for LinksBuddy to solve the chicken and egg problem on a small scale—to succeed we will need to attain "critical mass," which in the P2P business is referred to as "liquidity." True liquidity for out P2P platform business will occur when each golf host has the reasonable expectation of renting what they list to a golf traveler, and each golf traveler has the reasonable expectation of finding a golf host in a destination of their choice. As our platform grows and the more golf travelers and golf hosts it has, the more value it provides to all participants. This is due to a phenomenon called the "network effect," pursuant to which the value of participating in a network depends on the number of people already participating.

The Trust Issue: for a P2P marketplace where accommodation and personal service will be provided by peers on one side of the platform, trust and safety are essential to the business. Even Airbnb has faced challenges in obtaining and maintaining the trust of both their providers and users. Reputation will mean everything in the success of our P2P marketplace.

Legal Issues: we anticipate that LinksBuddy will likely have to face similar legal issues as those Airbnb is currently dealing with on a broad scale. These include consumer protection, taxation, health and safety, and zoning regulations that apply to businesses offering accommodation.

Current Lack of Financial Resources:

Our Strategy to Succeed:

A Unique Value Proposition and Business Model that have been Tested and Validated: LinksBuddy is by no means starting from scratch. We have spent the last six months creating, testing and validating our business model and the P2P platform product we intend to launch. Through extensive field testing, we have identified and validated the optimum target customer segment for our platform and have discovered and verified their primary problems and needs. We have also tested and verified the optimum initial value proposition to solve those problems and satisfy those needs. As part of this process, we have tested and validated the best channels and types of customer relationships to obtain, maintain and grow our customer base on each side of our platform, as well as the optimum way to monetize our platform. We have zeroed in on the key resources and activities we need to be successful, as well as strategic partnerships that are necessary or desirable. Finally, we have identified and validated our cost structure and our financial business model, which of executed properly will by highly and sustainably profitable. Together, the integrated pieces of our tested and verified business model will allow us to effectively disrupt and re-segment the golf travel market.

A Tested and Validated Strategic and Tactical Plan to Clear the Chicken and Egg Hurdle and Reach Critical Mass: as part of our business model validation process, we created and validated a scripted expansion strategy and model for solving the chicken and egg problem and reaching critical mass as quickly as possible. We intend to initially focus on the golf host side of the market, providing incentives and making it easy for our initial golf hosts to list on our website before we open the platform to golf traveler bookings. In doing so, we will focus on a small number of destinations at launch and take advantage of the knowledge and network of persons already integrated into each local golf community. We will initially use local representatives in ten different destinations to recruit and list an initial flight of 10-20 golf hosts in each destination. We believe this will be possible by ensuring that the initial flights totaling at least 100 golf hosts will not be out-of-pocket any expenses, and by using our local representatives to instill a sense of community among each flight of hosts. With this number of golf hosts, we believe based on our business model testing and validation that we can use an intensive internet and public relations marketing campaign to attract a sufficient number of golf traveler customers to our website who will meet golf hosts online and choose to try our service as early evangelists. This will allow us to successfully launch our business. Over the following nine month period we will systematically add new destinations and flights of golf hosts while attracting large numbers of curious golf travelers to our website. We believe that we will hit critical mass of both golf hosts and golf travelers by the end of this period, at which time we will be on our way towards organic growth (where new flights of golf hosts request to organize themselves in new destinations), and the holy grail of the network effect (where the value of our platform catapults because customers on both sides of the platform believe they will find and obtain what they are looking for from our service).

A Tested and Validated Method of Attracting and Converting Golf Hosts and Golf Travelers: Our strategy for recruiting our initial flights of golf hosts will be to retain a local representative in each destination who is either in the golf industry, such as a local teaching golf professional, or someone who wants to be an accommodation provider. This person will be responsible for recruiting and listing the initial flight or accommodation providers. Our strategy for recruiting and converting golf travelers is to use a wide range of internet marketing techniques and public relations methods to drive golf travelers to our website, where we will convert them into traveling customers. Once we have obtained our initial flights of golf hosts, we will also use these marketing and public relations approaches to recruiting and listing new accommodation providers. However, we still intend to have a local representative in each destination. These methods have been tested and verified during our business modeling process. We currently have local representatives in six destinations, have more than 10 golf hosts in each destination who listed on our prototype website during our testing phase, have over 100 golf travelers who participated in our field tests by traveling to golf with a field test host, and have over 1,000 golf travelers who have expressed a strong interest in using our platform services once they become available.

Tested and Validated Financial Model: Our path to profitability and beyond is based on our chicken and egg problem solving model. We will have a substantial upfront research and development cost in completing our platform software and website. In addition, we will have significant pre-launch costs in building our flights of accommodation providers at each location. Once those two assets are in place, assuming we launch new destinations on schedule as described above, our operating expenses as a percentage of revenues will decrease over time, as will our cost of customer acquisition, while at the same time our revenues are rising dramatically as each quarter we are operating a substantially greater number of locations. We expect to achieve both break even cash flow positive after one year of operation. Shortly thereafter, however, we expect to expend a significant amount of cash and see profitability temporarily dip as we launch our European operations. Once our transnational operations are in place, however, we believe the skies the limit in terms of revenues and net profits. For the first fiscal year, we expect to generate $$$ in total revenue with a net profit margin of %%%. By then end of the second fiscal year of operations, we expect to generate $$$ in total revenues with a net profit margin of %%%, and for the third fiscal year $$$ in total net revenues with a net profit margin of %%%.

Experience, Vision and Motivation of our Founders: Steven Duffer has long-term experience with almost every aspect of the golf industry, and Martin Marketer has long-term experience in the golf travel and hospitality industry, as well as internet marketing, provided them with a solid foundation of relevant experience. In addition, lead seed capital investor and board member Peter Programmer has launched several successful start-up companies and invested in many others.

Core Competencies and Competitive Advantages: each of the strategic plans described above will result in a long-term core competency and competitive advantage for our business. These include:

- A unique value proposition

- A verified, repeatable and scalable business model that can be applied to other sports travel niches

- Proprietary software and website containing all the key features and functions, which can also be adapted to other sports travel niches

- Established international golf community, as well as a community building model that can be replicated in any destination, as well as in other sports travel niches

- The "LinksBuddy" brand, which will signify and instantly evoke the worldwide golf community created through our platform, as well as the golfer's values of integrity in the pursuit of excellence that we ascribe to.

- An international network of dedicated local representatives

- Critical mass of golf travelers and golf hosts

- The network effect

CHAPTER 14:
DISCUSSION OF THE BUSINESS ENVIRONMENT

Chapter Overview

Industry Analysis 251
Market Analysis 254
Competitive Analysis 257
LinksBuddy Case Study 260

CHAPTER 14

DISCUSSION OF THE BUSINESS ENVIRONMENT

In the "Description of the Business" section you convinced your audience that you have identified an important consumer problem worth addressing, supported this assertion with facts that you discovered and validated during the process of creating your Business Model Canvas, and described how you would provide a better solution to that problem than the competition. In other words, you've shown your readers that there is a market opportunity for your product.

But that begs the question: How big is that opportunity? Is it big enough to support a profitable business for you as the founder, and drive the rates of return your investors are looking for? What other companies have identified the same opportunity and are pursuing it as well? Is the market expanding rapidly enough that it will be big enough for you and your competitors? If not, can you capture sufficient market share to compete with the others? Your business plan audience will expect answers to these questions, so you need to address them.

Therefore, in this section of your business plan you should describe the size and nature of your opportunity, and in order to do so you should provide an analysis of the industry, the overall market, your target customer segment, and the competition.

The industry you will be competing in and the market for your products or services are not the same thing: an industry is a group of sellers, while a market is a group of buyers. It is possible that a market for a product is attractive at the same time the industry supplying that product is not, and vice versa. For example, there may be a large market for a particular product, but the industry providing that product has substantial barriers to entry that only a few well established companies can overcome, all but precluding start-up businesses from gaining a foothold. So you need to understand both your industry and your market in order to assess the opportunities and challenges each present for your business.

In addition, as you already know from our discussion of "customer segments" in Chapter 4, it is critical that you drill down deeper than the overall market for your product, identify and analyze what segments exist within that market, and choose the best customer segment or segments to target. The audience for your business plan will be sophisticated and well aware that you will have limited resources to communicate with potential customers and convince them to buy, so they will first want to make sure you are targeting the persons who are most likely to be quality customers and who will give you the largest market share and generate the highest profit. They will then want to make sure that the segment you have targeted is large enough and has the right potential for future growth to make their return on investment goals reachable—and you will concurrently want to do to make sure the goals you have set for your business are reachable through this target segment.

Business is not conducted in a vacuum, however, and therefore your market analysis should not be as well. So you also need to collect, analyze and present information on your competition. In addition, you need to identify and understand trends in the market and forces external to the market—such as government regulation or the introduction of new technology—which may have an impact on your ability to compete and execute your business model.

Industry Analysis

An industry consists of sellers offering products or services that are similar or substitutable for one another. Therefore an industry can be very broad, such as the automobile industry, but it can also be divisible into segments the same as a market can be. For example, an industry can be segmented by markets, customer segments, products, geography, etc. The entertainment industry includes many segments such as film, television, radio, music, theater, dance, and literary publishing, each of which is a large industry unto itself, and each of which can be further segmented as well. Businesses in each of these entertainment segments compete for consumer dollars not only within their individual segment, but among all entertainment industry segments, and their business strategies and marketing plans must take this into account in order to be successful.

It is important that you understand, and your business plan reflects, the size, characteristics and trends of both your overall industry and your specific industry segment (and geographic sub-segment, particularly if you are a local business). Some of the factors you will want to analyze and discuss in this portion of your business plan (with respect to both your industry and each industry segment you will participate in), include the following:

- Current and projected size in terms of revenues, profits, profit margins, etc.

- Current and projected growth rate

- Principal costs of doing business and trends with respect to those costs

- Composition of the participants, including their:

    - Revenues, net profits, profit margins, growth rate, market share, location, etc.

    - Current product offerings and amount of differentiation between those offerings

    - Customer base characteristics

    - Key channels and primary types of customer relationships

    - Business models

- Degree and nature of fragmentation/concentration:

    - Number of participants

    - Combined market share of the three largest participants

    - Trends: whether your industry and segment are becoming more or less fragmented

- Degree and nature of segmentation:

    ☐ Number of segments

    ☐ Nature of the segments

    ☐ Amount and degree of competition between segments

    ☐ Trends—whether your industry and segment are becoming more or less segmented

- Importance of technology; the rate of introduction of new technology; and the rate of change in key technology

- Rate of product innovation, marketing innovation, operational innovation, business model innovation, etc.

- Critical success factors

- Main barriers to entry and strength of those barriers

- External trends that have potential impact:

    ☐ Economic

    ☐ Social

    ☐ Regulatory

    ☐ Technological

    ☐ Political

Normally, an industry is *concentrated* if either a large amount of capital is required to enter industry or a substantial amount of consolidation has taken place leaving only a few participants. An industry is *fragmented* if a low amount of capital is required to enter the industry or it is in the beginning stages and many companies are able to enter and compete.

In analyzing and presenting information about your industry, you can use numbers, charts, graphs, etc. But as with all the information you choose to include in this section, take care to present those numbers in the context of your business model, and use them to support your strategy and goals.

For example, you can use your industry analysis to understand:

- Opportunities and threats

- Where your business and product offering/value proposition will fit within the industry

- What kind of future participants will it most likely attract

- Whether the industry can support new entrants

In writing your industry analysis keep in mind that it should lay the foundation for rest of the rest of your business plan to follow, including your market and competitive analysis. Select and present the most relevant industry information that will lay that foundation.

Market Analysis

The market analysis you will provide in this section is very different from the analysis contained in the "marketing plan" section discussed in Chapter 15. The "market analysis" focuses on your overall market and your target market segment(s)—meaning the customer segments you identified in your Business Model Canvas—and the potential sales and market share you can gain in your chosen segment(s). It provides an indication of the growth potential within the industry, and this will allow you to develop your own estimates for the future of your business. The marketing plan, which will be based in large part on your market analysis, focuses on how you will go about achieving the sales and market share you believe are possible, with descriptions of your classic marketing strategies regarding product, price, promotion, and place, as well as your internet marketing strategy and plan.

As we learned in Chapter 4 on "customer segments," a market consists of a group of consumers having the desire and ability to buy a product to satisfy a particular type of want or need. In addition, within every market for a product, different consumers have different needs, get different benefits from the product, respond differently to marketing messages, are in different locations, etc. As a result, it would not be efficient to communicate with and sell to each potential customer in the same manner. So as we discussed in connection with identifying your customer segments for your business model, it is therefore in the interest of every business to segment the market into manageable groups that can be efficiently targeted.

The goal is to identify a target customer segment that consists of the people most likely to buy your product who are within your marketing and distribution reach. Properly identifying this target segment will be the key to your business success. The reason is that if you understand who your primary potential customers are, what they want, and how and when and why they buy, then every component of your business—from product development to marketing to sales to distribution to customer service—can be geared towards satisfying their desires and convincing them to purchase what you have to offer at a price that allows you to make a profit.

The good news is that as part of creating your Business Model Canvas, you have already done most of the work and have identified your target customer segments. However, you should also have an understanding of all the customer segments in your market, not just your own target customer segment.

The biggest mistake that people make when selecting a target market is to define their market too broadly or to try to target too many segments simultaneously. Startups are usually best served by zeroing in on a specific target market. It's simply too difficult and expensive, in the vast majority of cases, to adopt a more aggressive strategy, at least initially.

A useful customer segment has the following characteristics:

- Size you can manage
- Customers you can identify
- Customers you can reach
- Large enough to be profitable

In addition to size and reach, you will want to check and see whether you have selected the segment that represents the best prospects for entry. You also might consider whether the customer segment you have chosen is consistent with your founders' passions and/or core competencies. Many founders normally select the target market that represents the best fit for them both professionally and personally, as will be reflected in their vision, mission and values statements.

Once you have officially identified your target market, you can analyze and describe the opportunity within that market that you have for sales and growth. But estimating the size of a target market and growth potential can be a tricky proposition. The first rule of thumb is to not make frivolous predictions.

In the end, you should be able to understand and describe in your business plan the following with respect to both your market and target market segments:

- The size and nature of the market where demand for your product exists
- The size and nature of the market segments within the overall market
- The size and nature of the market segment where demand for your product is highest and target customers are most likely to buy (your target segment)
- What product features and benefits your target segment want and value the most
- The degree of differentiation among products being purchased
- Where, when, and how your target segment want the product delivered
- The demographics and buying habits of your target segment
- The tastes and expectations of your target segment with respect to the type of product you wish to offer
- The price elasticity of your product within the target segment; and how important price is in the buying decision
- The value proposition/unique selling proposition that you can offer to differentiate yourself from the competition

- The SWOT components: the strengths and weaknesses of your product, as well as the opportunities and threats you will face in the marketplace

- Trends with respect to the market and target customer segments, including with respect to customer demand

- Growth and projected growth of the market

- The presence of an untapped market or market segment for your industry

- The amount of product substitution by customers

- Whether it is necessary to reach a critical mass of customers and/or sales

- Whether there is room for new entrants in the market

- Whether the market can expand to include new entrants

- Barriers to entry

- Seasonality

- Cyclicality

Although you will already have most of the information you need from the Business Model Canvas process, you may need to conduct some additional market research using the primary and secondary methods described in Chapter 2.

Competitive Analysis

An additional benefit of market segmentation is that it helps you identify and understand who your real competition will be. That competition can be broken down into:

- **Direct competition:** companies that sell the same or similar products to yours within your target market

- **Indirect competition:** companies that solve the same problem or meet the same needs as your product, but with different products that can be substituted for your product

- **Future competition:** potential direct and indirect competitors

Keep in mind that indirect competitors are likely candidates for becoming direct competitors in the future. In fact, don't take any potential future competition for granted. Additional competition could come from many different directions, including another company expanding their current product line, customers and/or suppliers deciding to produce a product similar to yours, the acquisition of a competitor by a larger company with more resources, etc.

For purposes of your business plan, indentify the following with respect to each of your main competitors:

- Market share and projected market share

- Size and projected growth in terms of revenue, profits and profit margins

- Strengths and Weaknesses of their organization, business model, product offering/value proposition, management team, customer base, etc.

- Core competencies and competitive advantages

- Goals and strategy

- Degree and manner of product differentiation

Once you've assessed your competition, you need to have a strategy regarding how you will compete with them, particularly in how you develop and position your product and company to effectively compete in the marketplace. For example, your research may show customer dissatisfaction with some aspect of a competing product, and if you design your product to address that dissatisfaction, you may be able to capture market share from your competitor. Your research may also reveal that a large company which previously did not compete in your market is about to enter the fray, and therefore allow you to design a strategy that differentiates your product not only from existing competitors, but such new competitors as well.

Look once again at the opportunities and threats presented by the competition and determine the following:

- What has made the most successful companies so successful?

- Why have the unsuccessful companies failed?

- What are they lacking?

- Where are they most vulnerable?

- How can we develop a skill that they lack?

- What are the critical success factors in competing with them?

- What strategies would provide you with a competitive advantage?

- How will you develop and maintain a competitive advantage?

- Most importantly, how will you differentiate your product offering/value proposition from theirs?

- How will set your product or service apart from your competitors or strategic groups?

Once you have finished collecting and analyzing the information required for your industry, market and competitive analysis, you should have a solid foundation for determining the goals and objectives of your marketing program and the strategies and tactics you will use to meet those goals and objectives.

> **LinksBuddy Case Study**
>
> # Chapter 14
> # The Business Environment
>
> **Industry Analysis**
>
> When Steven and Martin first sat down to conduct secondary market research in preparation for creating their business model, they realized that while LinksBuddy sat squarely within the golf tourism industry, it would be part of a substantial number of different industries and industry segments: the leisure industry and its golf industry segment; the hospitality industry and its accommodation segment; the tourism industry and its sports travel segment; and the multi-sided market industry, its P2P segment, and the accommodation sub-segment. Peter emphasized to them how important it was to understand their place in each of these industries, the keys to success in each industry, trends and potential competitors, and other factors that could have an impact on their business. So in developing their business plan, Steven and Martin first focused on the aspects of each industry that were most relevant to their business.
>
> For example, with respect to the leisure industry and the tourism industry in general, it is important for Steven and Peter to understand the impact that the economic downturn had on these industries and current trends as far as growth and revenues. It is also important for them to understand how customers in these industries are allocating their discretionary spending dollars and the share that each industry, and each industry segment, is capturing. It is also important for them to identify key participants in these industries that could be considered indirect competitors to LinksBuddy in terms of competition for discretionary leisure and travel dollars. With respect to the accommodation industry, Steven and Martin focused on the type and standard of accommodation that seemed to be trending with people traveling on holiday, as well as accommodation providers that could be considered in competition with LinksBuddy. This brought them to the P2P sub-segment of accommodation providers. Here it is important for Steven and Martin to understand virtually everything about this segment and the key players

involved, particularly Airbnb. Doing so will not only identify potential direct and indirect competitors, but also issues they will face and solutions that other companies have used to address those issues—for example the legal issues faced by Airbnb.

The golf industry segment consists of several different sub-segments, including golf course operation, equipment, and golf tourism. Golf equipment and golf course operations have experienced some severe challenges over the last decade, with slowed golf course development growth and slowed growth in number of golfers and number of rounds played. Equipment sales have also been extremely slow. This contrasts with more steady growth in golf tourism, and it's very important that Steven and Martin understand this dichotomy, the factors involved, and what current trends portend for the future, because all will have a direct impact on their business operations and their strategy needs to directly address these issues. With respect to potential investors, Steven and Martin realize that they will have to explain clearly and compellingly why an investment in a golf industry company makes sense at this time given the depressed industry indicators. Their case will rest on many factors, including the positive trends in golf tourism combined with the exceedingly positive trends in the P2P travel accommodation sector fueled by Airbnb and the increasingly rapid embrace by consumers of the sharing economy

With respect to their specific industry segment, golf tourism, Steven and Martin produce a full-blown industry discussion. They collect current financial information and identify trends in revenue growth, costs and margins, as well as customer demographics, geographic breakdowns in terms of destinations and customer origin, barriers to entry, etc. They also and identify all of the major participants and seek to understand their business models inside and out. Last but not least, they zero in on all of the important trends in the industry.

Market Analysis

"For outside investors, this will be one of the most important sections of your business plan," Peter tells Steven and Martin. "You need to convince them in a completely credible manor that your market opportunity is big enough to get them the kind of returns they're interested in. And that's not going to be an easy thing to do."

Steven and Martin identify three key aspects to their market analysis that they need to understand completely and communicate convincingly to potential investors. The first, and easiest, is why investors can believe that the total available market of golf travelers will remain strong even though the market of golfers in general has shown weakness—particularly with respect to the US market. In order to do so, Steven and Martin collect and organize all of the key statistics and trends for the golf tourist market that support their thesis that this large market of golf travelers will grow considerably for the foreseeable future.

Now comes the hard questions that investors are sure to ask: How do you know that there is a large percentage of golf travelers who will be willing to change their consumer habits and stay in private accommodation in primarily non-resort locations? How can we be sure that this market can be disrupted and re-segmented as you propose? Is the size of your genuine SAM really big enough to warrant our investment?

In terms of financing their business, this is one of the key areas where the business modeling process will really pay off for Steven and Martin. They now realize that if they had not gone through that process, not only would they not have a validated business model to present to their potential investor, but any answer they would give to these crucial market opportunity questions would be seen as pure unsubstantiated speculation. Fortunately, following their field tests, Steven and Martin come armed with hard data to back up their reasoned deductions based on secondary market research. First, they now have the results of hundreds of interviews, both in person and on their prototype website, showing strong interest by golf travelers in their service. Second, they have the results of their calls to action and other marketing tests they ran as part of their field tests. And third, they have demonstrated the ability to attract real customers for their trial runs in six different locations, and have positive follow-up reports from the more than one hundred golf travelers who participated in these tests. These results validate their hypothesis that there is a substantial niche of golf travelers who would be willing to use LinksBuddy as their primary golf travel facilitator. This will be a key selling point of their business plan.

The other hard question comes with respect to the golf hosts: Even if you can recruit a critical mass of golf travelers, how do you know you can find enough accommodation providers in each golfing destination to service the market? Again, if Steven and Martin had not gone through the business modeling process, they would have no way to credibly answer that question. But since this question has already been asked, and the answer validated by their testing process, they can present solid evidence that this market exists and is ready to jump onboard the LinksBuddy platform.

So who are these golf travelers and golf hosts that make up the LinksBuddy target market segments? Once again, the business modeling process has validated their final hypothesis about the best segment of golfers to target.

Competitive Analysis

With respect to golf travelers, LinksBuddy will be in direct competition with golf tour package companies despite the fact that they will offer a very different value proposition. As such, Steven and Martin identify the top golf tour companies who operate in the United States and learn everything possible about them, including their business models, target market, marketing message, financial results and trends, strengths and weaknesses, etc. What they pay particularly close attention to are their strengths and weaknesses in order to find the best ways to differentiate LinksBuddy from its primary competitors and pull market share from those businesses. In addition, they look for target market customers who would participate to a much larger extent in the golf travel experience if they were offered a value proposition such as what LinksBuddy intends to offer. They also assess which if any of the tour companies could pivot and create their own P2P marketplace and compete on a head to head basis with LinksBuddy in the future.

With respect to the golf host/accommodation provider side of the platform, Steven and Martin see both the golf tour operators' accommodation partners and Airbnb being their primary competition. The accommodation partners of the tour operators are examined to determine their offering to golf travelers and how LinksBuddy can differentiate its private accommodation offering in a way that most appeals to their target customers. Airbnb is closely analyzed to understand its business model strengths and weaknesses that can be adapted or avoided by LinksBuddy (and explain each to potential investors), as well as the method it used to solve the chicken and egg problem. Airbnb is also viewed as a current indirect competitor as some golfers already arrange their own personal golf travel experience using Airbnb accommodation, and LinksBuddy wants to capture those persons' business by offering a comprehensive value proposition. In addition, Airbnb can be seen a potential future competitor as it continues to expand its operations into tangential business segments.

CHAPTER 15:
THE MARKETING PLAN

Chapter Overview

Conducting Market Research and Analysis..267
Setting Marketing Goals..267
Developing Strategies and Tactics to Acquire, Retain and Grow
Customers 269
Product..269
Price..270
Place..271
Promotion 271
       Advertising 272
       Public Relations 272
       Sales Promotion..273
       Personal Selling...273
Internet Marketing..275
Budget and Analytics..278
LinksBuddy Case Study..280

CHAPTER 15

THE MARKETING PLAN

Now that you have completed your industry analysis, market analysis, and competitive analysis, you can use the results to develop a marketing plan that allows you to locate and get the attention of the consumers in your target market segment; communicate with them about how your product/value proposition will benefit their lives; convince and motivate them to buy; deliver your product to them at a satisfactory place and time; retain them as loyal customers in the future; and get them to buy even more. All of this while maximizing long term profit and cash flow.

If that sounds like a large chunk of your business operations, it's because it is. And the best way for all of these steps to happen successfully is to develop a comprehensive marketing plan for your business and then execute that plan. Remember, if you cannot think through and explain how you will efficiently and effectively market your product, then your business will not succeed. You can have the best product in the world, but if nobody knows about it, or the people that do know cannot be convinced to buy, the product has no meaning.

The steps involved in putting together a good marketing plan include:

- Conducting market research and analysis (which you have already done in large part)

- Setting marketing goals

- Developing strategies and tactics to achieve your marketing goals

- Budgeting

- Measuring effectiveness and return on investment of your marketing plan

Because the marketing plan is an integral part of your business plan, it must be developed to work in tandem with all aspects of your business and help achieve the overall goals of your organization.

Conducting Market Research and Analysis

At this point, you should have already conducted most of the necessary market research as part of your initial market research and all of the iterations you went through while testing and validating your business model using the Business Model Canvas. Now you can put all of the information you collected and analysis you performed to good use while creating your marketing plan. Inevitably, however, as you get into the details of the marketing plan there will be certain areas that require more research and validation. Fortunately, you should be well-versed in this process at this point, and can use the same tools and methods you used in the Business Model Canvas.

The next step in creating your marketing plan is to use your market research to once again analyze and understand the persons who make up your target segment: who they are, how they act, what may motivate them to purchase your product, and how, when, where, and at what price they would buy. This will allow you to determine how to position your product with respect to the competition, how to find and communicate with potential customers, the best price to offer your product, and where to offer your product. In other words, it will allow you to create a set of marketing goals, as well as strategies and tactics to meet those goals.

Setting Marketing Goals

Your initial instinct might be to say that the goal of marketing is to generate as much revenue and make as much profit as possible. In the long run, this may be true. But the path to realizing those two goals may not be a straight line. In some cases, focusing on other goals such as building a brand and gaining market share may result in lower profits in the beginning, but ultimately lead to a more profitable and sustainable business over the long term.

In addition, keep in mind that your marketing goals should mesh with the goals embodied in your vision, mission, and values statements, pointing not only towards profits, but also towards the type of organization and reputation you wish to build in the marketplace and the community. In the long run, this will also add value to your business.

Therefore, in addition to generating revenue and producing positive cash flow and a profit, the goals of a marketing program can include:

- Brand Building
- Product Positioning
- Product Differentiation
- Market Share
- Market Penetration
- Customer Loyalty and Retention and Growth
- Return on Marketing Investment

At the end of the day, you will always want to establish a brand, properly position and differentiate your product, gain as much market share as possible, develop customer loyalty, get a good return on your marketing dollars, generate positive cash flow, and make an acceptable profit. But in marketing, focus is important. Different goals may involve different, and sometimes conflicting, strategies and tactics. And as a small business, especially in the start-up phase, you will likely have limited marketing resources. So concentrating on one or more goals at a particular point in time is often the best way to efficiently allocate resources and achieve all of your goals in the long run.

Developing Strategies and Tactics to Acquire, Retain and Grow Customers

Your marketing mix consists of the strategies and tactics you will use to acquire, retain and grow customers and to accomplish your other related marketing goals. Traditionally, a company's "marketing mix" has been centered on the "Four Ps of Marketing":

- Product

- Price

- Place, and

- Promotion

These are the aspects of marketing that are within a company's control, as opposed to external factors—such as the tactics of competitor—that can be addressed and managed using the Four Ps but cannot be controlled.

Over the last decade, marketing strategies and tactics have been revolutionized by the Internet, which allows companies to get their message out to a large number of people at a relatively low cost. The impact has caused many marketing managers and experts to reassess the applicability of the Four Ps in today's technology-driven economy, especially since Internet marketing strategy and tactics, and even goals, can be different than those of traditional marketing. However, in one form or another most businesses must still pay attention to the original Four Ps, and work to integrate their traditional promotions with those available on the Internet for a comprehensive marketing program that combines traditional marketing and new marketing strategies and tactics.

So let's first take a more detailed look at the Four Ps and then get an overview of what new marketing on the Internet entails.

Product

As we discussed in great detail in Part II covering the Business Model Canvas, it does not make sense for a business to develop any product, or product feature, unless you have identified an important need or desire for that product/feature in the marketplace. And once you know what your target market wants and needs, it does make business sense to develop and produce a marketable product that contains features that satisfies the desires of your target segment while differentiating you from the competition. Therefore, as you learned while creating your Business Model Canvas, in designing and developing your product it is critical to keep in mind your value proposition and the important problems and needs of your customer segment that it addresses. Even though this will in large part have taken place already as part of the business modeling process, your marketing plan should take into account features that may be added in the future, and be flexible enough to adapt to what you learn as the product is introduced and you get feedback from real purchasing customers.

Price

Pricing a product is a delicate balance between generating revenue and maximizing profit margins, while at the same time realizing your other marketing goals. A low price point may increase sales, generate higher revenues, and increase market share, but at the expense of profit margins. A high price may increase profit margin while helping you establish a premium brand, but at the expense of losing revenue from customers who are unwilling to pay that price, and therefore losing market share.

Pricing will also be impacted by forces outside your control, such as how competitors are pricing their products and general economic conditions. At this point you may need to conduct some additional market research, focused on collecting information on the price points of competing products and what target customers are willing to pay, as well as their price sensitivity. This will give you a sense of the price range you can charge depending on the goal you want to achieve. Taking all of this into account, you should price your products at a point you think will best help you achieve your marketing and business goals.

For more information on pricing, go back to our discussion of this subject in Chapter 8 on revenue streams.

Place

Place involves where and when your customer will purchase your product, as well as where, when and how you will deliver it to the customer. This involves both marketing strategy and operations logistics, which we discussed in Chapter 6 on channels and will again be covered in Chapter ___ on your operations plan. The former is geared towards what your customers want and need; the latter is geared toward providing it to them in the best manner possible.

Your marketing strategy must determine whether your customers wish to purchase directly from you or from intermediaries, whether they will place orders online or otherwise and have them shipped, or take possession of the product at its point of sale. The first key is to determine where and when your potential buyers will expect to purchase your product, and make the purchase available to them in that location at that time. The second is to determine how, when and in what quantity your customers will expect to have the product delivered to them, and devise an efficient and cost-effective manner of doing so.

Promotion

Promotion is what most people typically think of when they hear the term "marketing." It is the communication of information to your target market in an attempt to get them to buy your product both now and in the future. The four major types of promotion typically integrated into a marketing strategy are:

- Advertising
- Publicity
- Sales promotions, and
- Personal selling

Your promotional mix should be designed to reach as much of the target customer segment audience as possible in a manner that gives you a good return on your investment of money, time and other resources—i.e. best achieves your marketing and business goals.

Advertising

The key to a successful advertising campaign is to assess which mix of marketing vehicles will reach the greatest number of likely buyers at a time and in a place where it is possible to influence their behavior. Each vehicle available for advertising entails its own set of goals, strategies, and tactics that must be understood and integrated to be effective.

Advertising vehicles include:

- Internet
- Print Media, such and newspapers and magazines
- Broadcast Media, such as radio and television
- Direct Mail
- Brochures, Flyers, and Postcards
- Catalogs
- Newsletters
- Billboards

Public Relations

Public relations entails the use of free media—such feature articles about a company or product in a magazine, or related interviews on television talk shows—to spread the word to the target audience.

Public relations vehicles include:

- Articles
- Events
- Press Releases
- Grand Openings

- Networking
- Trade Press
- Industry Analyst Coverage

Sales Promotion

Sales promotion allows the business owner to target both the consumer as well as the retailer, which is often necessary for the business to get its products stocked.

Sales promotion vehicles include:

- Free Samples
- Coupons
- Contests
- Rebates
- Point of Sales Promotions

Personal Selling

Personal selling, which refers to face-to-face or telephone sales, usually provides immediate feedback for the company about the product and instills greater confidence in customers. Personal selling also allows the business owner to collect information on competitive products, prices, and service and delivery problems.

It's a statement of the obvious to say that a company needs sales in order to survive and thrive. But what's not so obvious is the best way to generate and optimize those sales. As the founder of a new company, you may think that you should just go out and hire some experienced sales persons, tell them to do their thing, and wait for the orders to roll in. But in most cases you would be wrong, and you'll probably be surprised to learn that the best person to sell your products at the start-up stage is actually—now look in the mirror—you.

In the start-up phase, it is important for many reasons that the person running the business is out presenting the products and having personal interactions with customers. Going out and pitching your product to customers gives you the ability to connect directly with your first buyers and develop long-term relationships. And most importantly, it provides the opportunity to receive direct customer feedback at a crucial time for your company. You may have a business plan and a marketing plan that provide substantial information on your target customers and their needs, but until you sit down with customers in a genuine sales presentation, ask questions as any top sales professional would do, and listen directly to your customers desires and concerns, your information will still be incomplete.

The reason for this is that despite your best pre-launch efforts, it is almost impossible to develop an exact match between your product and your customers' needs before the product is out there in the marketplace. When you're the one in the sales meetings, personally demonstrating your product, gauging your customers' reactions, asking questions and listening to their answers, you get the most valuable information possible about how to improve both your product and your message—especially when you start hearing the same responses from many customers.

Your goal should be to develop a sales strategy and process that you can teach others as you grow and scale your organization. The goal should be to codify all of the knowledge you gain from your start-up sales and use it to establish standard operating procedures and train your sales team going forward.

Once the product, business model, and marketing strategy have been refined, then it will be time to bring on a salesperson or two to give you the bandwidth for growth. Then, once you're ready to significantly scale the business, you can look to hire a sales manager and create a sales team for him or her to manage.

If done properly, adding salespeople can free you up to spend time and energy on other tasks, as well as result in increased sales by expanding your pipeline of leads and creating the bandwidth necessary to qualify those leads and close sales. But always remember, your sales team will be responsible for more than just generating revenue—they will be the persons with the most direct and frequent contact with your customers. Therefore, hiring the wrong salespersons, handing them the wrong strategy, or using an ineffective and/or un-scalable process could actually damage both your brand and your sales.

Internet Marketing

The Internet provides businesses with the ability to reach large numbers of target customers in an interactive, real time, collaborative online environment. As a result, Internet marketing will allow your new business to combine mass marketing, public relations, sales promotions, and personal selling into one promotional forum. In some cases, it also allows for the actual distribution of your product as well.

The first step in establishing your Internet marketing program will be to design and create a website, which we will cover in detail in Chapter 16. A basic website will contain information regarding your business, a description of the products you offer, and promotional material related to those products. With a more advanced website, you can optimize your Internet marketing potential by providing informative content such as articles and blogs. And if you wish to engage in e-commerce, which we will also cover in Chapter 16, your website will include an online shopping store as well.

Once your website is established, you need to create an online promotional mix that reaches your target market, attracts their attention, draws them to visit your website, and converts them as customers. Reaching your target customer segment involves determining which websites they visit regularly, when they visit, and how they use the sites. Once you've found where your primary potential customers reside online, however, they have to find you.

The techniques for getting the attention of your target customers and drawing them to your website fall into one of two categories: "inbound marketing" and "outbound marketing." Inbound marketing vehicles such as content creation and social media engagement take human effort and cost money to produce and maintain, but no unaffiliated third party is paid. With outbound marketing vehicles, you pay a third party for placing an advertisement, sponsored link, or the like on their website.

Inbound marketing is also called "earned" marketing. It is a manner of drawing visitors and generating leads through a combination of content and links to your website. While inbound marketing is free of media costs, there are significant organizational and human resource costs to executing this strategy successfully. It takes concerted effort to create, publish, maintain, and refresh content that gets the attention of a large number of quality viewers and draws them to your website. That being said, in the long run the cost of drawing visitors to your website using inbound marketing techniques tends to be less than using paid outbound marketing techniques.

An inbound marketing strategy will take longer to put in place than simply paying for sponsored links and advertisements on other sites, which can be launched very quickly. It takes time to build interesting and informative content, establish and grow social networks, increase website authority, and acquire high quality links. Once created, however, your online content will have a much longer life than traditional promotional material and draw higher quality visitors—i.e. those visitors most likely to be converted into customers—to your website. And unlike outbound marketing methods, which disappear once you stop paying for them, inbound marketing content will remain available online for a long time.

Inbound marketing methods include:

- Website Content
- External Online Content
- Social Media
- Referrals (Links)
- E-Mail
- Public Relations
- Online Customer Service

Content is king in today's Internet marketing environment. The method of content marketing has been around for a long time, but it has exploded as more and more people look to the Internet as their primary source of information on products and services they want to buy.

Content marketing is a method of getting "found" by your customers, promoting your products, and creating brand awareness indirectly without a direct interruptive sales pitch. The idea is to create informative content that is highly ranked by Internet search engines, so people who are looking for that information will find either content located on your website, or content that you have created and placed on another site with links back to your website. The goal is to build product and brand awareness and reputation with your content and generate sales by enticing a large number of high quality visits to your website. High quality content also develops valuable customer relationships, establishes credibility, and builds a trustworthy reputation.

Types of inbound marketing content include:

- Articles
- Blogs
- Social Media
- Video
- Podcasts
- Research/White Papers
- Forums
- Q&A
- Webinars
- Infographics
- Newsletters
- Press Releases
- Public Relations Placements and Mentions
- Online Business Directories

You can create content such as articles, blogs, forums, white papers, and Q&A for your own website, but don't stop there. To give you the optimum opportunity to get found by potential customers, place high quality content you have created on other websites, and link that content back to your own website.

Social media networking has become a key ingredient in the Internet marketing strategy of many businesses. Sites such as Facebook, Twitter, Tumblr, Pinterest, Instagram, LinkedIn, Google+, and Digg provide a platform both for placing your content and interacting with your target market. Video hosting websites such as YouTube or Metacafe have also been a benefit to little known businesses. Creating a video that goes viral can make millions of people aware of your business in a very short time.

All of your sources of content can interact with each other through links and search results, and should be coordinated as such.

The key to all of this, however, is that your content must be discovered by your intended audience and drawn to your website. The best way to ensure that happens is to rank high in Internet search results. And the best way to get a high ranking is employ search engine optimization ("SEO") techniques such as keywords and tags and creating quality relevant content that is regularly refreshed.

The other important SEO technique is to place and generate as many high quality links to your site and content as possible, because the more such links you have and the higher quality they are, the higher you will rank in the search engine results. So the more links the better, especially from sites relevant to your business.

When you create your own content, you can embed links in whatever you create, whether it resides on your website or that of a third party. But you also want to generate what are known as referrals, which are links on third party sites and embedded in content created by third parties such as articles, product reviews, and discussion forums. You can seek free links at news sites, industry-related sites, local business directory sites, and the like.

Links can also be paid for, as can search results, and this is where you enter the realm of outbound marketing.

Budget and Analytics

One of the most difficult parts of creating a marketing plan is setting a budget. It is very easy to get carried away and spend too much, resulting in paying for promotions that do not give you a good return on investment. But it is also easy to short shrift the importance of marketing by spending too little, resulting in missed opportunities to sell your product, gain market share, and build your brand.

There are two key aspects to setting a marketing budget: how much money to spend and how to allocate those funds.

How much you spend will be determined by the resources you have available and the nature of your business. If your resources are limited, don't abandon marketing as a priority, just educate yourself on all of the less expensive marketing opportunities available to you, such as some of the Internet marketing techniques we just discussed, and take advantage of them as much as possible. If you do have adequate resources, see if you can get information on the percent of revenues that companies in your business typically spend on marketing. You may, however, need to spend a higher percentage than your competitors at the outset, until your business and products become known by your target market.

When you're coming up with an annual figure for marketing costs, don't forget about related expenses such as market research, attending functions and trade shows, training yourself and others, and hiring experts to help you with special projects. And always allow a bit extra for the unexpected.

The key is to get the biggest bang for your marketing buck, and in order to do so it's important that you track and measure how successful your marketing programs have been.

LinksBuddy Case Study

Chapter 15
The Marketing Plan

In creating their marketing plan, Steven and Martin realize that the nature of the LinksBuddy business will dictate a multi-faceted plan with the need to set strategies and goals that address challenges many businesses do not face. For example, one of the primary goals of their marketing plan must be to overcome the chicken and egg problem and reach a critical mass of golf host and golf traveler participants in a time frame that allows their business to succeed. Any marketing strategy that does not accomplish that goal, even if it succeeds in its own right, will contribute to the company's failure. In addition, it is critical that Steven and Martin face head on the fact that they are attempting to re-segment an entrenched market and change consumer behavior in that market—i.e. convincing golf travelers to abandon the traditional form of golf travel in favor of a new value proposition. So their marketing strategy must include tactics designed to accomplish that goal. Finally, their marketing plan must be in sync and designed to accomplish their goal of a systematic roll out of new destinations. If they create a general marketing plan that does not directly assist in the successful launch of these specific locations in a specific time frame, it will be a wasted effort. Their marketing plan and operational plan must be completely integrated.

Steven and Martin identify other critical marketing goals as well. At the top of that list is to build a successful brand that connotes in every customer's minds their vision for the golfing community it is their mission to create. This means that every use of their brand name "LinksBuddy" must engender integrity and trust, comradery and community, a shared love of the game of golf, and the opportunity to realize golfing dreams. Any marketing activity that advances that brand image can be considered, all others avoided. A related goal to changing their customers' current golf travel behavior must be clear differentiation of the LinksBuddy brand and value proposition from what is currently available to golf travelers. All marketing activities should be designed to demonstrate clearly why the LinksBuddy golf travel experience will be superior to a traditional golf travel experience through a tour operator. All of these goals wrap into an additional goal of attaining a high level of customer retention and growth. It will be crucial for LinksBuddy to get early evangelist customers to remain customers after their first travel experience and form the core of the golfer community that Steven and Martin intend to create. Accomplishing this goal will become a key tactic in accomplishing the goal of attaining critical mass in the right time frame, and will also be key to accomplishing a final goal of steadily reducing the cost of customer acquisition and increasing the lifetime value of customers over time. A final goal of their marketing plan will to make sure that each tactic helps drive a high level of traffic to their website, and that once there a high percentage will be converted to active customers.

The strategy and tactics that Steven and Martin adopt with respect to the 4Ps of product, price, place and promotion, as well as all other aspects of their marketing plan, must be designed to accomplish their stated goals. They first take a close look at their value proposition and assess how will it integrates with these goals, and how they can use the different aspects of their value proposition to differentiate themselves from traditional golf tour operators, build their brand image, establish trust, etc. They also assess whether they should tweak their value proposition in order to best achieve their marketing goals. In the end, they focus on a strategy of communicating the most important features of their value proposition in all of their marketing efforts to differentiate their product, build their brand, and change customer behavior: Community; Comradery; Hospitality; Unique Local Experience; Convenience; Course Access; Cost-effectiveness. These features will each be promoted with the goal of convincing their target market that LinksBuddy offers them everything they receive from a golf tour package operator and so much more. The "so much more" is "membership" in a worldwide community of golfers, a new golfing friend with local knowledge and access to a top-tier golf course, a travel experience that is personal and hospitable rather than impersonal and sterile, and provides the ability to enjoy the destination with a local who knows where to go and what to do.

The price that LinksBuddy intends to charge its golf traveler and golf host customers has already been validated during the business model testing process. But for purposes of their written business plan, they will need to give investors a clear explanation of their pricing model and the reasons behind it. For example, they will explain how they derived the percentage they will charge each side of the platform based on a combination of factors, including the price necessary to cover projected expenses and achieve an adequate margin, the price charged by relevant comparable companies such as Airbnb (and justification for their markup over Airbnb prices based on the personal service offered by golf hosts to golf customers), and the ceiling they place on their pricing model based on customer perceived value. These same explanations they will give potential investors will be communicated in different form to customers in order to convince them they are receiving good value for the benefits they receive. In addition, as part of their marketing strategy to solve the chicken and the egg problem and gain critical mass, Steven and Martin intend to offer their initial flights of golf hosts discounted fees or fee waivers for a period of time. This will constitute a cost that must be factored into their projected financial results.

The channels that Steven and Martin will use in their marketing program are divers as well. In order to attract and convert golf hosts they will use local promotional channels, beginning with the local representative they retain in each location. This will be supplemented by targeted public relations in each location to generate awareness and interest, driving potential golf hosts and golf travelers to the website or to contact the local representative directly.

On top of that, Steven and Martin will engage in an intensive internet marketing and public relations campaign generate awareness and buzz about the new LinksBuddy travel experience that is geared towards achieving all of their marketing goals. Steven will head up the public relations effort, lining up online interviews, podcast interviews, traditional radio and television interviews, setting up booths at golf courses and tournament events, etc. For customers that arrive on the website, Steven and his assistant will be there in the form of blogs and other content, and ready to engage directly in hosted forums on LinksBuddy golf travel and other golf related subject. He will also travel to each new destination to recruit and train local representatives, enlist golf course partners, meet with golf hosts, and spread the message of their new and unique offering. Each method he employs will include calls to action that pull potential golf travelers and golf hosts to the website, and obtain contact information from customers as well.

Martin will employ all of the internet marketing techniques he has at his disposal, focusing on those for which costs will be mostly in terms of his and his assistant's sweat equity rather than paid methods. Social media will be a big focus, including Facebook, Twitter, Instagram, Snapchat and YouTube. Their website content will include a variety of blogs, videos, forum, articles on golf and golf travel, information about destinations, etc. designed to draw viewers to the site, keep them there and convert them as customers. But just as importantly, the website will be designed to create community. The goal, in fact, is to make LinksBuddy the default homepage and leisure time online entertainment venue for its community of golf enthusiasts, and to use that community to organically attract new members and create viral effects. Martin will also employ a variety of outbound online marketing techniques, but in doing so will keep a close eye on data collection which validates that the methods he employs will achieve a good return on marketing dollars invested.

CHAPTER 16:
WEBSITE AND E-COMMERCE PLAN

Chapter Overview

Creating a Website 286
    Domain Names 287
    Websites 288
    Web Site Design and Development 289
    Buying a Website 291
Engaging in E-commerce 291
LinksBuddy Case Study 294

CHAPTER 16

WEBSITE AND E-COMMERCE PLAN

Websites have become an integral part of running almost any line of business in today's technology-driven economy, and anybody reading your business plan will understand that. Although in some cases it may still be possible to do business the old fashioned way based on print and broadcast advertising, as well as word of mouth, it is almost guaranteed that a properly conceived, established, and managed website will deliver a good return on the time and money invested. For that to be the case, however, the website must be created and operated in the right way, and you must take advantage of the internet marketing techniques we spoke about in Chapter 15, or the beneficial results you anticipated could be reversed.

If you're going to go further and actually sell your products using the Internet, then the stakes and your required knowledge and skill base are even higher. You will not only need a well-designed and smoothly functioning website, you will need to be able to receive, process and protect orders over the Internet, and potentially even deliver your product that was as well. There is a vast graveyard of businesses that have failed because their founders thought they had a great idea for selling their products via the Internet, but failed to master the art and craft of doing so.

The investors reading your business plan will be well aware of this, and you need to be aware as well. If you want to go into e-commerce and have never done so before, you have a lot to learn if you want to succeed. But it can and has been done by many successful entrepreneurs.

Creating a Website

The first step in establishing a website is the same as the first step in starting a company—you have to select a name and then take the right measures to secure the use of that name. The name of a website, which also acts as the primary portion of its Internet address, is called the "domain name." Every domain name must be registered and placed in an international database. Unlike trademarks, where the same mark can apply to different types of products, every domain name is unique.

Simultaneous with selecting and securing a domain name, you can be designing the layout and user interface that will make up the look and feel of your website and drive the overall user experience. Once that is accomplished, the computer code that will operate the website and turn the design into a reality must be programmed. Both the design and development of a successful website require specialized skills. So if you or the employees in your business don't have experience in this area, it is a good idea to hire a professional website designer and developer (if necessary) to perform these important tasks for you.

As with any form of business, one other option is always just to buy what you need. It may even be possible to purchase a registered domain name, a functioning website, and all of the associated assets as a package. But in most cases, you will want to either start from scratch or use a template and tailor your website to your particular business.

In your business plan, demonstrate that you have taken the necessary steps to establish a website that will attract and retain customers and add significant value to your business.

Domain Names

Your domain name will be one of the primary marketing tools of your business, and should be chosen with the same care that you use in choosing the trademarks attached to your products and services. Factors to consider include:

- How effective the domain name will be in driving Internet searches by your target audience to your website

- How memorable the domain name will be for your customers.

- Whether it will be possible to register the domain name as a trademark

- Whether it may infringe the trademarks of another person in places where you intend to do business

Unlike trademarks, domain names are not technically owned by the user. Domain names must be registered in the domain name system ("DNS") database, upon which the registrant is granted the "right to use" the name. Therefore, once you've chosen the domain name (or names) that you want to register, first go to any well-known registrar's database and see if the name is available. This may take some time, because hundreds of millions of domain names have already been registered.

Since there are so many domain names that have already been registered, you may also have difficulty finding one that you are satisfied with for your business. And even if you do find an acceptable domain name, you may see a better one that has been registered and is for sale. In these situations, you may want to buy a domain name rather than registering a new name yourself.

Websites

A website consists of content accessible through the Internet. The website of a local seafood restaurant could be as simple as a single homepage displaying the business name and logo, a photograph of the restaurant's exterior, a few menu items, location, and contact information. The website for a multinational consumer products corporation could include entire catalog for several product lines, interactive graphics, forums, shopping services, databases, and whatever else is required to conduct the entire business online.

Regardless of how big or small, complex or simple a website is, there are certain steps that need to be taken to get it up and running, make it successful, and maintain it going forward. First you need to think through exactly what you want to accomplish with the website and who the target audience will be. For example, will you use the site purely for informational purposes, or do you want to sell products over the site as well?

Then you need to visualize how the website will look and feel, and how you would like visitors to interact with the available content. Are static photographs sufficient, or are interactive graphics and animation required? Do the customers need to perform pricing and other forms of calculation?

Every function of the website needs to be identified and analyzed for it to be successful. If this is not done upfront, then your site could turn away as many customers as it attracts.

Once this basic description of the commercial requirements of the site is in place, then the technical work begins. The entire website needs to be designed and developed to realize your commercial vision. This includes an interwoven system of software programs that operate the website, including the user interface and all of the text, graphics, and sounds that will be included on the site. Then content must be developed or otherwise obtained and added to the site.

Finally, the programs and content that make up the website must be hosted on a server. This is where the website will reside and be maintained, and where your visitors will be directed via your domain name to view your website content. Typically, websites are hosted on servers owned by external hosting companies, who have the resources to cost-effectively maintain servers of sufficient bandwidth in a safe and secure environment.

There is one last thing to keep in mind when creating and launching a website. Both in the development of the computer programs operating the website, and with respect to the content that appears on the site, care must be taken to ensure that applicable intellectual property, consumer protection, and other laws are adhered to.

Web Site Design and Development

Your website is the first impression that many potential customers will have of your business. For that reason, it is crucial that the site be visually appealing, easy to navigate, and function quickly and smoothly. With a well designed and developed website, visitors will linger, browse, and come back often. A poor website will have the opposite effect, sending customers racing out the virtual door, often never to return.

Although often used interchangeably, website "design" and "development" are technically two different terms. Website design refers to how a site looks and operates on the surface—its graphic appearance and usability. It also entails making the website "search engine friendly," i.e. using key words and other techniques that cause your site to appear prominently when customers are searching the Internet for what you sell.

Website development refers to the underlying computer code that allows the website to look and operate the way the designer intended. The software that must be programmed to operate a website is extensive. It must control everything from the ability to enlarge a photograph to links to other websites to accepting credit cards.

As a result, most businesses that are just starting out don't have the technical capability or capacity to program website software, but fortunately they don't have to. For a simple website, downloadable design software is available for which the development work has already been done. For more complex sites, there are many website designers and developers available and willing to perform the service for a fee.

If your business has limited resources and you just want a very basic Internet presence that will simply perform the function of making potential customers aware of the goods and services you offer, as well as provide your location and contact information, then you may want to go online and download a proven website design software package to create your own site.

Be aware, however, that even a website design program that performs all of the functions you desire will require a significant amount of thought, as well as trial and error, if you want your site to be a successful marketing and sales tool for your business. You will need to consider carefully the appearance of the site and how the visitors will interact with the information you provide. To realize the importance of this, just think about some of the websites you have visited that had poor graphics and were difficult to read text, or were complicated and counter-intuitive to interface with. This type of website screams out "unprofessional" and reflects poorly on the business involved.

For these reasons, even if you are starting a new business it is probably worth the investment to hire an experienced website designer to help you create an easy to use site that will attract and retain customers, as well as a developer if you intend to write the software code for your own site rather than using a template. Keep in mind when looking at candidates that you need a person or a team who can perform both the design and development functions. A website designer who dabbles in development, or vice versa, is not good enough. You need an expert in both areas.

Buying a Website

In some cases, rather than recreate the wheel it may be a good idea to buy an existing website. This would make the most sense if you want to enter the business already being operated on the website, or if you find a site for sale that could easily be altered to suit the needs of your own business.

Website owners offer sites for sale directly or through brokers. In addition, you can search the Internet for sites that appear to be dormant and attempt to contact the owner to make an offer to buy. The other instance where websites are purchased and sold is in connection with the sale of an ongoing business.

Engaging in E-commerce

If you decide to use your website as more than just a marketing tool and actually sell your products via the site, then you have entered the exciting but very challenging world of e-commerce. Doing so successfully will require that you not just become familiar with, but actually master, all of the aspects of Internet marketing we touched on in Chapter 15 and website design we discussed in this chapter. In addition, you will need to develop detailed knowledge of every function involved in selling products over the Internet. Therefore, in this section we will simply highlight the areas that you need to research thoroughly and understand completely.

With an e-commerce website, you will be able to promote and sell your products all over the world 24 hours a day/7 days a week while avoiding the high-cost of leasing and staffing a retail store. You will be able deliver large amounts of information to your customers, allow them to compare products and prices almost instantaneously, and make a purchase without leaving their home or office. However, in order to take advantage of these positive aspects of e-commerce, you need to be better than the competition at driving potential customers to your website, convincing them to make a purchase when they arrive, and bringing them back as repeat customers. This is much easier said than done.

In the previous sections we discussed the basics of website design and development that you must know in order to get a site up and running. But an e-commerce website requires all of that and much more. The elements of a successful e-commerce website/business include:

- An Internet marketing strategy that is comprehensive, integrated, and drives a high volume of qualified traffic to your website

- A customer conversion strategy and related techniques that turns a high-percentage of viewers into customers, and then repeat customers

- A user experience that keeps customers on your website and keeps them coming back for more

- A competitive and effective online pricing strategy

- A profitable business model

- A navigation system that is easy to use, consistent, and intuitive

- A hosting solution that is high performance, feature-rich, and reliable 24/7

- An order mechanism/shopping cart system that is fast, easy to use, and functional

- A payment gateway that is fast, efficient, and accurate

- A merchant account that is professional, reliable, and cost-effective

- Security software that protects your customers' payment/transaction details

- A privacy policy that protects your customers personal data

- An order management system that efficiently tracks sales, orders, and inventory

- A fulfillment/shipment system that quickly, cost-effectively, and accurately delivers products to customers and handles returns

- Excellent pre-sale and post-sale customer service and technical support

- An integrated M-commerce (mobile commerce) and F-commerce (Facebook commerce) strategy

- Measurement tools for tracking and analyzing key performance indicators

If you are going to rely on online sales to drive your business, you must become an expert in every area listed above. This is true regardless of whether you decide, as you likely will, to use an e-commerce hosting solution to host your website.

While third-party solutions provide many, or even all, of the necessary tools and applications you will need to start an e-commerce business, you will have little chance of success unless you understand the most effective way to utilize those tools and applications. In addition, you need to understand every element of e-commerce in order to select the best hosting solution and applications for your business.

If you don't get it right, customers who are accustomed to shopping with ease on popular e-commerce sites will depart quickly and never return to your site. However, if you do get it right, you will have increased your marketing and sales reach exponentially, and the world will literally become your economic oyster.

> **LinksBuddy Case Study**
>
> ## Chapter 16
> ## Website and E-Commerce Plan
>
> The LinksBuddy platform software and website will be the key asset and key to success of the business. It will be called the "LinksBuddy Clubhouse" and will be Steven and Martin's business command central—the hub through which their business is conducted and which integrates all aspects of their business model and operations. Steven and Martin have to get this right, and they have to communicate clearly to investors exactly how they will do so. While Steven and Martin already have a prototype website that was used to test and validate their business mode, it is by no means the final MVP platform they intend to launch. So the completion of the design and development of their platform software and website is a critical aspect of their business plan, both in terms of technology development, value proposition, and budget.
>
> They begin by preparing a design and development plan for their platform software and website that includes specifications, milestones and budget. They had employed a friend of Martin's to produce the prototype using a common webpage development tool, but the final product will require a highly talented and experienced developer and designer—which will probably be two different people. Their key strategic and tactical decision involves whether to purchase a P2P white label platform from a third party, hire an in-house designer and/or developer to create their own, or hire a third party contractor(s) to do the work. After creating the specifications for the platform, soliciting bids, and comparing costs and benefits of their three options, they choose to go the third party contractor route. In their business plan, they will explain clearly to potential investors their reasons for going this direction, the costs involved and the risks involved.
>
> The functions, features and content of the platform they intend to develop will be the core of their value proposition, and it must function in an optimal manner and integrate all key value proposition and business transaction functions. Steven and Martin name those key functions the "10 Cs" because they consist of the following: Content (information that attracts, converts and retains customers and creates community);

Creation (the ability of golf hosts to create and build their own attractive listings); Community (the ability of golf hosts and travelers to interact both in group and one-on-one online settings); Curation (filtered search and matching functions for both golf travelers and golf hosts; Communication (ability of golf hosts and golf travelers to communicate, exchange information and arrange travel plans); Collaboration (a peer review system that allows the fair review and rating of golf hosts and golf travelers in a manner that instills trust and furthers the sense of community); Calls to Action (built-in methods of converting customers to become members of the community, golf hosts and frequent golf travelers); Consummation (of booking and travel arrangements and all financial aspects of the e-commerce transaction); Customer Service (via chat on the website, email or telephone); Collection of Data (methods of collecting valuable and usable data regarding customers and customer activity on the website; will include a sophisticated CRM system and integration of CRM software into the platform).

Because they intend to create a website that actually does function as a virtual clubhouse, it will be critical that Steven and Martin work with their platform developer and designer to not only get the functions and features right, but also optimize all of the website intangibles that will make their customers online experience enjoyable and efficient. This means they will need to take a complex set of functions and features and embed them in an exceedingly easy to navigate and intuitive user interface system that satisfies all of the customer's needs in an efficient manner. The analogy that Steven uses is of the staff of a five-star golf resort: they need to be there and provide all of the services you require without your ever noticing what they are doing. In addition, in order to make this the same as a clubhouse and entice customers to make it their personal homepage, they will want to embed access to external content on the site, such as links to golf and news websites, search bars, etc.

In order to not only develop the website, but get it up and running and operate it going forward, Steven and Martin will need to recruit, manage and budget for a number of partners as part of their business plan. They will need a web hosting solution that is capable of handling their initial operations and expanded operations in the future. The selection of this partner is very important, as they will require high performance and not be able to afford any risk of their website going offline for any reason. They will also need to purchase and integrate back office software that performs the accounting functions, and most likely either a contractor or in-house staff person to manage those functions. They will need to select and integrate merchant partners and a payment gateway to make it efficient and easy for customers to pay online for the LinksBuddy services. And they will need security software that protects their customers' payment/transaction details to ensure the important value proposition elements of trust and integrity is integrated into the transactional aspects of their business as well.

CHAPTER 17:
OPERATIONS

Chapter Overview

Product Design and Development Plan	300
Production	301
Suppliers	302
Distribution	303
Service and Support	305
Service Businesses	305
Organization	306
Location and Facilities	308
Choosing the Right Location	309
Property Lease	310
Capital Equipment	311
Legal Environment	311
External Influences	311
LinksBuddy Case Study	312

CHAPTER 17

OPERATIONS

With respect to your business plan, "operations" consists of everything necessary to convert your idea into a product in your customer's hands and to run your business. In other words, it is how you will execute your business model on a daily basis. This includes the product development, purchasing, production/manufacturing, packing and shipping, and distribution processes. It also includes all of the human and other resources and activities required to perform these functions.

So in this section of the business plan, you should demonstrate that you have a firm grasp of the process necessary to develop your product and bring it to market in an efficient and cost effective manner that ensures the level of quality and profitability you desire. But the main value of this section, and the analysis that goes into it, is identifying the areas that must be concentrated on to succeed in your business—in particular those areas where you can develop a core competency and/or gain a competitive advantage. Therefore, after providing a process overview you should focus on the aspects of each functional area that are either essential to the success of your business—i.e. key activities and critical success factors—or that set you apart from your competitors.

Conversely, you need to identify the areas where you may currently lag behind the competition, and develop a plan for either getting up to speed or compensating for your weakness.

The detail required with respect to individual areas of product development and operations will depend on the nature of your business. If you are developing new software that has not been finalized, product development milestones and schedules should be included in the business plan. If you will require a distribution partner in order to effectively access and distribute to your target market, your plan for obtaining such a partner, and the anticipated terms of the arrangement, should be laid out. If specialized machinery will be required to manufacture your product, then you should discuss whether you will purchase the equipment or outsource the entire process. Accounting systems and controls may seem like a very basic function of running a business, but if your system cannot effectively handle orders, collections, and payments, you may find a potential profit turning into a loss.

The descriptions in this section don't need to be overly detailed—just enough for the readers to understand how the business will operate and its key operational components. The bottom line is that you need to assure both yourself and your investors that you have thought through the entire process of running your business, not just the sexy part that revolves around marketing and sales.

One way to get started in this section is to provide an operating model, possibly including a flowchart, that clearly describes your operations from start to finish and the key functions, activities and processes involved. In addition, you can provide a description of the key elements of your operations strategy, goals and objectives, including the basis for the operational choices you have made. As always, you need to make sure that each aspect of your operations plan and strategy is in support of your overall business strategy and goals, and can be linked directly back to them.

Once you've provided an overview via your operations model, you can then break it down into its component parts and give a description of each, again focusing on what is most critical to your business operations while at the same time demonstrating that you understand how all the pieces work and fit together.

Components of operations can include the following:

- Product design and development
- Production/manufacturing and quality control
- Suppliers and vendors
- Inventory control and management
- Physical sales and distribution

- Terms of sales (credit terms, discounts, and return policies)
- Customer service and support
- Administration and support functions: accounting; human resources; legal
- Business location
- Facilities and equipment
- Technology
- Organization
- Legal environment
- Service business

Keep in mind that depending on the nature of your business, some of these functions such as product development, technology, and distribution may require a plan of their own, as well as a dedicated section of your Business Plan.

Product Design and Development Plan

Whether you need a product design and development plan, and if you do the contents of that plan and how it will be described in your business plan, will be dictated by the type of business you have and the status of your product development efforts. If you are developing an entirely new or mostly new product, then you will need a product development plan for sure. If your product and its development process are complex and/or critical to your business, then you may want to devote a separate section of your business plan to product development and not bury it in the "operations" section.

The purpose of the design and development plan section is to provide investors with a description of the product's design, chart its development using key milestones through to production, create a product development budget, and do all of this within the context of the marketing plan and other top-level business strategies and goals.

Many new businesses never even launch because product development turns out to be more difficult, take more time, and/or be more expensive than anticipated, or the product becomes more difficult or expensive to produce in sufficient quantity. Therefore it is critical to make an honest and critical assessment of what it will take to develop and produce your product.

Your description of your product design and development plan should include:

- Development Schedule (including tasks, milestones and status)
- Development Costs
- Potential Difficulties and Risks Involved

The development schedule should include all of the key development tasks and activities, as well as the different stages of development and key milestones. It should be tied directly to the development budget. You should not be shy about identifying the challenges and risks involved in product development. But you should also describe how you intend to overcome those obstacles should they arise.

Production

Once you have a product that has been developed and tested and ready to go to market, you need to produce your product in sufficient quantity and of sufficient quality and on a cost efficient basis. If you are launching a new toy for the children's market, then your production may include the manufacturing process. If you are offering a service, it may include all of the preparation that goes into being able to offer that service.

What you need to do in this section is to provide an overview of the production process that includes a description all of the key resources—including materials, skills, facilities and equipment, and intellectual property. State the primary source of those key resources, as well as key activities or processes, key partners and their role in the production process, critical success factors, challenges and risks, and costs involved in producing your product.

Suppliers

Nearly every business needs suppliers. If you manufacture products, you need raw materials and components. If you run a restaurant, you need food and beverages. If you own a retail store, you need inventory of the goods you sell. And the success or failure of your business could turn on your relationship with your suppliers and their ability to deliver the quantity of goods you need at the quality you desire, on time, and at a predictable price.

For that reason, it is always a good idea to have alternative sources of supply for everything that is critical to your business; otherwise the success of your business will depend entirely on the success of your supplier's business, which you have no control over. Even if you own a small manufacturing business you may want to have more than one source of raw materials. If for any reason your supplier is unable to deliver on time, it will mean the cancellation of orders and the loss of customers. This could damage your business reputation in a way that no indemnification could remedy.

Plan reviewers want to know who are your key suppliers and that you've established relationships with your suppliers of good repute and that there's a high level of assurance that you'll be able to get what you need to establish or continue your business, and you'll get it of sufficient quality. They also want to be told about the terms of your agreements and the quality and reliability of what you plan to buy.

Having good relationships with your suppliers can help you manage your inventory effectively, which is a key operations concern for many businesses. It's also important to explain how you will manage your inventory. If you have too much inventory, you're wasting money; if you have too little, you're losing out on sales (and possibly customers, if they perceive your business as unreliable).

Pricing is an important feature of the relationship with suppliers. You need to tell your reader whether you expect to pay standard prices or receive special discounts as a result of quantity or some other criteria. Payment terms, return policy, and so on are also important. And note if any letters of credit will be required, especially for international shipments. Will they extend credit to your business, and if so, how much and on what conditions?

Distribution

The ultimate goal of all your product development, marketing, and sales efforts will be to get your product into the hands of the end user, because it is the end user who will drive product demand. You can have the best product in the world and thousands of eager buyers, but if you can't get your product to your customers where and when they want to buy, none of it has any meaning. While direct sales are one way to accomplish this goal, it is not the only or necessarily the best way to do so. Your strategy should be to sell to the person or organization in the distribution channel that will best deliver your product to the end user.

Distribution includes the entire process of moving the product from the factory to the end user. The type of distribution network you choose will depend upon the industry and the size of the market. The distribution strategy you choose for your product will be based on several factors that include the channels being used by your competition, your pricing strategy and your own internal resources.

A distribution channel is the chain of individuals and organizations involved in getting a product or service from the producer to the consumer. There are many factors to consider when selecting the appropriate distribution channel for a given product. You need to fully understand who it is you are planning to market to and select distribution routes that will make the most sense for those targets.

Depending on the type of product your start-up offers, the best distribution channel may be obvious, or you may have multiple viable routes to choose from. Keep in mind, however, that while increasing the number of ways in which a consumer can find your product has the potential to increase sales, it also creates complexities that can make distribution management difficult and costly. In addition, the longer the distribution channel, the less profit you might get from the sale.

In addition to direct sales, the basic distribution alternatives are:

- Wholesalers
- Distributors

- OEM (Original Equipment Manufacturer)

- Manufacturer's Representatives

- Online Sales

As opposed to a sales agent, a distributor buys products from the manufacturer, stores them, and resells them to retailers, end users, or customers. Most distributors also provide marketing, technical support, and other services that benefit the supplier. The strength of your distribution network can make or break your business, and it is often more effective and efficient to have distribution performed by third parties that are familiar with the local market and close to the customers. This will especially be the case when you are selling products outside of your home state, or the United States for that matter.

It also makes sense to hire businesses that specialize in distribution because they will have the infrastructure and systems in place to most efficiently get your product in the hands of your customers, and will often be responsible for marketing in their assigned region as well. In addition, distributors will be responsible for warehousing and shipping and will take on credit risk for uncollectible accounts receivable.

Distributors need to make a profit as well, however, so in return for shouldering these responsibilities the distributor may request preferable terms for the purchase of your product. In addition, the distributor might demand exclusive rights to the territory they cover, which will add a whole new level of negotiation when it comes to the distribution agreement.

In fact, many of the most important parts of a distribution agreement will be driven by whether or not exclusive rights are granted. These clauses include the efforts the distributor must make to sell your products, the territory covered by the agreement, and the termination provisions. In an exclusive distribution deal, you will want to clearly spell out the marketing and distribution efforts that you require from the distributor, the level of organization it must maintain, and minimum sales targets for the area covered. You do not want to get locked into an exclusive arrangement with a distributor who is either not using its best efforts to promote your product or who is simply not up to the task, so the default, cure, and termination provisions are very important.

In addition, the territory covered by the distribution agreement should be specifically defined, because you don't want to end up in breach of another exclusive distribution agreement if one distributor strays into the territory of another. You also don't want a distributor with insufficient reach attempting to sell your products where it cannot provide the appropriate level of customer service. On the other hand, the distributor will want the ability to "cure" any failure to meet minimum sales targets as long as it is using its best efforts to meet the goals.

It is very important to thoroughly investigate a distributor and the local market before any distribution agreement is signed. In many respects, the distributor will be the face of your company with respect to your customers, and the distributor's reputation will become your reputation. Make sure your distributors have the business skills and resources to represent your company well and deliver on their promises to customers.

Service and Support

In some businesses, after-sales service and support are important. This is especially true of more complex, technical products. Customers who buy computers, copying machines, or automobiles need to have someone to call when the products break and for periodic maintenance. Important service issues include pricing, parts inventories, travel expense, dispatch, and training. If this is a key activity for your business, your strategy in this area should be covered in your business plan.

Service Businesses

The Operations Plan for a service business, or for a business that offers a combination of products and services, will have some different/additional considerations that need to be addressed. You should describe the following:

- How the service will be performed and delivered

- Where it will be performed (your location, customer's location, other)

- The size of the territory where you will perform the service
- Who will perform the service
- When the service will be performed
- What special qualifications are required to provide the service
- What facilities and equipment are required
- What technology will be required
- How you will price the service

Entrepreneurs are often ignorant of the calculations needed to price services correctly. As a result, improper pricing is a common cause of failure in service-oriented start-ups. Therefore, it is important that plans for service businesses examine the pricing calculation in some detail. Readers will want to be assured that you're charging enough to cover all your costs but not so much that you'll be uncompetitive. In the service sector you need efficiencies to provide good value and s make profit.

Organization

A business is only as good as the people who perform its operations. However, the critical task of finding, hiring, training, and retaining good people is one of the most difficult and time consuming responsibilities of an entrepreneur.

Before embarking on a recruitment spree for your new business, you first need to identify the business operations that need to be performed by people, both now and in the future. Once you have identified those functions, you will then need to assess whether they should be undertaken by a full-time or part-time employee of the business, or whether it is better to retain an independent contractor to do the work. In doing so, you should analyze whether the service is an integral part of operating your business that will be required for the foreseeable future, or whether it is a temporary need either to get your business up and running or improve its operations.

The organizational plan and chart shows how you will structure your company by functional area, the various responsibilities and tasks assigned to each functional area, and the management and staff personnel required to carry out the tasks assigned to each functional area. If your plan anticipates hiring a large number of people, you should make a brief statement about how you plan to attract, select, hire, and retain employees.

Although every company will differ in its organizational structure, most can be divided into several broad functional areas that include:

- Marketing and sales (includes customer relations and service)
- Production (including quality assurance)
- Research and development
- Administration

Keep in mind that not every business can be divided in this manner. In fact, every business is different, and each one must be structured according to its own requirements and goals. For example, a product-oriented organization implies that people are responsible for particular product lines, and within those product lines, they accomplish all of the required functions. A geographic organization is appropriate when operations are to be spread out over considerable distances, and it doesn't make sense to try to manage from afar. Widely dispersed selling and distribution operations are typically organized geographically.

The organizational structure provides a basis from which to project operating expenses. This is critical to the formation of financial statements, which are heavily scrutinized by investors; therefore, the organizational structure has to be well-defined and based within a realistic framework given the parameters of the business. You should then include a description of your compensation and benefits plan.

Location and Facilities

According to the famous axiom, the three most important rules in business are location, location, and location. This holds true whether you are in the retail, restaurant, manufacturing, or almost any other line of business.

The business plan should indicate whether the company plans to purchase or lease property. If a property is to be purchased, readers will want to know the price and how it's to be financed. If it will be leased, they'll need to be made aware of the rents, term, and any other conditions or restrictions that come with the agreement. Most companies in the start-up phase will find it impossible, impractical, or inefficient to purchase property in the right location, so almost all end up leasing commercial space to meet their business needs.

Normally, a commercial property lease will comprise one of the largest single operating expense items of running a small business. As a result, the choice of where, for how long, and at what price to lease commercial property is one of the most significant start-up decisions you will make. It is therefore critical to think strategically about your long-term business plans before signing a lease, taking into account both the current and future needs of the business.

Choosing the right property is a difficult proposition, and one of the trickiest aspects of this decision is the length of the lease. If you sign a long-term lease for more commercial space than you presently need and your business does not "grow into" the space as expected, then the burden of the lease could collapse the entire business. However, if you sign a short-term lease and/or lease property that is insufficient to meet the future needs of your business, you may end up spending important capital on improving a property that you don't use for long and paying brokers' fees and moving expenses for a second time in quick succession—not to mention confusing your customers by changing location.

Ideally, you would rent sufficient space to meet your current needs, at least for the initial two years, with adjacent space available that you can expand into when your business grows in the future. But of course this type of space is hard to come by in a good location, so at the beginning you may need to either rent more space than you initially need, or sign a shorter lease with a plan in mind for moving to a larger space in the future. Much of this will depend on the nature of your business—the key is to have a plan.

Along with location and term, price is the other most important factor in deciding what property to lease. In determining how much you can afford, look to what percentage of your annual revenues the rent will entail. If it's more than 10 percent, it's probably too much. But remember, for many businesses it is worth paying more for a better location that will drive higher sales. Check the rents on comparable properties in the area to get a feel for whether a particular property is over, under, or at market price. Keep in mind, however, that many factors can impact the rent, and hidden costs may be involved, so look closely before making any judgment.

In searching for an acceptable property, first identify the best general location and then analyze each available property within your price and term range, weighing all of the important factors that can make or break a particular location.

Choosing the Right Location

Issues to consider when analyzing a commercial space include the following—note that the majority of them deal with location in one form or another:

- Nature of the desired property and neighborhood—retail, commercial, or industrial

- Condition and appearance—are major repairs required?

- Layout conducive to your business

- Adaptability: can leasehold improvements be made that meet your needs?

- Availability of additional space for future lease

- Proximity to and ease of access for target segment customers

- Proximity of complementary businesses that attract your target customers

- Proximity to and ease of access for pool of employees

- Proximity to and ease of access for suppliers

- Location of competition

- Zoning restrictions and other applicable ordinances

- Site image, history, and reputation: Is the location consistent with the image you want to maintain?

- Neighborhood safety and building security

- Parking for customers, visitors, and employees

- Sufficiency and cost of utilities—electric, plumbing, heating and air-conditioning

- Availability of municipal tax and other incentives

- Does the site allow you to meet your business goals?

In your business plan, provide the address where your business will be located. Describe the surrounding area and explain why this location will be effective. Also, note any disadvantages or possible problems presented by your location and what, if anything, you have done or will do to counteract these negatives. If you have a virtual business, you should explain why you have chosen to operate this way.

Property Lease

Once you have identified the right location at an acceptable price, you need to look carefully at the terms and conditions of the lease. Remember that renting commercial property is in effect a "buyer beware" proposition. The type of consumer protections available to persons who lease residential property will not protect those who lease commercial properties. On the contrary, it will be assumed that a business owner is sophisticated enough to understand the provisions of the lease, and if not will retain a professional adviser. So if the base monthly rent seems much lower than for comparable properties, look carefully at the details of the agreement, because the deal you've been offered might in fact be too good to be true.

In your business plan, provide details such as the square footage of the property, how your facility is laid out, what type of loading area it has to receive merchandise (if applicable) and the number and location of parking spaces. Also provide data about vehicle and pedestrian traffic, accessibility from major roads and highways, related nearby businesses and anything else that affects your location. If your business has more than one location, be sure to describe each one. Also discuss the major fixtures and equipment your business requires and how they work with your space. Note whether you are likely to outgrow the space, and if so, how you plan to handle a move/expansion.

Regardless of whether a business is complex or simple, its plan should have a thorough description of the facility it is to occupy. A number of specific issues need to be addressed. The square-foot space requirements of the business should be described for the near term and the longer run. The current or planned facility is then discussed in terms of how well it meets those requirements. An important issue is always whether or not the present facility is expandable to meet projected future needs.

Capital Equipment

Most businesses need a certain amount of equipment to operate. Capital equipment refers to large, more or less permanent items that the business retains and uses for a number of years. Capital items need not be immovable or permanently stuck to the ground. Thus capital equipment includes vehicles as well as machines, computers, and certain changes and additions to the facility.

Legal Environment

Describe the following in this section: licensing requirements, permits, any special regulations covering your industry or profession, zoning or building code requirements, insurance coverage, trademarks, copyrights, and patents (pending, existing, or purchased).

External Influences.

In many businesses there are important issues outside of competition that influence performance. A business plan should demonstrate that the author is aware of these forces and has a plan to cope with them. Typical external influences include the following: Government Regulation. The Technological Change.

> ## LinksBuddy Case Study
>
> ## Chapter 17
> ## Operations
>
> From an operations standpoint, the LinksBuddy operations will be much more complex than a normal e-commerce website business. This flows from the facts that is a multi-sided platform, involves value being created and exchanged by persons who are not employed by the business, and involved significant offsite operations in a large number of destinations. For this reason, having a plan to make sure their operations are efficient, cost-effective, replicable, and well-integrated with their business model and marketing plan is very important to LinksBuddy's success.
>
> For planning purposes, Steven and Martin break down their operations into component parts, with the goal of developing efficient, cost-effective and replicable processes for each component. With respect to their golf destinations, they need perform many different integrated functions. The key will be recruiting and training local representatives who can manage many different local operational functions. The local representatives need to run point on recruiting and training golf hosts and helping them post attractive listings and become valuable hosts. They need to handle logistics such as tee times, additional golf partners, etc. And they also need to be involved in hosting the golf traveler and making sure the experience is a good one, and they need to be Steven and Martin's eyes and ears for feedback from customers on both sides of the platform. Also at the local level, LinksBuddy needs to form associations with the golf course management teams in order to gain efficient access, gain discounts, and explore cross-promotional opportunities. And their operations do not end with the golf experience, because a key part of their value proposition is that golf travelers can enjoy a more diverse golf travel experience than with ordinary package tour operators. So they will want to form strategic alliances with transportation providers, restaurants and entertainment venues, etc. that their customers can enjoy along with their golf hosts. Finally, they will need to manage the local legal landscape in terms of licensing and other legal issues involved in doing business in that community. The key to achieving their strategic goals will be to turn all of

this into a replicable process, a core competency, that they can efficiently duplicate in each new destination.

The goal of operations in the San Francisco home office will be to remain as lean and efficient as possible. The strategy will focus on which operational functions to bring in-house and which to contract out. At the outset, the balance will tilt towards outsourcing most support functions and several key functions such as platform software and website design and development. Operations will be located in a small office, near the airport due to the amount of traveling that Steven will be required to do in order to open and manage new destinations. From that office, the following operational activities will be performed and managed: platform and website development; website content; marketing and public relations; customer support; accounting and other back office functions; human resources activities; and legal.

From and organizational standpoint, Steven will be the President of LinksBuddy and Martin will be the Chief Operating Officer and Marketing Executive. Steven will oversee all of the local representatives, who will be independent contractors. He will also have a destination development manager and an administrative assistant reporting directly to him. As the organization grows, the business will hire a northern and southern regional manager to oversee development and management of destinations. Martin will oversee the independent contractors performing platform software and website development, and will hire a webmaster with IT skills as the development nears completion. He will also have a marketing manager and two customer support representatives reporting to him, as well as an administrative assistant. He will outsource but oversee the human resources, accounting, and legal functions at the outset. While there will be only a handful of employees to manage, there will be quite a few people performing the necessary operational functions, and it all adds up.

Steven and Martin look at their operations flowchart and organizational chart, and then estimate costs and compare them to the cost estimates they made in the business modeling process. They can see that even with a lean organization, cost control is going to be a key to their initial success. This will require a high degree of efficiency in launching each new destination, and put a premium on the quality of their local representatives. It will also make it imperative for Martin to make sure that platform software and website development comes in on time and on budget. Cost of operations will also make it extremely important that Steven and Martin achieve their strategic goals in terms of destination launch and golf traveler visits per golf host—i.e. they cannot afford to miss their targets for attaining critical mass.

All of this demonstrates how important to the success of LinksBuddy each piece of the puzzle will be. Operations might not be sexy, but efficiency will determine the success or failure of their business.

CHAPTER 18:
THE MANAGEMENT TEAM

Chapter Overview

Forming Your Management Team 317
       Sales 319
       Marketing..319
       Product Development 320
       Technology..320
       Finance and Accounting..321
       Human Resources 322
Board of Directors 322
LinksBuddy Case Study..324

CHAPTER 18

THE MANAGEMENT TEAM

When analyzing your company, investors will not only look to see whether you have a good idea and a large target market, they will closely assess whether you and your management team can execute on that idea and build a valuable business around it. They know that without the right people, even the best business idea will wither on the vines and their funds will go down the drain. In fact, many investors and others who read business plans look first at the executive summary, and then go directly to the management team section to assess the strength of the people starting the firm. This practice stems from the prevalent belief that unless a proposed new venture has a strong management team, little else matters. Good ideas never succeed on their own.

Begin this section by providing background on each member of your senior management team, including their educational and employment history. In addition to your managers, assess what other essential jobs are there in your company, and which key employees will perform them. Focus, however, on what their roles and responsibilities will be in your business and what qualities they bring to the table that will help you succeed. Highlight past achievements and talents and tool sets that will them a key asset in your business. Most plans also include an organizational chart to show who will be reporting to who in your company. The organization should always try to build on people's strengths and minimize the effect of their weaknesses or lack of experience.

The second thing to review as you write the management team section of your business plan is to clearly describe how the team will evolve. Almost all new ventures have gaps in their management teams at the business plan stage. That's normal. What's important is to describe where the gaps are and how they'll be filled.

If you have formed a corporation, then also provide background on your board of directors. Highlight why they were chosen to sit on the board and any unique experience they have that will add value to your business.

Finally, identify who the business owners are and the percentage of the corporation or partnership they own. In the case of a corporation, show all outstanding equity, as well as all stock options or warrants, and describe the terms of any classes of preferred stock.

Forming Your Management Team

No business person can be an island unto him or herself. While everyone knows the legends of those famous companies that had their beginnings as one individual with a great idea working out of a home office or garage, the reality is that the founders of those businesses had to assemble teams to help them turn their initial ideas into profitable realties. Just like the Bill Gates and Steve Jobs of this world, you too will need to build your team.

Whether you put your management team and board of directors in place all at once or over a number of years will depend on the trajectory of your business plan and the specific circumstances you encounter while trying to implement that plan. But even if you put your team together over time, you need to have a hiring strategy in place so that you compile a cohesive group that includes individuals who collectively possess the mix of skills and traits that will best contribute to the success of your business.

In forming a management team, it is important at first to take a step back and visualize how your organization can run most effectively in the future. In doing so, you should review your personal strengths and weaknesses, keeping firmly in mind the values, vision, and mission you foresee for your business, and then identify the key success factors that will make or break your desired outcome.

In visualizing your future business operations, place in the foreground the fact that you will, by necessity, have to let go of the reins at some point and manage your team rather than perform even the most important tasks yourself. Even if you can perform a particular task better than anyone else, it will most often be less efficient overall for you to do so rather than delegate. This means that you must have complete faith and trust in every manager you hire.

In addition, there will be many areas of the business where you can hire somebody to perform and manage the tasks better than you could yourself. In these situations, you must be secure and confident enough to hire the best and the brightest you can find and afford, even if they know more about a particular area of expertise than you do. As the leader of the organization, you want to assemble a team that brings more to the table than you personally have to offer, and are willing to voice their professional opinion rather than simply agree with whatever you say.

That being said, you also want to look for team players that have genuinely bought into your vision and mission for your new organization, and the values you want that organization to represent. While you will want to secure independent thinkers who take the initiative and can manage their functional areas without constant oversight, you also need to avoid hiring mavericks that refuse to follow strategic direction and operate without regard for the success of the business as a whole.

There is also a tension between the need to get a management team on board in a timely manner and making sure you hire the right people. While you want to have your team in place early enough to capture the business opportunity you have identified, do not compromise on your management hires just to have a warm body overseeing a particular area of your business. It is critical that every manager has the skills and experience to meet the needs of your business. As with every team, if one member is unable to perform his or her role adequately, the entire group falls apart.

Finally, look closely at the roles each member of the management team will play in the business and try to assemble a team with a diverse mix of backgrounds that complement each other. What you want to create is a synergistic environment where putting people with different experiences and skill sets together leads to a high level of creativity in determining and implementing the strategies, goals, and objectives of the business.

Ultimately, your team will most likely include managers overseeing sales, marketing, product development, technology, operations, finance and accounting, human resources, and possibly business development and legal matters. At the beginning, two or more of these areas may be managed by a single individual, and some may be handled by outside professionals, but as the business grows they will most likely require a designated vice president, or at least someone at the management level. The priority of these hires will depend on the specific needs of your business and the timeframes included in your business plan.

Sales

In most successful businesses, the person running the sales department is treated like royalty. This is for good reason. Even if you have the best product in the world, the only way your company will make money is if enough people buy that product at the right price, and it is the sales manager's responsibility to get them to do so.

Everyone knows the stereotypical slick salesperson, but the best are those that are focused like a lazar on closing the deal with the customer at a price that earns the best possible profit. Remember, however, that what you need in a sales manager is not just a good salesman, but a good manager of people and accounts, and a good strategic thinker that understands how his team fits in with the rest of the organization. If you find that person, he or she will be worth their weight in gold—and will probably demand it in salary and incentives.

Marketing

While sales and marketing go hand in hand, they are by no means synonymous. And while from a cost standpoint you may combine sales and marketing under the same manager when your business is in its infancy, eventually it is a good idea to have separate management for the two functions. This is true first of all because the skill set required is not the same, and second because it is good to have a healthy tension between the two departments so that they push each other to greater heights.

More so than any other member of senior management, your marketing manager should be able to help you understand, analyze, and think strategically about how to capture the business opportunity that you started your company to capitalize on. He or she will be responsible for building the brand, differentiating the product, and getting the message out to potential customers in a manner that makes the sales team's job as easy as possible. In many cases, marketing will also drive product development by identifying the benefits consumers want and working with the development team to incorporate features into your product that provide those benefits.

Product Development

The product development manager has the difficult and unenviable task of making sure the product works perfectly and contains all the features that marketing and sales need to sell the item, while at the same time ensuring that the development timetable is met and there are no cost overruns. This means that the best developer does not always make the best product development manager, the same as the best salesperson does not always make the best sales manager.

You do need someone that understands the technology, otherwise it can become easy for the development team to pull the wool over the manager's eyes as to whether milestones will be met on time or not and whether or not key product features can be incorporated to meet the requirements of the marketing team. However, in addition to understanding the technology, it's just as important to have a good manager in place; someone that can motivate the development team to meet the equally important goals of quality, timeliness, and cost effectiveness.

Technology

In today's economy, there is hardly any business that gets by without the use of technology. Therefore, someone in your organization will need to have the competence to manage and implement your technological requirements.

One difficulty with start-ups is that the company often can't afford the technology managers that it really needs, and often end up making hires whose capabilities are soon outgrown by the pace of business innovation and development. The key to managing this process is thinking through the short, medium, and long-term technological needs of your business, recognizing that this bridge must likely be crossed down the road, and preparing the organization for the transition from an initial technology manager to a top-level chief technology officer and/or chief information officer.

One of the keys in doing so will be to create a specific job description for this position, both now and in the future. This will allow you to determine what skills the technology manager must bring to your organization during its early stages and what skills you might look for in a technology manager a little further down the road. The specific requirements will depend on the nature of your business and your organization. Companies whose technology needs are mostly internal may hire a chief information officer to be responsible for the technology necessary to run the company in the most efficient and profitable manner. Companies who sell technology-driven products may also be in need of a chief technology officer, who will be in charge of developing technologies for commercial purposes.

In preparing the job description for a chief information officer and/or a chief technology officer, keep in mind that your chosen person will be a member of your management team and will therefore need to be able to think strategically as well as technically, having the ability to understand the dynamics of the business and the competitive environment in which it operates.

Finance and Accounting

If you don't have much experience in business, it is easy to fall into the trap of believing that all you need in this position is a bookkeeper—someone to make sure the accounts are kept in order. At the very beginning this may be true, but as your business grows the person in charge of finance and accounting will become a key strategic member of your management team.

From a practical standpoint, the person you hire must have the experience to be able to put in place systems and controls that produce accurate records and ensure your accounts will meet the highest level of scrutiny. At the next level, your finance and accounting officer will take on the essential role of financial forecasting and budgeting, which will affect every aspect of your business's decision making process, especially your cash flow needs, and serve as the benchmark for whether your business is progressing as planned. A good finance officer will help make sure that costs do not exceed budgeted amounts and every dollar you spend in every area of your business produces a good return on its investment.

Finally, this person will be your point person on dealing with lending institutions and investors, helping them understand the financial statements and projections, and reassuring them that the financial foundation of your company is solid and its goals are attainable. If investors and lenders don't have faith in the person in charge of your finances, they will not have faith in your business.

Human Resources

Even more so than finance and accounting, it is easy to be lured into thinking that human resources is simply a recordkeeping function. But a good human resources manager can be the person that fuels your organization by recruiting talented new hires, keeping those hires happy by effectively resolving grievances and managing benefit programs, and protecting you from unwanted distractions such as lawsuits. The right human resources manager can be the glue that holds your company together and keeps everyone motivated to achieve its goals.

Board of Directors

A well-assembled board of directors can be a great asset to your business, providing you with experienced practical advice and strategic direction, as well as with valuable contacts in the commercial world. A dysfunctional board, however, can be a company's worst nightmare, resulting in deadlocks and tensions that can drag your business to a standstill, or worse. So take your time and put together a board of directors that both adds value to your business and can work well together amongst themselves and with your senior management team.

As with putting together a management team, the assembly of a board of directors should be driven by the needs, challenges, and opportunities of your business. The key is to find directors with complementary experience, skills, and perspectives who can work together as a group. But the tricky part is to find members who are sufficiently independent so that they challenge you and your business to perform at the optimum level, while at the same time supporting the vision that you have for your business.

From an experience standpoint, look to enlist a couple of people who have already been where you want to go and done what you want to do, i.e. built a start-up company into a sustainable and profitable enterprise. They will have faced the same challenges you are about to face, understand your needs as an owner-manager, and be able to offer specific advice about how to grow the business and overcome threats and obstacles.

Also look for people who have an in-depth understanding of your business and industry. They will likely be able to provide insights into the market you are entering and the competition you will face, and provide related strategic advice that goes beyond the experience level of you and your management team. They may also be able to provide contacts in the industry and help you recruit talented managers, employees, and strategic partners from within the industry.

If you obtain financing from venture capital or angel investors, they will almost surely require seats on your board of directors. This is not a bad thing, because most will bring a breadth of experience of working with start-up companies and will be highly aware of the factors that lead to success or failure. They will also force you to keep your eye firmly on the goals of profitability, positive cash flow, and return on investment. However, their priorities may not always be the same as yours, and you will also want some independent directors that can bridge any tensions between you and your investors, as well as give you a sense of whether you are on or off track in the arguments you are making when those tensions arise.

Another practical consideration in selecting board members is their availability. Someone running a large company and sitting on multiple boards may seem appealing, but they may not be able to devote enough time and attention to your business to give you more than superficial advice. In addition, you may find yourself in a logistical nightmare trying to arrange board meetings that fit their schedule, if they are available to attend at all.

Finally, take into account personality types. Persons who are bullies or overly dominant tend to shed more heat than light on an organization and inhibit good advice from other board members. On the flip side, even if you think it would be nice to have a rubber stamp board, if you go this route you will have missed a great opportunity to gain strategic advice and obtain a helpful gauge as to whether you are heading in the right direction.

Generally, you should think in terms of a three to five member board. For obvious reasons, you will want an odd number to avoid a stalemate in the decision making process. That being said, a board consisting of three members will run the risk of two people always taking sides against the other. However, that is something that you may need to contend with and manage at the outset. In most cases, it is best to start with a three-person board and increase it when you raise money from investors who require board seats, or as you grow and can attract new and better qualified candidates.

> **LinksBuddy Case Study**
>
> ## Chapter 18
> ## The Management Team
>
> This seemingly easy section of the business plan is not so easy for Steven and Martin after all. The first reason is that it requires them, at Peter's suggestion, to take a hard look in the mirror at where they are right now. The second reason is that it requires them to take a hard look at where they're heading.
>
> "Serious investors do not only invest in the business model, market opportunity, etc. They invest in the people who they will depend on to execute that business model and capitalize on the market opportunity," Peter tell Steven and Martin. "So when they meet the two of you, will they be sold that you have all of the qualities necessary to do so?"
>
> "You do want to sell yourself," he continues. "Confidence and passion are indispensable in starting a new business. But you don't want to disguise obvious weaknesses. By doing this you not only deceive your investors, who will simply walk away. You deceive yourselves and decrease your chances of success."
>
> Steven and Martin each put together a CV that focuses on their experience, capabilities, and role in their new enterprise. They highlight their experience in the golf tourism industry and familiarity with customers' problems and needs, as well as the participants in the industry. "We are our own target customers," Steven notes in one or their sessions. They also seek to communicate their passion and commitment to their vision, mission and values. Finally, they highlight Peter's presence and include a testimonial that marks his seal of approval of them as a competent team of founders.
>
> Afterwards, however, they take that hard look in the mirror and identify the areas of weakness they have as a start-up team. The key weaknesses are that they have no start-up, P2P or financial management experience. Having identified those weaknesses, they seek to build a strategic vision that would address them. Peter's participation as an advisor and on the

board of directors is the first step in that process, as he has extensive experience in start-up businesses and financial management. But he does not have direct P2P experience, or even multi-level market experience. Steven and Martin, therefore decide to recruit another board member and advisor with direct P2P experience. They will also seek to retain an attorney and an accountant to handle their basic legal and accounting needs, but who also have extensive experience with start-up companies and, if possible, with P2P companies as well. Finally, they determine that the new hires they have to make in the near future will focus on people with P2P experience who have the qualities necessary to thrive in a start-up environment. These current weaknesses and their plan to address them are clearly communicated in the written business plan.

This partially answers the second question of where they are heading in terms of assembling a winning management team. But a difficult portion of that question still remains: how lean do they want to remain, and for how long?

While Steven and Martin want to bring in value-added personnel to round out their portfolio or talent and capabilities, they do not want to become bloated either from a cost or decision-making perspective. And they do not want to bring in people whose capabilities will quickly become obsolete as the company expands, and have to be replaced. The strategy they develop is to address this conundrum in a balance fashion. They will recruit at least one management team member with extensive P2P experience, most likely on the marketing side. Having filled and likely paid more than they otherwise would want to in order to fill the gap in their team, they will be satisfied with lower level and less expensive personnel in other areas, such as Steven's assistant. Overall, however, their strategy is to stay lean as described in the organizational chart they produced for their operations plan. They need to be able to control costs, pivot quickly if necessary, and bring in heavier hitters in terms of sales and marketing, IT and finance after their business gains traction, further validates their business model, and is primed to expand. That is the time they will fill out their management team.

The other strategic decision they make with respect to organizational structure at the management level is with respect to the non-traditional structure they have adopted. By its very nature, they have a double business with two different (but overlapping) target customer segments, value propositions, etc. So instead of fighting that problem, they decide to embrace it in the nature of their organization and create an environment of friendly competition among the two sides of the business. Steven will head the golf host team, and Martin will head the golf traveler team. The strategic goal is for each of them to push the other

CHAPTER 19:
FINANCIAL PLAN AND PROJECTIONS

Chapter Overview

Types of Financial Statements and Reports 330
Balance Sheet 331
    Current Assets 331
    Fixed Assets... 331
    Intangible Assets 331
    Other Assets.. 331
    Current Liabilities... 331
    Long-Term Liabilities 332
    Owner's Equity 332
Income Statement 332
    Sales 332
    Cost of Goods Sold.. 333
    Gross Profit... 333
    Operating Expenses... 333
    Operating Profit 333
    Depreciation.. 333
    Other Income and Expenses.. 333
    Net Profit Before Taxes 333
    Net Profit After Taxes... 334
Cash Flow Statement.. 334
    Net Cash Flow from Operating Activities 334
    Net Cash Flow from Investing Activities 334

    Net Cash Flow from Financing Activities 335
    Net Change in Cash and Marketable Securities 335
The Financial Planning Process 335
Assumptions 335
Financial Forecasts 336
Revenue Forecasts 336
Expenses 338
Gross Profit Margin 338
Net Profits 339
LinksBuddy Case Study 340

CHAPTER 19

FINANCIAL PLAN AND PROJECTIONS

Last, but definitely not least, is a description of your financial plan and projections. This is where you provide the projected financial results of putting your business plan into effect, and discuss the meaning and ramifications of those numbers for your business.

As with the rest of the business plan, the most important reason for putting together these financial projections is for your own internal planning purposes. They can serve as the basis for your budget, allow you to gauge how much extra cash you need to raise, and provide a measure of how you are doing with respect to your plan once actual results start to flow in. In addition, like the business plan itself, going through the process of preparing your pro forma financial projections may be as valuable as the projections themselves.

In addition to becoming the primary barometer of your internal planning process, the financial projections you create for your business plan will allow potential investors and lenders to analyze whether your business idea, if properly executed, will provide them with a sufficient rate of return on their investment. If the business will not generate sufficient cash, reach profitability soon enough, or create enough value to make an exit strategy viable, they will wish you good luck and move on. But if your forecasted financial results will achieve these three goals, you may find yourself with a feeding frenzy of investors at your door.

It's extremely important that all of a firm's pro forma financial statement be prepared as accurately and realistically as possible. Potential investors also ask detailed questions about the assumptions that are behind the projections. If your business plan does capture the attention of an investor or banker, your financial statements will be gone over very carefully as part of the "due diligence" process. Entrepreneurs who present business plans to investors must be thoroughly conversant with what their financial projections are saying. An entrepreneur who doesn't understand his or her own financials is in trouble.

The guts of your financial plan section will be pro forma income statements, balance sheets, and cash flow statements for the next 3-5 years (the standard is three years but banks will sometimes require five), supported by a break-even analysis and relevant financial ratios. These are not financial accounting statements that reflect verifiable historical results. They are financial forecasts: an educated prediction of future results based on sales and expense forecasts, which in turn are based on a set of assumptions about your business, the market, the industry, and the economy.

If the business being planned already exists, however, the plan document should also contain actual statements for the last three years. Banks and investors like to see this historical information by month to see what the cash "burn rate" has been—how much cash you are spending a month and then compare it to the forecast and note the changes. Also, for both existing and start-up businesses, at a given monthly expenditure level, include how long the requested amount of loan/equity will last and then what your funding alternatives are.

If your plan has been built in the manner described in this book, most of the hard work has already been done. You'll find yourself referring to earlier sections in your business plan frequently while you prepare your financial projections. For example, you already prepared your sales forecasts, a marketing budget, and a schedule of the salaries of your initial management team. These numbers, along with others, flow directly to the financial projections you develop in this chapter. If you are doing this business plan for yourself, you can have several cases— most likely, pessimistic and optimistic.

Types of Financial Statements and Reports

Financial statements collectively summarize all of the information recorded in the general ledger and present the results of operations and the financial position of the company. At minimum, the financial statement projections you include in your business plan should include the big three: a balance sheet, income statement, and cash flow statement.

Balance Sheet

The balance sheet provides a snapshot of your company's financial position at a point in time, and does so in a format reflecting the accounting equation. A pro forma balance sheet therefore has three major sections: assets, liabilities, and equity at a specific point in time. Assets list the total resources of the business, liabilities list claims against the business, and equity lists the amount left over after the claims are deducted from the resources.

The key components of the balance sheet are:

Current Assets

These are the assets that can be converted into cash in one year or less. They include cash, accounts receivable, and inventory.

Fixed Assets

These are the tangible assets of a business that will not be converted to cash within one year during the normal course of operations. They include land, buildings, equipment, and vehicles.

Intangible Assets

These are assets that have no physical properties but still have value. They include intellectual property (such as patents) and goodwill.

Other Assets

Some company's include this category of assets in their balance sheet in order to break certain assets, such as life insurance and long-term investments, out from their other asset categories.

Current Liabilities

These are the obligations of the business that are due within one year. They include accounts payable, accrued expenses (such as payroll), amounts due on lines of credit, and current amounts due on long-term debt.

Long-Term Liabilities

These are the obligations of the business that will not come due for at least one year. The most common long-term liability is bank debt.

Owner's Equity

This figure represents the total amount invested by the stockholders plus the accumulated profit of the business.

Note that the excess of current assets over current liabilities is called "net working capital." For most companies, current assets should be twice as much as current liabilities. This is to protect against unexpected bad debts, declines in inventory value, unanticipated liabilities, etc. that could cause the company to become insolvent.

Income Statement

The pro forma income statement shows the financial performance earnings and profitability of your company over a specific period of time—it presents the projected flow of revenues, costs, and expenses through your business during that given period, and whether your business will be making a profit or experiencing a loss for that period. If you created a balance sheet at the beginning of the specified period and at the end of the period, the income statement would show how you got from the financial position depicted on the first balance sheet to the next. The bottom line of the projected income statement is net income, meaning the actual profit your business is projected to earn during the period in question.

The key components of the income statement are:

Sales

This number constitutes the gross revenue generated from the sale of your product, net of any returns and discounts allowed.

Cost of Goods Sold

This is the direct cost associated with producing your product. These costs include materials costs, direct factory labor, and factory overhead costs.

Gross Profit

Your Gross Profit equals Sales minus Cost of Goods Sold. Here you can see the amount of direct profit generated by the production of your product, before other indirect income and expense items are included.

Operating Expenses

These are the selling, general, and administrative expenses incurred in running your business, such as marketing programs, rent, and salaries.

Operating Profit

Your Operating Profit equals Gross Profit less Operating Expenses. This tells you the amount of profit you have earned from normal business operations.

Depreciation

Depreciation results when a company purchases a fixed asset and expenses it over the entire period of its planned use. Depending on the type of asset, depreciation expense is included either in operating expenses or cost of goods sold.

Other Income and Expenses

Other income and expenses report transactions that did not take place occur during the normal course of business. Capital gains income and interest expense on debt are included in this category.

Net Profit Before Taxes

This is the earnings of your business before you pay taxes. The amount is calculated by adding/subtracting the amount of Other Income and Expenses to/from Operating Profit.

Net Profit After Taxes

This is the "bottom line" earnings of your business—your net income for the period being measured.

Cash Flow Statement

The cash flow statement is one of the most useful and important tools in running your business. This statement shows all of the sources and uses of cash and cash equivalents during the period measured. It also details the overall change in the total of cash and cash equivalents during that period. Many of the readers of your business plan will consider your pro forma cash flows to be the most valuable of your financial statements. The cash flow statements provide an indication of whether a firm will be able to maintain a sufficient cash balance to get up and running successfully. This issue is critical enough that you should prepare your cash flow on a monthly basis, at least for the first two years of your firm's existence.

Normally, the cash flow statement measures cash flow from three major sources: operating activities, investing activities, and financing activities. In order to do so, the statement is prepared by converting the accrual basis of accounting used for the income statement and balance sheet back to a cash basis.

Once again, two time periods of comparative balance sheets are examined in order to prepare a statement of cash flows, and the statement is divided into four categories:

Net Cash Flow from Operating Activities

Operating activities are the daily internal activities of a business that either generate cash or use it. Items contributing to this category include cash collected from customers and cash paid for operating expenses, interest, and taxes.

Net Cash Flow from Investing Activities

Investing activities are discretionary investments made by management. These primarily consist of the purchase (or sale) of plant and equipment.

Net Cash Flow from Financing Activities

Financing activities are those external sources and uses of cash that affect cash flow. These include sales of common stock, changes in short or long-term loans, and dividends paid.

Net Change in Cash and Marketable Securities

The results of the first three categories are then used to determine the total change in cash and marketable securities during the period being measured.

While understanding historical sources and uses of cash is important, even more important is to understand future cash flows so you can plan your operations to grow in an optimum manner without ever running short on cash. Good financial management, therefore, requires the preparation of a budget.

The Financial Planning Process

Financial projections are built up by addressing financial statements one line at a time, usually starting with revenue based on projected unit sales. Once sales and the production required to meet those sales are established, the various statement line items can be developed one at a time. The forecasting procedure then works down the income statement through the cost and expense lines. It also projects the line items of the balance sheet, working through the left side until a figure for total assets is reached and liabilities are projected down to long-term debt.

Assumptions

It is highly advisable to have an introductory page in your financial plan noting the key assumptions you financial projections are based on and how each one was determined. These assumptions should be well thought-out and easily explainable and supportable. Some assumptions will be based on general information, and no specific sources will be cited to substantiate the assumption. In many instances, the assumption sheet references earlier portions of the business plan.

For example, from the marketing section, you have the sales forecast and pricing and the marketing budget. From the management team and organization section, you get the staffing—number of people and pay rates. From the operations section, you have buildings/equipment used, rentals, utilities, and other facility costs. Also make assumptions on costs going into costs of goods sold, inventory, accounts receivable and collections, etc. It's impossible to overemphasize the importance of conveying to your reader that your statements are built on good data.

Financial Forecasts

Once you have established your base assumptions, use them to forecast sales on a monthly basis for the first year, quarterly for the second and third years, and annually for the fourth and fifth. Take into account seasonality and buying trends in your industry. The most important thing is to be as realistic as possible—not overly optimistic and therefore not believable, but not overly pessimistic either.

From these sales forecasts—together with any other sources of income, amounts you plan to raise, and assumed taxes and expenses—you can create the required pro forma income statements, balance sheets, and cash flow statements.

Revenue Forecasts

Revenue forecasts are the cornerstone of the budgeting process. The main component of forecasted revenues will be from sales, but the forecast should include all sources of revenue for your business. Forecasting revenue is also the most difficult aspect of budgeting, especially for a business in the start-up phase. Clearly identify all assumptions you are making and don't be overly aggressive in your estimations.

Start with the number of units of your product you expect to sell at what price. There are four basic ways for a new firm to estimate the number of units you will sell and the resulting revenues you will receive. All of the methods produce estimates—there is no way to precisely predict the sales of a new business. More than one method should be used if possible. The most important thing is to come up with an estimate that is based on sound assumptions and seems both realistic and attainable.

The first way to estimate the sales for a new business is to contact the trade associations in your industry and ask if they track the sales numbers for businesses that are similar to the business you plan to start. If the trade association doesn't track actual sales numbers for comparable businesses, ask if there are other rules of thumb or metrics that help new companies estimate sales.

The second way to estimate a new firm's sales is to find a comparable firm, or a company that's selling a comparable product. Many financial experts feel that this is the most effective approach. For example, if you are planning to open a woman's clothing boutique, try to find a boutique that is similar to the one you are planning, and simply call the owner and ask for a chance to talk to him or her about the business. You should try to find a store out of your trade area so the owner doesn't see you as a potential competitor.

The third way to try to estimate sales is to conduct Internet searches to try to find magazine and newspaper articles that focus on firms in your industry. On occasion, the articles will talk about the sales experiences of a similar early stage firm. If you know of a firm that's comparable to your firm,

The fourth way to estimate a startup's sales is to use a multiplication method to try to arrive at a reasonable number. Startups that plan to sell a product on a national basis normally use a top–down approach to arrive at this number. This typically involves trying to estimate the total number of users of the product, estimate the average price customers pay, and estimate how much of the market their business will garner. Startups that plan to sell locally, such as a restaurant or clothing boutique, normally use a more bottom–up approach. This approach involves trying to determine how many customers to expect and the average amount each customer will spend. The numbers are usually computed on a weekly, monthly, and yearly basis.

Start with the bottom-up approach, since this will give support for the assumptions, and then compare these results to industry norms to see if they are realistic. So start with the basics. List your products and services, note how much you can produce/provide, and through the rigorous development of your marketing plan, state how much you can reasonably expect to sell.

The ideal scenario for startups is to use all four methods of estimating initial sales and then compare the estimates. The key is to arrive at your estimates by following a clear rationale and to present numbers that appear to be both realistic and obtainable.

Expenses

Here you must identify all the costs and expenses that you will have to incur to earn the forecasted revenues. Forecasted expenses can be divided into fixed, variable, and semi-variable costs.

- Fixed Costs are those expenses that remain the same regardless of the level of sales you achieve. They include rent, salaries, and insurance.

- Variable Costs are directly related to sales volumes. These include the cost of raw materials and shipping costs.

- Semi-Variable Costs are fixed costs that can be variable when influenced by volume of business. These can include some salaries and advertising.

To determine expenses, write down a list of every functional department that will be required to do business. Then write down a list of all the equipment and inventory that will have to be purchased, including the facility to be occupied. Finally, decide how many people you're going to hire and what materials, equipment, and services you will buy.

Gross Profit Margin

This requires an estimate of your cost of your goods sold, which is then subtracted from your forecasted sales revenue.

Net Profits

You can either end with the bottom line or begin with it. Many believe it makes sense to begin with the net profit percentage you wish to achieve and believe is possible, then do a sales forecast, and then create your expense budget to achieve the desired bottom line results. The budgeting process will then flesh out whether this is possible.

Once you have a set of financial statements that are consistent with all the research and components of your business plan, take a pause and conduct a "reality check."

Ask questions such as:

- Is there any business seasonality, and is it reflected in the monthly income and cash flow numbers?

- Are your gross/net margins in the competitive range? If not, why not?

- Are growth in number of customers and revenue supported by action plans and consistent with industry growth rates, or is all your growth achieved by taking business away from others?

- What are the risks to achieving your projected sales, income, and cash flow? Are these reasonable risks? Should contingencies be included?

- Is the amount of any requested funding supported by the needs shown in the financial statements?

LinksBuddy Case Study

Chapter 19
Financial Plan and Projections

With all of the building blocks in place, Steven and Martin at last sit down to make their financial projections and determine whether the initial projections they made as part of the business modeling process still held true, or whether they had changed necessitated planning and/or business model iterations. To begin the process, they sat down and listed all of their key assumptions. This required them in turn to put their strategic destination development plan into concrete terms.

Their first assumption was the time it would take to officially launch their platform and the expenses they would incur during that period. These expenses, broken down individually, included: platform software and website design, development and final validation; destination development including recruiting and training of local representatives and at least 10 golf hosts per destination; marketing costs including online marketing and PR; salaries and third party contractor expenses; travel expenses (significant since Steven will spend time at each destination); rent; and professional fees.

They then identified the number of destinations they assumed they would offer upon official launch of their platform (10 in the southern region), and the minimum number of golf hosts listed for each destination (also 10). Matched with this was their assumption about the average number of golf travelers who would visit each location per month, and the average revenue that LinksBuddy would derive per golf traveler visit ($100). Steven and Martin assumed that for each month of the first quarter, they would achieve 50 golf traveler visits per destination, or 500 total golf traveler visits resulting in $50,000 per month in total revenue. The "number of golf traveler visits" and "average revenue per golf traveler visit" would be their basic standard of measurement going forward, broken down further as necessary.

Steven and Martin then made an assumption as to the number of additional destinations they would have available to launch by the beginning of the second quarter (10 more in the southern region for a total of 20 destination, each with an average of 10 golf hosts for a total of 200 hosts). This would double their monthly revenue to $100,000 per month.

In the third quarter, Steven and Martin assumed they could launch 10 destinations in the northern region, each with an average of 10 golf hosts. However, the number of available destinations in the southern region would decrease to 10 due to seasonality. Therefore their monthly revenue would remain steady at $100,000 per month.

In the fourth quarter, they believed they could add another 10 destinations in the northern region for total of 20, have 10 destinations still available in the southern region, and generate $150,000 in total monthly revenue.

This is when things would begin to get exciting. In their fifth quarter of active operations they assumed they could add 10 more destinations in the southern region for a total of 30 (all of which would be open), that the average number of hosts per destination would grow to 12, that they would still have 10 destinations operating in the northern region, and that the number of monthly golf traveler visits per destination would grow to 60. This would result in 40 destinations, 480 hosts, 2,400 golf traveler visits, and $240,000 in monthly revenue.

In the following quarter they would reach add 10 additional southern destinations, and the quarter after that 10 additional northern destinations. At this point, with 70 total destinations, they assumed they would reach critical mass where any golf traveler visiting the site could find a destination he was interested in and an acceptable host at that destination. They also assumed that they would have created a large international online golf community that would propel them toward the network effect. And finally, they assumed that the following quarter they would be able to launch their operations in Europe.

But these assumptions only represented half of the equation. What about costs? Steven and Martin already had most of their cost assumptions at their fingertips in the form of their marketing, platform design and development, and operations plans.

They state their assumption regarding the time and cost of developing their platform software and website. Then they stated their assumption on the average cost of launching each new destination. Then they stated assumptions regarding headcount and salaries by month, including third party contractors such as the local representatives. Then they stated their assumptions regarding the trajectory of marketing costs and cost of customer acquisition on each side of the platform. Finally they pulled it all together and matched their assumptions regarding monthly revenue with assumptions regarding monthly costs, broken down by income statement category.

With these assumptions and the supporting material and figures in hand, they sat down and created financial statement projections for their first three years of operation. These statements revealed that if their assumptions were correct, then Steven and Martin would create a highly profitable P2P business, and have validated that their business model was sustainably profitable, repeatable and scalable. At that point, the sky would be the limit—because they would be primed to expand into any sports travel market that they so desired.

CHAPTER 20:
FUNDING SOURCES

Chapter Overview

How Much Cash Do I Need?	345
Should I Raise Money?	346
Who Should I Raise Money From?	347
Friends and Family	348
Angel Investors	348
Venture Capital Investors	349
Banks and Other Lending Institutions	349
SBA Loans	350
Basic 7(a) Loan Program	350
CDC/504 Loan Program	351
7(m) Microloan Program	351
Crowdfunding	351
How Much Money Should I Raise and When?	352
Seed Financing	353
Series A Round	353
Series B Round	354
Series C Round	354
What Ownership Interest Should I Give to Equity Investors?	355

CHAPTER 20

FUNDING SOURCES

Starting a new business involves an inherent tension between two famous adages: "Run your business on a shoestring" and "You have to spend money to make money."

Regarding the first adage, it's important that you run your new business lean and on-budget, making every dollar count until you have achieved sustained profitability and positive cash flow. This is important not only from a current cash flow standpoint— but also because it sets the right tone for running your business successfully in the future.

On the flip side, cash generally fuels business growth. If you don't inject enough cash into achieving the key milestones that your business must hit to be successful, your business could either stagnate or fail—with better capitalized competitors simply passing it by.

So it is vital that you determine at an early stage how much cash your start-up will need to get to a sustained level of positive cash flow from where it can finance itself through revenues generated by sales. Once you know how much you need, you should then plan how you will raise the necessary funds to get the business to this self-sufficient level. This will involve either funding the initial operations with your personal assets, raising debt financing from lenders, or having investors contribute equity capital to your business.

To develop such a plan, you can begin by asking yourself five basic questions:

- How much cash does the business need?

- Should I raise money from outside sources?

- Who should I raise money from?

- How much money should I raise and when?

- What ownership interest should I give, if any, to equity investors?

How Much Cash Do I Need?

The one phrase a business owner never wants to hear is: "We're out of cash." Fortunately, if you've prepared a business plan you already have a strong idea of how much cash your business will need to achieve a sustained positive cash flow, as well as how you will obtain that cash. So you should never hear those words unless something unexpected happens. If you haven't prepared a business plan, you now have one of the best reasons to do so, because having a firm grasp of your business's current and future cash needs is one of the most important aspects of successfully running a business, and having a handle on your business's cash needs is extremely difficult without having considered those needs properly.

To determine how much cash your business will need in excess of that which it is likely to generate from sales, and when you will need it, look at your business plan and compare your cash flow projections with your milestone schedule. By doing so, you will be able to determine how much additional cash you will need in order to achieve all of your major milestones up until your business has become cash flow positive.

In addition, check your monthly and quarterly cash flow forecasts to make sure that you will not run out of cash at any specific moment in time. For example, if you can foresee abnormally high negative cash flow during a certain period, perhaps because your business is seasonal, or because it will need to make a large capital expenditure for equipment, then you may need to secure additional funding to cover the shortfall during that period.

Finally, it is important to include a buffer in your cash flow projections. If your product launch or business opening is delayed a couple of months and you run out of cash as a result, or if the economy takes a downturn just when you projected your business would take off, it could be disastrous. So it's a good idea to add a minimum of a twenty percent—and up to a fifty percent— cushion to your expected cash needs for the next two to three years.

Should I Raise Money?

The answer to this question depends first on whether you have the ability to self-finance your business, and secondly on the nature of the business itself. If you can swing it, then self-financing your business allows you to maintain absolute control over your operations and gives you the maximum amount of flexibility in the future. This, however, requires you to take a close and clear-eyed look at your personal financial situation and the assets you have available, or can leverage, to contribute to the business.

Just as you don't want your business to run out of money, you don't want to personally run out of money either. Both could have a drastic effect on your new business and your life. Therefore, manage your personal finances the same way you manage your business, and start by creating a personal balance sheet and cash flow forecast in order to see clearly what assets and liabilities you have and what your monthly personal cash needs will be for the foreseeable future.

Make sure you have enough cash or other liquid assets to pay your living expenses until the time that your business can contribute regularly to your income. At a minimum, you probably want to be able to cover one year's worth of living expenses, with a buffer for unforeseen circumstances. Unless you are independently wealthy, it will almost certainly be necessary to cut many corners during your start-up period, but try not to add the stress of not being able to pay your own bills to the already stressful situation of starting a new business.

Even if you personally have the cash necessary for your business to get started, depending on the nature of your business and the industry in which you will be competing, you may want to raise money from outside sources. This is especially true in high growth businesses, where additional cash may help scale the business much more quickly and successfully, and in industries where competitors have more capital resources and can spend their way to market share.

However, if you are contemplating going this route, ask yourself whether you are prepared for the implications of raising money from outside investors. The most obvious implications are that you will give up a percentage ownership interest in your new company and perhaps some control as well, with investors likely gaining a seat on your board of directors or at least looking over your shoulder to protect their investment. Their goals may not always be the same as yours, and you may find yourself in a position of having to compromise on the type of organization you want to create.

Raising money from outside investors may also affect your ability to raise money from other sources in the future, or to exit the business as and when you would like. For example, taking a $20 million offer to buy your business may seem like a dream come true to you, but your investors may block the deal in hopes of a much bigger payoff down the line. Conversely, you may wish to hold onto a business that you have built from the ground up, but your investors may want to force a sale to cash out on their investment.

If you do decide to raise money from outside sources, you should thoroughly understand the process and have a long-term fundraising strategy in place before you take the first dime.

Who Should I Raise Money From?

Who you raise money from will be highly dependent on the nature of your business, because the nature of your business will dictate your options. Most angel investors and all venture capital investors will require the possibility of very high rates of return on their investment, so if your business does not have high growth potential leading to an exit strategy for the investor in 3-7 years, then angel and venture capital money will not be an option. For less scalable businesses, a loan may be a possibility. But most banks will require the proven ability to cover the loan payments and hard assets as security, so new businesses without a track record and significant assets may not be able to secure a loan.

Depending on the type of new business you are starting and the point at which you need to raise money, your basic financing sources will include:

- Friends and Family

- Angel Investors

- Venture Capital Investors
- Banks and other Lending Institutions
- Small Business Administration Loans
- Crowdfunding

Friends and Family

If you cannot finance your business yourself, then friends and family can be both your best and worst sources of funds. On the positive side, you may be able to borrow money from friends and family on favorable terms without having to give up much (if any) equity or control. But if your business goes sour and you are unable to repay the money you borrowed, or the equity in your business loses its value, it could harm some of the most important relationships in your life.

If you have no choice but to borrow money from friends and family, or if other options are not palatable for one reason or the other, the key is to do so professionally. Handshake deals are the primary recipe for disaster. Therefore, treat whoever is providing the funds as an arms' length lender or investor, providing them with your business plan to analyze, answering their questions, and drawing up legal documents that make clear whether the money is being provided as a loan or an investment, as well as the exact terms on which that money is provided.

Creating the proper expectations is the key to maintaining the relationship that led to the money being handed over in the first place. This applies whether your business succeeds or fails.

Angel Investors

Angel investors are typically high net worth individuals who provide funding to businesses at very early stages in exchange for a share of that business. Many angels have started, ran, and sold successful businesses of their own, and are now investing in other start-up companies. Often, angel investors form groups, where they pool their resources and spread their risk by investing small amounts in many start-ups.

Angel investors may be the best option when you need a limited amount of capital, anywhere between $20,000 and $1 million, and are still at the stages of developing your concept and proving it will be viable in the marketplace. However, most angel investors will expect the possibility of a very high return on their investment in exchange for the high degree of risk they are taking with their money. They may also seek significant levels of control over your business.

Venture Capital Investors

Venture capital investors are distinguished from angel investors by the amount of money they invest, where their money comes from, when they invest, and the manner in which they invest.

Venture capital funds raise large amounts of money from institutional investors and high net worth individuals, and then "manage" that money by investing in high growth companies. Venture capital investors typically invest at an early stage, but not as early as an angel investor. Normally, they require a higher degree of certainty that the product will actually be brought to market and have a strong probability of success.

Venture capital investors will normally want to invest between $2 million to $10 million, and even beyond, in today's market. They will not make smaller investments because they require the potential of a very large return on each investment. In addition, they require a more hands on approach with their investments than an angel investor, and therefore do not want to spread either their financial or human resources too thin.

Banks and Other Lending Institutions

It is notoriously difficult for a small business to get a loan from a traditional bank, especially in a poor economic climate. Banks typically receive no equity upside to the money they lend, and are therefore interested solely in whether the new business can repay the principal and interest on the loan. Because a much higher percentage of new businesses default than do established businesses, in general start-up businesses are not considered a good risk for a bank. This is true even if the borrower can provide adequate collateral, because banks do not want to be in the liquidation business.

The best way to secure a bank loan is to have a historical record of positive cash flow that would cover the loan amounts due, as bankers are much less interested in projections than are equity investors. In addition, either your business will need asset coverage of the loan, which is unlikely in a start-up situation, or you will have to pledge your personal assets in order to secure the loan. In most cases, it will probably need to be both.

As an alternative to a loan, it may be possible to secure an overdraft facility with your bank— which is a credit agreement allowing you to use or withdraw more than you have in your account up to a maximum negative balance. This can help cover short term cash flow deficiencies. But once again, this will probably require a personal guarantee.

SBA Loans

Another potential financing option is to borrow money via the U.S. Small Business Administration ("SBA") loan program (http://www.sba.gov/loanprograms). These loans are normally accessed through your local bank, credit union, or non-profit financial intermediary, and often require a personal guarantee. The three most relevant SBA loan programs are the Basic 7(a) Loan Program, the CDC/504 Loan Program, and the 7(m) Microloan Program. The 7(a) and 504 programs are restricted to small businesses with less than $7 million in tangible net worth and less than $2.5 million in net income.

Basic 7(a) Loan Program

The 7(a) is the SBA's most popular loan program. Start-up companies who qualify can get up to $750,000 from their local 7(a) lender. 7(a) loans are typically used for working capital, asset purchases, and property improvements.

Personal guarantees are required from all the business owners holding an ownership stake of 20 percent or more in the borrowing company.

CDC/504 Loan Program

The 504 loan program is intended to supply financing for major fixed asset purchases, such as equipment or real estate. The asset purchase is normally funded by a loan from a bank or other local lender, along with a second loan from a certified development company ("CDC"). The CDC loan is funded with an SBA guarantee for up to 40 percent of the value of the asset. Personal guarantees are also required from company owners for 504 loans.

7(m) Microloan Program

The microloan program provides loans of up to $35,000 that can be used for a broad range of purposes. The loans under this program come directly from the SBA and are provided to business owners via non-profit community-based intermediaries. All new businesses are eligible to apply for the microloan program.

Crowdfunding

Crowdfunding is the process of raising capital from many individuals who each make a small contribution towards funding a project or new business. In order to raise money in this manner, entrepreneurs normally select a crowdfunding platform, establish fundraising goals, create a page on the platform's website describing the business or project being funded, and then use social media and other means to publicize the campaign and raise the money.

There are two main types of crowdfunding—donation-based and investment-based. The concept began and first caught fire on the donation-based model, where funders donate money to finance a project in return for products or rewards. Investment-based crowdfunding, on the other hand, is where businesses seeking capital either sell shares in their company or take money in the form of a loan. In this model, individuals who fund become stockholders or lenders and have the potential to make back more than their original investment.

There are hundreds of crowdfunding platforms available, but the vast majority of funds are raised through the most popular sites such as Kickstarter, Indiegogo, and Crowdfunder. All platforms are not the same, however, so compare them carefully before making a choice. For example, some platforms only support donation-based crowdfunding, not investment-based, and some require you to make your fundraising goal or the funds must be returned.

A crowdfunding platform also serves as an excellent marketing tool and provides a forum from which you could receive valuable feedback about your product. However, be aware that crowdfunding exposes a new business idea or product to the public early on in the development stage, creating the possibility that a better capitalized competitor will take the idea and beat you to the market.

Until recently, there were significant securities law restrictions on the ability of new businesses to raise money from large numbers of investors in the form of crowdfunding. However, in 2012 the Jumpstart Our Business Start-ups Act (the "JOBS Act") came into effect, changing the start-up fundraising equation. The JOBS Act provides a new securities law exemption allowing start-ups to sell shares to a large number of investors through investment-based crowdfunding, so long as the offering meets the criteria set forth in the JOBS Act and any rules and regulations promulgated thereunder. Before getting started on an investment-based crowdfunding strategy, make sure you familiarize yourself with this new law.

How Much Money Should I Raise and When?

If you do have a business with the growth potential necessary to raise money from angel and/or venture capital investors, you should be aware that most companies in your position raise money in stages rather than all at once, and become familiar with how the process normally works.

The stages of financing, named after the series of preferred stock that are typically issued to investors, are:

- Seed Capital

- Series A Round (First Round or Start-up Stage)

- Series B Round (Second Round or Expansion Stage)

- Series C Round, etc. (Third Round or Later Stage)

During each of these stages, entrepreneurs typically only raise a portion of the total amount they will need to raise during their company's first 3-5 years of existence. The reason is that the earlier the stage they raise money, the larger the equity percentage they will have to give away per investment dollar because of the higher degree of risk involved. Therefore, most start-ups companies will raise enough to achieve a significant milestone, and then raise another round on better terms for subsequent milestones, and so on.

Despite the fact that your business is at its initial stages and may be several years away from the prospect of multiple rounds of financing, it is important to understand the process, because how you raise money at the early stages affects how and whether you raise money at later stages.

Seed Financing

Typically, seed financing helps a start-up company hire its first few employees, develop the product it intends to offer, plan for the product's introduction, fine-tune the business model, and possibly launch the first product in the marketplace. A seed financing round typically raises anywhere from $10,000-$2 million, but for high growth start-ups the amount is normally in the range of $250,000-$750,000. The investors are usually angels and early stage venture capitalists.

Series A Round

Once your product has been developed and you are either preparing to launch or have already gained some traction with the target market, a Series A round can be raised for purposes of successfully rolling out your new product, as increasing your marketing reach in order to significantly grow sales, capturing additional sources of revenue, and hiring senior level management and prime technology talent. The amount typically raised used to be $2 million to $15 million, with a median of $3 million to $7 million. But Series A round financings have risen dramatically in recent years, and the $7 million to $15 million rounds have become more common. Venture capital investors typically lead a Series A round.

Series B Round

At this point, the development of your initial product should be complete and you should be generating steady revenues under a working business model. The funds raised will normally be for the purpose of developing follow-on products, further expanding sales and marketing efforts into new territories, supplementing operations, and the like. Sometimes a Series B round is used to raise funds to buy other companies as well. The round normally raises anywhere from $7 million upwards. Often the Series B round is led by the same venture capital investor who led the Series A round, but at this stage the company also may attract investors who focus on later stage deals.

Series C Round

The Series C round is often used by a company for big ticket items such as acquisitions, major capital expenditures, international expansion, development of new product lines, etc. that will give the company the additional revenues necessary to become IPO (i.e. initial public offering) ready. The amount raised can range from tens to hundreds of millions. At this stage, the venture capital investors may wish to step aside and allow an investment bank or other later stage financier to lead the round as a bridge to, and in preparation for, an IPO or strategic merger.

At each stage of financing, there is a tension between the inclination to "raise as much as you can, while you can" and the desire to avoid undue dilution. In any event, however, you should at least try and raise enough cash to get you through a couple of major milestones, plus a cushion of six months or so that would allow you to close the next round at a much higher valuation than the last.

What you want to avoid is attempting to raise money when running out of cash, because then all the leverage you gained by accomplishing the last milestone may fly out the window. And you definitely want to avoid a rushed "bridge" round that plugs a cash gap but can be very expensive and send a bad message regarding your cash management capabilities. This means, once again, that you must have a firm grasp of your future cash needs and stick to your budgeted amounts to avoid running dry prematurely.

The other thing you want to avoid is a "down round," i.e. a round of financing at a valuation lower than the last. This introduces yet another tension — that between wanting to obtain as high a valuation as possible from your investors and not overvaluing the business so that future financings become more difficult.

What Ownership Interest Should I Give to Equity Investors?

The amount of equity that you give away will be tied to the valuation of your business. However, even though valuation techniques are used to value the business, it is the market conditions, the lead investor's experience, and the amount of interest in the company that ultimately dictates the terms of investment and equity levels sought. As a business owner it's important to be familiar with how this process works so you don't end up giving away more than you need to.

As discussed in the previous chapter, there are many valuation techniques, and the technique or combination of techniques an investor uses will depend on the nature of your business and its stage of development when the funding occurs. These techniques include the discounted cash flow method and market and transaction comparables method. However, the discounted cash flow method does not work well for early stage companies because accurately predicting future cash flows without the benefit of historical sales is too difficult, and because the model is extremely sensitive to the discount rate chosen.

In fact, valuations at the "seed stage" are driven in large part by subjective factors, because the company at that time is either at or just past the concept stage, with no proven results of any kind. These subjective factors include the abilities of the CEO and management team, value and strength of the company's intellectual property, how long it is expected to take for the company to launch a product, how long it is expected to take for the company to be profitable, estimated capital needs and burn rate, and volatility of the particular industry. In post-seed investing, achieving milestones such as demonstrating proof of concept will factor strongly in valuation determinations. After a company launches a product, more quantifiable data on revenue and cash flow is available and can be used to value the company.

Taking all of this into account, what many venture capital investors do in valuing an early stage company is the following—or something similar thereto:

- Estimate the future exit value of the company based upon comparable companies that have done an IPO or been sold.

- Determine the rate of return that the investor requires based on the degree of risk of the investment compared to other possible investments.

- Determine the amount of money to be invested in the current and future financing rounds.

- Determine the ownership percentage the investor needs to receive in order to realize the desired rate of return.

Most venture capital investors will require a rate of return that will give them a minimum return of 10x cash on exit, or a compounded rate of return of approximately 38% per annum.

All of these calculations are done through financial modeling based on certain assumptions, and then tweaked based to take account of the market conditions that the target business is operating under in order to gauge the probability that a lucrative exit will actually be achieved.

Needless to say, you need to negotiate a high value for your business so that you end up selling as little equity as possible. But come armed with good arguments and be careful of what you ask for, because if investors cannot achieve the required target returns they will simply walk away and invest in another opportunity.

A

Accounting systems, 299
Advertisers, 161
Advertising, 272
Aggregators, 128
Airbnb, 71–72
Amazon.com vision statement, 29
Analytics and budget, 278–279
Angel capital investors, 202
Angel investors, 348–349
Assumptions, 335–336
Auctions, 159
Audience, 250, 251

B

Balance sheet, 331–332
Banks, 349
Basic 7(a) loans, 350–351
B2B business, 12
Bookstore, key activities of, 13
Brainstorming, 105–106, 199, 200
    and idea generation, 52–53
Brochure, 60
Budget and analytics, 278–279
Bulk buying, 185–186
Business description, 19, 226
    business ownership, 235
    case study, 236–247
    company background
        basic information, 226–227
        legal structure, 227
    competitive advantages, 230–231
    core competencies, 230–231
    critical success factors, 234
    financial business model, 232–233
    funding requirements, 234–235
    nature of business, 228–230
    strategic goals and objectives, 233
    value chain description, 231–232
    vision, mission and values statement, 227–228

Business environment, 19, 250
    case study, 260–264
    competitive analysis, 257–259
        for business plan, 258
        direct competition, 257
        future competition, 258
        indirect competition, 258
        opportunities and threats, 259
        strategy for competition, 258–259
    customer segment, 251
    industry analysis, 251–254
        entertainment industry, 251–252
        external trends, 253
        fragmentation, 252–253
        participants, 252
        segmentation, 253
        segments, 251
        usage of, 254
    industry and market, 250–251
    market analysis, 254–257
        goal of, 254
        market and target market segments, 255–256
        and marketing plan, 254
Business function, 217
    strategy and action plan, 200–201
Business, goal of, 4
Business model, 28, 34
    and business plan, 194
        overlap between, 21
    components of, 4–5, 7
    creation of, 7–8, 217
    definition, 4
    description of, 19
    discovering, 50–51
    economic viability of, 121
    financial. *See* Financial business model
    identifying, 5
    integrated, 52
    key activities. *See* Key activities
    key resources. *See* Key resources
    modeling technique for creating, 6–7
    operational planning, 200–201

profitability of, 14
prototype. *See* Business model hypothesis
purpose of, 182
step in creating, 76
SWOT analysis, 196–199
taking time to create, 5–6
Business model canvas, 139
    brainstorming and idea generation, 52–53
    building blocks of, 7–8, 51
        channels, 12
        cost structure, 14
        customer relationships, 12
        customer segments, 10–11
        key activities, 13
        key partnerships, 13
        key resources, 13
        revenue streams, 12–13
        value proposition, 11–12, 51
    business model, 51–52
    business model hypothesis. *See* Business model hypothesis
    distribution of product, 124
    downloading, 49–50
    goal of, 51
    physical layout of, 9
    sale of product, 124
    secondary research material, 36
    significance of, 7, 48
    value proposition, 9
    vision and mission statements, 50–51
    visualizing process of, 50–51
Business model hypothesis
    case study, 69–73
    executing, 67–68
    initial, selection of, 53–55
    revising of, 64–65
    testing of, 55–64
        customer problem, 57
        direct personal customer interaction, 58–59
        framework for, 55
        overarching questions for, 55–56
        prioritization, 57
        problems and needs, 56
        sequence for, 56–57
        solution, 57
        test development for, 56–64
        value proposition hypothesis, 56
    validating, 64–67
Business modeling and planning process
    market research. *See* Market research
    mission statement for, 29
    value statement for, 29–30
    vision statement for, 28–29
Business modeling team
    formation of, 38–40
        for customer development, 40
        key employees, 39–40
        for product development, 40
        for small business, 39
Business model recipe, 5
Business nature, 228–230
    and competition, 229–230
    customer's problem, identification of, 228–229
    product information, 229
    profile customer and product offering, 228
    value proposition, 229
Business ownership, 235
Business periodicals, 35
Business plan, 250
    audience of, 201–203
        business types and, 202–203
        management team, 201
    benefits, 16
    business description. *See* Business description
    and business model
        overlap between, 21
    business model as, 194
    case study, 22–26, 205–208
    components of
        business environment, 19
        description of business, 19
        executive summary, 18

financial plan and projections, 21
management team, 20
marketing plan, 19–20
operations plan, 20
creation and documentation of, 217
e-commerce. *See* e-commerce
executive summary
    case study, 218–224
    contents of, 211–215
    importance of, 210
    length and style of, 215–216
    when to write, 216–217
financial projections, 16–17
finding flaws in, 15–16
forms, shapes and sizes of, 15
importance of, 194
layout and content, 18
length and style of, 17
length of, 203–204
as marketing document, 17
operational planning, 200–201
operations. *See* Operations
purposes of, 14
reasons of writing, 15
strategy and goals, 195–196
SWOT Analysis
    brainstorming, 199
    importance of, 196
    opportunities and threats, 198
    prioritized lists, 199
    process of performing, 199
    in strategic planning and goal-setting, 199
    strengths and weaknesses, identifying, 197–198
synthesized, benefits of, 204
tailored to intended audience, 17
Business planning, 196–199
    vs. business model, 15
    components of, 14–15
    market research, 16
    process, 15–16

Business process elements, 7
Business strategy, 19

C

Calls to action, 59
    positive responses to, 61
Capital equipment, 311
case study, 236–247
Cash flow
    and costs, 186
    forecast, 346
    statement, 334–335
Channel hypothesis, making
    customer service and support, 129
    distribution of product, 124
        distribution channel, 125
        physical distribution alternatives, 125–127
        virtual distribution alternatives, 127–128
    promotion of product, 123–124
    questions for, 130
    sale of product, 124–125
Channels for customer service, 129
Channels of communication, 12
    case study, 133–136
    choice for business model, 121–122
    customer feedback on, 131
    and customer relationships, link between, 138
    definition of, 120
    economic model, 129–130
    iterating, 132
    marketing platforms and vehicles, 12
    revising, 132
    sales and distribution channels, 12
    and satisfied customer, 121
    selection for business model, 129–130
    types of
        direct channels, 123
        indirect channels, 123

physical channels, 122
virtual channels, 122–123
validating, 132
Chicken and egg problem, 71–72
Commercial property lease, 308
Company background
basic information, 226–227
legal structure, 227
Competition, 298
market and, 17
strategy for, 258–259
Competitive advantages, 213, 230–231
Competitive analysis, 19, 257–259
for business plan, 258
direct competition, 257
future competition, 258
indirect competition, 258
opportunities and threats, 259
strategy for competition, 258–259
Competitive environment, 213
Competitive pricing, 159
Computer-aided canvases, 50
Content marketing, 276–277
Core competencies, 214, 230–231
Cost driven *vs.* values-driven business, 185
"Cost of acquisition," 121
Cost plus markup, 158
Cost structure, 14
associated key activities and key resources, 182–184
case study, 187–189
cash flow and, 186
control, 185
economies of scale, 185–186
economies of scope, 186
fixed *vs.* variable, 184–185
importance in business model, 182
Critical success factors, 215, 234, 298
Crowdfunding, 351–352
Customer acquisition costs, 142
Customer development, 40
Customer feedback

on channels, 131
learning from, 64–65
Customer feedback on value proposition, 106–112
competitors' offerings, 111
follow-up questions, 111
goal of, 109
product prototype, 107
product/ solution presentation outline, 109–110
qualitative and quantitative, 111
questions to customers, 110–111
visual aids, 108
brochure, 108
data sheet, 108
3D product mock-up, 109
landing page, 109
product packaging, 108
product prototype, 109
storyboard, 108
video, 109
website, 107
Customer feedback summaries, 89–90
Customer job, 10
Customer journey
channels of communication. *See* Channels of communication
definition of, 120
stages of, 120–121
Customer lifetime value, 159
Customer problem, 228
Customer problems and needs
identifying, 10
Customer profile, 78–80
creating, 84–85
of Value Proposition Canvas, 78–79
Customer profile hypotheses
revising, iterating, and validating, 89–91
testing of, 85–89
interview questions, 87–88
interviews with customers, 87–89
product prototype, 87, 88

steps of, 86–87
Customer relationship proposition
　creating
　　automated services, 141
　　channel and business objective, 141–142
　　customer acquisition cost and, 140, 142
　　customer communities, 141
　　customer profiles, 139–140
　　dedicated personal assistance, 141
　　investment analysis, 142
　　lifetime value, 140
　　personal assistance, 140–141
　　questions for, 139
　　self service, 141
　customer feedback on
　　customer acquisition cost, 147
　　customer acquisition tactics, 147
　　questions, 146–147
　revising, iterating, and validating, 148
Customer relationships, 12
　case study, 149–151
　and channels, link between, 138
　goal in selecting type of, 142
　importance of, 138
　interaction with customers, 138
　spectrum of, 138–139
Customers
　acquisition, 142–144
　growing, 145–146
　retaining, 144–145
　strategy for, 214
Customer segments, 10–11, 228
　case study, 92–97
　characteristics, 255
　customer profile. *See* Customer profile
　customer profile hypotheses. *See* Customer profile hypotheses
　definition of, 76, 82
　goals of, 10–11
　group of potential buyers, 82–83
　identifying, 82–84
　importance of, 82
　market segmentation, 82–84
　problem/need of, 212–213
　problems and needs, 77
　　customer profile, 78–80
　　testing and understanding, 85–86
　problem/solution fit, 77, 100
　process of identifying, 76–77
　product/market fit, 77, 100
Customer service and support, 129
CVS Corporation vision statement, 29

D

Data sheet, 60
Daycare center, value proposition canvas of, 105
dealer, 126
Design experiments, 61
Direct channels, 123
Direct competition, 257
Direct personal customer interaction, 58–59
　contacting potential customers for, 62–63
　generating list of potential customers for, 61–62
Direct sales, 125, 126
Distribution
　agreement, 304–305
　alternatives, 303–304
　channel, 303
　distributor, 304–305
　network, strength of, 304
Distribution channel
　alternatives, 125–126
　definition of, 125
　factors to be considered for selection of, 125
　physical distribution alternatives, 125
　　dealer, 126
　　direct sales, 126
　　distributor, 126

independent sales agents, 126
   mass merchandisers, 127
   OEMs, 127
   retailers, 126–127
   systems integrators/VARs, 127
   wholesalers, 127
  virtual distribution alternatives
   aggregators, 128
   e-commerce sites, 128
   flash sales, 128
   free-to-paid channel, 128
   mobile-app commerce, 128
   owned website, 127
   social commerce, 128
Distribution intermediaries, 129
Distribution network, strength of, 128
Distribution partner, 298, 299
Distributors, 126, 128, 304
Double company problem, 71–72
Dynamic pricing, 159

E

"Earned" marketing, 275
E-commerce, 286
E-commerce website/business, 128
   advantages of, 291
   case study, 294–296
   elements of successful, 292–293
   third-party solutions, 293
Economies of scale, 185–186
Economies of scope, 186
Email to potential customers, 62–63
Evernote, 12
Executive summary, 18
  case study, 218–224
  contents of, 211–215
    competitive advantages, 213
    competitive environment, 213
    core competencies, 214
    critical success factors, 215
    expected return on investment, 215

financial business model, 214
funding needs, 215
key milestones, 215
management team, 214
opportunity, 213
problem/need of customer segment, 212–213
product differentiation, 214
revenue streams, 214
solution/value proposition, 213
strategy for customers, 214
  importance of, 210
  length and style of, 215–216
  when to write, 216–217
Expenses, 338
Experiments, 37
External influences, 311

F

Face-to-face interviews, 58–59
   contacting potential customers for, 62–63
   generating list of potential customers for, 61–62
Feedback, 38
Financial business model, 214, 232–233
Financial forecasts, 330, 336
Financial plan, 21, 329
   guts of, 330
Financial planning process, 335
Financial projections, 21
   assumptions, 335–336
   for internal planning process, 329
   potential investors and, 329
   preparing, 330
Financial resources, 174
Financial statement, 329
Financial statements and reports
   case study, 340–342
   financial planning process, 335
   gross profit margin, 338
   net profits, 339

types of, 330
    assumptions, 335–336
    balance sheet, 331–332
    cash flow statement, 334–335
    expenses, 338
    financial forecasts, 336
    income statement, 332–334
    revenue forecasts, 336–338
Financing. *See* Funding
Fixed costs, 14, 184
Fixed pricing
    competitive pricing, 159
    cost plus markup, 158
    customer lifetime value, 159
    definition of, 157
    freemium model, 159
    methods of setting, 157–158
    portfolio, 158
    product feature dependent, 158
    return on investment, 158
    volume-base pricing, 158
    volume oriented, 158
Flash sales, 128
Focus groups, 37–38
Follow-on purchases, 121
Freemium
    model, 159
    strategy, 162
Free-to-paid channel, 128
Friends and family, 348
Funding
    business growth and, 344
    needs, 215, 234–235
    requirements for business, 345–346
    sources, 347
        angel investors, 348–349
        banks, 349
        basic 7(a) loans, 350–351
        crowdfunding, 351–352
        friends and family, 348
        lending institutions, 350
        504 loan program, 351
        microloan program, 351
        SBA loans, 350
        venture capital investors, 349
Fund raising
    cash and liquid assets, 346
    from outside investors, 346–347
    self-financing and, 346–347
    stages of, 352
        seed financing, 353
        Series A round, 353–354
        Series B round, 354
        Series C round, 354–355
Future competition, 258

G

Gain creators, 11, 105, 112
Gains of customers, 79–80
Goals and objectives, 233
Good business idea, components of, 76
Gross profit margin, 338

H

Human resources, 174

I

Idea generation, 52–53
Inbound marketing
    cost of, 275–276
    definition of, 275
    methods, 276
        external online content, 277
        links, 278
        social media networking, 278
        website content, 276–277
    vs. outbound marketing, 275
    strategy, 276
Income statements, 330, 332–334
Independent sales agents, 126

Indirect channels, 123
Indirect competition, 258
Industry
    analysis, 19, 251–254
        entertainment industry, 251–252
        external trends, 253
        fragmentation, 252–253
        participants, 252
        segmentation, 253
        segments, 251
        usage of, 254
    vs. market, 250
Information collection and analysis, 32
Information for market analysis, 31
Information sources, 34–36
Integrated revenue stream, 161–162
Intellectual property assets, 174
Intellectual property protection key activities, 172
Internal planning process, 21
Internet businesses, 162
Internet marketing
    importance of, 275
    program
        inbound marketing. *See* Inbound marketing
        online promotional mix, 275
        outbound marketing, 276
        website, 275
    strategies and tactics, 269
Interviews, 37, 58–59
Inventory management, 302
Investors, 329
Iterating testing, 64–65

J
Jobs of customers, 78–79, 85

K
Key activities, 13, 170, 298
    associated costs, 182–183
    case study, 177–180
    factors influencing, 172
    general categories of, 171–172
    identifying, 170–171, 173
    intellectual property protection, 172
    on local level, 172–173
    for software development, 172
Key employees, business modeling team, 39–40
Key milestones, 215
Key partners, 170
Key partnerships, 13
    case study, 177–180
    for outsourcing, 175
    with third-parties, 175
    types of, 176
Key resources, 13, 170
    associated costs, 182–183
    case study, 177–180
    categories of, 173
    financial resources, 174
    human resources, 174
    identifying, 173
    intellectual property assets, 174
    physical assets, 173–174

L
Legal environment, 311
Legal structure, 227
Lenders
    business plan for, 17
    traditional, 202–203
Lending institutions, 350
Lifetime value, 140
504 loan program, 351
Location and facilities
    property lease, 308, 310–311
    rent, 308–309
    right location selection, 309–310

INDEX | 365

right property selection, 308

M

Management team, 20, 214, 316
   board of directors, 322–323
   case study, 324–326
   formation of, 317
      finance and accounting, 321–322
      future business operations visualization for, 317
      human resources, 322
      marketing, 319–320
      product development, 320
      right people hiring, 318
      roles of member, 318
      sales, 319
      technological requirements for, 320–321
   significance of, 316–317
Market
   and competition, 17
   definition of, 81
   identification of, 81
   vs. industry, 250
   for music recording industry, 81
   for product, 254–255
   and target market segments, 255–256
Market analysis, 19, 81–82, 254–257
   goal of, 254
   market and target market segments, 255–256
   and marketing plan, 254
Marketing
   goals of, 267–268
   place, 271
   pricing, 270. *See also* Revenue stream
   product, 269–270
   promotion, 271
      advertising, 272
      personal selling, 273–274
      public relations, 272–273
      sales promotion, 273
Marketing budget, key aspects to setting, 279
Marketing costs, 279
Marketing mix, 269
Marketing plan, 19–20
   development of
      budget and analytics, 278–279
      case study, 280–283
      Internet marketing, 274–278
      market research and analysis, 267
      place, 271
      pricing, 270
      product, 269–270
      promotion, 271–274
      setting marketing goals, 267–268
      steps involved in, 266–267
      strategies and tactics for customers, 269
   and market analysis, 254
Marketing platforms and vehicles, 12
Marketing program, goals of, 268
Marketing strategies and tactics, 269
Market opportunity, 250
Market research
   case study, 41–44
   definition of, 30
   direct personal contact, 38
   hypothesis testing, 30–31
   initial, 30
      information collection during, 32–34
      size and growth potential of market, 32
   marketing plan research, 31
   ongoing, 31
   primary
      experiments, 37
      feedback, 38
      focus groups, 37–38
      information collection and analysis, 32
      interviews, 37
      keys to, 37
      potential customers and, 31, 36

surveys and questionnaires, 37
secondary, 31
    information for market analysis, 31
    information sources, 34–36
    online research, 36
    purpose of, 34
    threshold questions, 34
Market research and analysis, 267
Market segmentation, 83–84. *See also* Customer segments
Mass merchandisers, 127
Merck value statement, 29
Microloan program, 351
Minimum viable product, 113
Mission statement, 29, 50–51, 227–228
Mobile-app commerce, 128
Mock-up of product package, 60
Multi-sided market
    customer feedback on, 163
    platform, 70
    revenue stream and pricing strategies for, 160–161
MVP. *See* Minimum viable product

N

Negotiated pricing, 159
Net profits, 339
Network effect, 72
New *vs.* existing markets, revenue stream and pricing strategies for, 160
New York Yankees, key resources of, 13

O

OEM. *See* Original Equipment Manufacturer
Online promotional mix, 275
Online retailer, 12
Online research, 36
Operating model, 299
Operational planning
    setting goals and objectives, 200
    strategy and action plan, 200–201
Operations
    capital equipment, 311
    case study, 312–314
    components of, 298–300
    distribution
        agreement, 304–305
        alternatives, 303–304
        channel, 303
        distributor, 304–305
        network, strength of, 304
    external influences, 311
    legal environment, 311
    location and facilities
        property lease, 308, 310–311
        rent, 308–309
        right location selection, 309–310
        right property selection, 308
    organizational structure, 306–307
    product design and development plan
        critical assessment of, 301
        development costs, 301
        development schedule, 301
        purpose of, 300
        requirements, 300
    production process, 301
    service and support, 305
    service businesses, 305–306
    suppliers, 302
Operations plan, 20
Opportunities and threats, 259
Opportunity, 213
Organizational structure, 306–307
Original Equipment Manufacturer, 127
Outbound marketing, 276
Outsourcing, 175
Owned website, 127

P

"Pain relievers," 11, 104–105, 112

Pains of customers, 79, 85
Peer-to-peer marketplace
  challenges faced by, 71–73
  critical mass of, 72
  examples of, 71
  functions of, 71
  liquidity in, 72
  and multi-sided market platform, 70
  success of, 72
Personal balance sheet, 346
Personal finances, 346
Personal selling, 273–274
Physical assets, 173–174
Physical channels, 122
Physical distribution alternatives, 125
  dealer, 126
  direct sales, 126
  distributor, 126
  independent sales agents, 126
  mass merchandisers, 127
  OEMs, 127
  retailers, 126–127
  systems integrators/VARs, 127
  wholesalers, 127
Portfolio pricing, 158
Potential customers
  contacting, for direct personal customer interaction, 62–63
  email to, 62–63
  list for direct personal customer interaction, 61–62
P2P marketplace. *See* Peer-to-peer marketplace
Pre-launch iterations, 113
Premium product., 161–162
Pricing of product offering, 157–162, 302
  customer feedback on, 162
  dynamic
    categories of, 159
    definition of, 159
  fixed
    competitive pricing, 159
    cost plus markup, 158
    customer lifetime value, 159
    definition of, 157
    freemium model, 159
    methods of setting, 157–158
    portfolio, 158
    product feature dependent, 158
    return on investment, 158
    volume-base pricing, 158
    volume oriented, 158
  new *vs.* existing markets, 160
  revising, iterating, and validating, 163–164
Primary market research
  experiments, 37
  feedback, 38
  focus groups, 37–38
  information collection and analysis, 32
  interviews, 37
  keys to, 37
  potential customers and, 31, 36
  surveys and questionnaires, 37
Product design and development plan
  critical assessment of, 301
  development costs, 301
  development schedule, 301
  purpose of, 300
  requirements, 300
Product development
  business modeling team, 40
  and operations, 298
Product differentiation, 214
Product feature dependent, 158
Product features, adding and deleting, 113
Production process, 301
Product/market fit, 77
Product promotion, communication channels for, 124
Product prototype, 61
  examples of, 60–61
  used in test, 59–60
Products and services, 11
Promotion

advertising, 272
definition of, 123
personal selling, 273–274
public relations, 272–273
sales promotion, 273
types of, 123–124
Promotional mix, 124
Public relations, 272–273
Purchases, "lifetime value" of, 121

R

Real-time markets, 159
Retailers, 126–127
Return on investment, 158
    expected, 215
Revenue forecasts, 336–338
Revenue stream, 12–13, 214
    advertising fees, 155
    asset sale, 155
    brokerage fees, 155
    case study, 165–168
    definition of, 154
    examples of, 154
    identifying, 12–13
    integrated, 161–162
    lending/leasing/rental fees, 155
    licensing fees, 155
    pricing of product offering. *See* pricing of product offering
    and pricing strategies
        for multi-sided markets, 160–161
        for new *vs.* existing markets, 160
        for single-sided markets, 160
    referral fees, 155
    service fees, 155
    subscription fees, 155
    types of, 13
    usage fees, 155
    web and mobile products, 156
Revenue stream proposition
    creating

market research, 156
    pricing strategy and tactics, 157
    questions for, 156–157
customer feedback on
    questions for, 162–163
    strategy to obtain, 162
    revising, iterating, and validating, 163–164

S

Sales agent, 304
Sales and distribution channels, 12
Sales promotion, 273
SAM. *See* Serviceable available market
SBA loans. *See* Small Business Administration loan
Search engine optimization ("SEO") techniques, 278
Secondary market research, 31
    information for market analysis, 31
    information sources, 34–36
    online research, 36
    purpose of, 34
    threshold questions, 34
Serviceable available market, 32
Serviceable obtainable market, 32
Service and support, 305
Service businesses, 305–306
Single-sided markets, revenue stream and pricing strategies for, 160
Small Business Administration loan, 350
Small business, business modeling team for, 39
Social commerce, 128
Software development, key activities for, 172
SOM. *See* Serviceable obtainable market
Sticky notes, 49–50
Storyboard, 60
Strategic goals and objectives, 233
Strategic partners, 203
    business plan for, 17
Strategyzer Web App, 49–50
Style points for executive summary, 215–216

Suppliers, 302
Supply, alternative sources of, 302
Surveys and questionnaires, 37
SWOT Analysis, 229
   brainstorming, 199
   importance of, 196
   opportunities and threats, 198
   prioritized lists, 199
   process of performing, 199
   in strategic planning and goal-setting, 199
   strengths and weaknesses, identifying, 197–198
Systems integrators, 127

T

Tactic, 233
TAM. *See* Total addressable market
Target market segments and market, 255–256
Third party, services and/or resources, 175
Total addressable market, 32

U

Uber value proposition, 100–101

V

Valuation
   of business, 355
      at "seed stage," 355–356
      techniques, 355–356
      by venture capital investors, 356
Value added resellers, 127
Value chain description, 231–232
Value proposition, 11–12, 34, 51, 111, 213
   annoyance reduction, 103
   case study, 115–118
   convenience, 102
   cost savings, 101
   customization, 102–103
   of daycare center, 101
   definition of, 11, 76, 101
   design, 102
   entertainment value, 102
   importance in business, 9, 100
   and key activities. *See* Key activities
   modification based on factors, 113
   parts of, 11, 100
   performance, 102
   physical and mental energy savings, 102
   quality, 102
   risk reduction, 103
   social status, 102
   time savings, 102
   Uber, 100–101
Value Proposition Canvas, 9
   brainstorming, 80, 105–106
   customer profile portion of, 78–79
   for customer segment, 105
   customers' jobs, pains and gains, 80–81
   of daycare center, 105
   downloading, 49–50
   gain creators section, 104, 105
   layout of, 10
   market, 80–81
   pain relievers section, 104–105
   products and services section, 104
   right side of, 10–11
Value proposition hypothesis
   assessing, 112
   customer feedback on. *See* Customer feedback on value proposition
   iterating, 112
   revising, 112–113
   stating, 103–106
   validating, 114
Values-driven *vs.* cost driven business, 185
Values statement, 227–228
Value statement, 29–30
Variable costs, 184–185
VARs. *See* Value added resellers
Venture capital investors, 202, 349

business plan for, 17
Video of business model, 61
Virtual channels, 122–123
Virtual distribution alternatives
    aggregators, 128
    e-commerce sites, 128
    flash sales, 128
    free-to-paid channel, 128
    mobile-app commerce, 128
    owned website, 127
    social commerce, 128
Vision statement, 28–29, 50–51, 227–228
Visual aids
    examples of, 60–61
    used in test, 59–60
Volume-base pricing, 158
Volume oriented pricing, 158

W
Web and mobile products
    revenue stream, 156
Web/ mobile markets, 160
Websites, 275
    creating, 286
        buying website, 291
        commercial vision, 289
        domain name, 287–288
        legal compliance, 289
        look and feel visualization, 288
        programs and content, 289
        requirement analysis, 289
        target audience, 288
        website design, 289–290
        website development, 290–291
    pages, 60
    significance for business, 286
Wholesalers, 127
Wireframe, 60

Y
Yield-based pricing, 159

Other Great Books from Enodare's Estate Planning Series

How to Probate an Estate - A Step-By-Step Guide for Executors

Make Your Own Living Trust & Avoid Probate

Make Your Own Living Will

This book is essential reading for anyone contemplating acting as an executor of someone's estate!

Learn about the various stages of probate and what an executor needs to do at each stage to successfully navigate his way through to closing the estate and distributing the deceased's assets.

You will learn how an executor initiates probate, locates and manages assets, deals with debt and taxes, distributes assets, and much more. This is a fantastic step-by-step guide through the entire process!

Living trusts are used to distribute a person's assets after they die in a manner that avoids the costs, delays and publicity of probate. They also cater for the management of property during periods of incapacity.

This book will guide you step-by-step through the process of creating your very own living trust, transferring assets to your living trust and subsequently managing those assets.

All relevant forms are included.

Do you want a say in what life sustaining medical treatments you receive during periods in which you are incapacitated and either in a permanent state of unconsciousness or suffering from a terminal illness? Well if so, you must have a living will!

This book will introduce you to living wills, the types of medical procedures that they cover, the matters that you need to consider when making them and, of course, provide you with all the relevant forms you need to make your own living will!

www.enodare.com

ther Great Books from Enodare's Estate Planning Series

Make Your Own Medical & Financial Powers of Attorney

Estate Planning Essentials

Funeral Planning Basics - A Step-By-Step Guide to Funeral Planning

The importance of having powers of attorney is often underappreciated. They allow people you trust to manage your property and financial affairs during periods in which you are incapacitated; as well as make medical decisions on your behalf based on the instructions in your power of attorney document. This ensures that your affairs don't go unmanaged and you don't receive any unwanted medical treatments.

This book provides all the necessary documents and step-by-step instructions to make a power of attorney to cover virtually any situation!

This book is a must read for anyone who doesn't already have a comprehensive estate plan.

It will show you the importance of having wills, trusts, powers of attorney and living wills in your estate plan. You will learn about the probate process, why people are so keen to avoid it and lots of simple methods you can actually use to do so. You will learn about reducing estate taxes and how best to provide for young beneficiaries and children.

This book is a great way to get you started on the way to making your own estate plan.

Through proper funeral planning, you can ensure that your loved ones are not confronted with the unnecessary burden of having to plan a funeral at a time which is already very traumatic for them.

This book will introduce you to issues such as organ donations, purchasing caskets, cremation, burial, purchasing grave plots, organization of funeral services, legal and financial issues, costs of pre-arranging a funeral, how to save money on funerals, how to finance funerals and much more.

www.enodare.com

Enodare's - Online Will Writer

Create Your Documents Online In Minutes

Enodare's secure Online Will Writer - Estate Planning Software enables you to immediately create, download and print documents such as wills, living trusts, living wills and powers of attorney from the comfort of your home and without delay! All documents are tailored in accordance with state laws!

Through the use of a simple question and answer process, we'll guide you step-by-step through the process of preparing your chosen document. It only takes a few minutes of your time and comprehensive help and information is available at every stage of the process. Of course you can always save you document and finish making it later; your information will remain secure. **Get Started Online Now!**

- ✔ Save Time and Money
- ✔ Created by Experienced Attorneys
- ✔ Secured with 256 Bit Encryption
- ✔ 100% Satisfaction Guarantee

Note: The documents are valid in all states except Louisiana.

Over 10 Years Experience providing Online Wills and Trusts

Ensure Your Family's Protected

www.enodare.com

Personal Budget Kit

Budgeting Made Easy

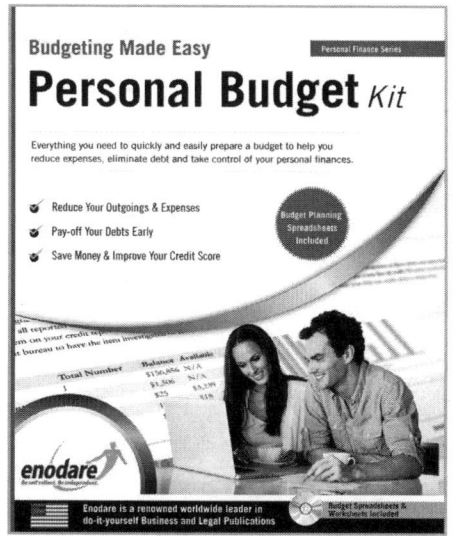

In this kit, we'll guide you step-by-step through the process of creating and living with a personal budget. We'll show you how analyze how you receive and spend your money and to set goals, both short and long-term.

You'll learn how to gain control of your personal cash flow. You'll discover when you need to make adjustments to your budget and how to do it wisely. Most of all, this kit will show you that budgeting isn't simply about adding limitations to your living but rather the foundation for living better by maximizing the resources you have.

This Personal Budget Kit provides you with step-by-step instructions, detailed information and all the budget worksheets and spreadsheets necessary to identify and understand your spending habits, reduce your expenses, set goals, prepare personal budgets, monitor your progress and take control over your finances.

- Reduce your spending painlessly and effortlessly
- Pay off your debts early
- Improve your credit rating
- Save & invest money
- Set & achieve financial goals
- Eliminate financial worries